PASS THE NEW POSTAL TEST 473E
2010 EDITION

Angelo Tropea

ISBN 1451559313

EAN-13 9781451559316

Published by Angelo Tropea, PO Box 26271, Brooklyn, NY 11202-6271

First paperback printing 2010

Please note that the addresses and forms in this book are fictitious
and are presented for instructional purposes only.

CONTENTS

Practice Tests

INTRODUCTION

You must score well on the Postal Test 473E to be considered for appointment.

Because of this, the aim of this book is to **keep it simple – and focused** on the actual test instead of complicating it with other information about the postal service and government jobs which does not contribute to attaining a higher score on the test.

The postal service has improved the process for applying and testing for certain postal positions. Generally, the application and testing process for the postal positions covered by this book has been computerized, as follows:

eCareers (Online application system)

Candidates for the following career postal positions who are required to take the new postal exam 473E (which has replaced the old 460 and 473 series of exams) now apply online at the USPS website:

http://www.usps.com/employment/

These postal positions are:

1. CITY CARRIER (Applicants must have a current valid state driver's license, at least two years of documented driving experience, and a safe driving record.)

City carriers deliver and collect mail outdoors and may carry a full mail bag up to 35 pounds on their shoulders. They also may be required to load and unload trays and containers and parcels up to 70 pounds.

2. MAIL PROCESSING CLERK

Employees who are mail processing clerks work with and monitor automated mail processing equipment and sometimes have to lift or transport containers that may be heavy.

3. MAIL HANDLER

Mail handlers transport mail within buildings and may have to lift and carry containers up to 70 pounds and push rolling containers within buildings.

4. SALES, SERVICES, AND DISTRIBUTION ASSOCIATE

Persons selected to be associates must successfully complete a job training program. Associates provide customer support, including in direct sales. They may also work distributing the mail.

5. RURAL CARRIER ASSOCIATE

Initially work less than a full week (part-time) and are not initially career employees. They work on a call-in basis and based on seniority may be offered a career rural carrier associate job when one becomes available.

_____

With eCareers candidates may apply AT ANY TIME and may apply for jobs in ANY STATE (nationwide).

In addition to career positions which require you to do well on the computerized exam 473E, you may also apply online for part-time or temporary jobs not requiring taking exam 473E.

To apply, you may follow these instructions:

1. Go to the website **http://www.usps.com/employment/** and first click on "Create your eCareer profile" which is found in the box on the right side of the web page. The process of creating your profile is explained in each screen. We suggest that you read carefully the requirements of each screen and answer appropriately.

The "eCareer profile" will be used by the online system to fill in automatically your information whenever you apply online for a postal position. The system will require you to create a "User Name" and "Password" and will also ask you for your e-mail address so that the postal service will be able to communicate with you.

2. Return to the website **http://www.usps.com/employment/** and click on "Search jobs online" which is found in the box on the right side of the web page. That will take you to the "Job Search" screen. If you wish to search for any open "City Carrier" positions, for example, you would type 'City Carrier' in the "Full Text Search, Keywords" box and then select the "Search Criteria for Employment Opportunities"

which may be a City (for example New York City), OR a LOCATION (for example, Alabama), OR a ZIP code (example 11201)

A screen showing "Search result" will appear. This screen will have a list of available positions in the area that you selected. To apply for a position click on the line which lists that position. This will cause a screen to appear which lists the details of that position. The positions covered by this book require that you take postal exam 473E. Other positions (temporary positions, casual positions) may not require an exam.

The 473E exam is comprised of 2 parts:

Part 1: A "Personal Characteristics and Experience Inventory" test which you take using the computer. This test is used to determine the suitability of candidates. Candidates usually take this test on their computer (or a computer in a library, or other facility where computers are available). This section of the test is explained further in this book. Candidates who pass this section of the test are notified to take Part 2 of the test in a supervised testing facility.

Part 2: A supervised testing facility is a place where there are a number of computers and where candidates take the test 473E simultaneously under supervision of postal representatives. Part 2 of the postal 473E has questions on the following areas:

1. Address Checking
2. Forms completion
3. Coding of addresses (by **referring** to a coding chart)
4. Coding of addresses (by **memory** of same coding chart in section 3, above)

All of these types of questions are explained in this book.

Although the 473E is administered using a computer at a testing facility, we believe strongly that in order to prepare for this exam it is wise to become completely familiar with the different types of questions that are asked and also to practice them with a book BEFORE you attempt to take any online practice versions of the test. The purpose of this book is to help transition you to the computer exam by taking away any uncertainty you may have regarding the exam content and test taking strategy.

To help you visualize the online format of the questions on the 473E test, we have provided a web site with sample online test questions. These sample questions are available for free at **http://www.postaltest.oom**

An interactive version of the questions is available for those with an Access Code (See bottom of page 83 for FREE INTERACTIVE Access Code)

This book and online sample test questions are designed to focus on the TEST. There are other good books on the market which focus on job descriptions, benefits, etc. You may also obtain all that information for free at the USPS web site at:

http://www.usps.com/employment

The information provided by the USPS is professional and complete.

Our aim is not to repeat what the USPS already says well, but to provide additional exercises and explanations and hints about the types of questions that are asked with the aim of enhancing your grade and thereby increasing your chances of being offered a job.

Among the topics covered at the USPS web site are:

Careers:

1. Sales and Marketing Jobs
2. Compensation and Benefits
3. Employment Opportunities
4. Career Development
5. USPS Employees
6. Let's Talk – How We Value Our Employees
7. Employment FAQ, including:
   A. USPS Online Job Application System – USPS Selection Process
   B. USPS Online Job Application System – Overview and Navigation
   C. USPS Online Job Application System – Search and Apply for Jobs
   D. USPS Online Job Application System – Assessment and Examination

<u>Other Eligibility Requirements</u>

In addition to the requirements listed below, the employment history of applicants is reviewed. Their military history is reviewed, if applicable, and a criminal records check is also made.

Age:

1. (with a high school diploma) must be at least 16 at time of appointment.
2. (without a high school diploma) must be at least 18 at time of appointment.

Citizenship:

1. U.S. citizen, or
2. permanent resident alien

English skills:

Must have basic competency for both speaking and reading.

Drug test:

Drug screening will be conducted.

Driving record:

For jobs requiring driving, like City Carrier, the driving record will be reviewed.

Selective Service:

Males born after 12/31/59 must be registered with Selective Service at age 18.

We believe that the combination of this book, the sample questions available **FREE** online, and a careful review and submission of job requests (at the postal web site http://www.usps.com/employment) will greatly enhance your chances of success. What will improve your chances even more are hard work and your desire to succeed.

The Postal Test 473E

The test consists of 5 timed parts:

1. Address Checking
2. Forms Completion
3. Coding
4. Memory
5. Personal Characteristics and Experience Inventory

Part	Time Allowed	Number of Ques.	Description of Question
1. Address Checking	11 minutes	60	Compare two addresses.
2. Forms Completion	15 minutes	30	Correctly complete forms.
3. Coding	6 minutes	36	Find correct code for an address.
4. Memory (of coding examples, above)	7 minutes	36	Memorize address codes (which are same as codes in the "Coding" section part of the test.)
5. Personal Characteristics and Experience Inventory	90 minutes	236	Tests for experience and job-related tendencies.

HOW TO USE THIS BOOK

If I escorted you and a group of other people to the front of a beautiful house and announced that the house would be awarded to the first person who opens the front door, there probably would be a mad rush for that door.

Of course, if the door were unlocked, the fastest runner would probably win the house. However, if the door were locked, then the person with the KEY - even if he or she was not the fastest person - would win the house.

What I am trying to stress is the following:

1. Do NOT be a part of the crowd of other applicants who runs into the test unprepared.

2. Practice with this book and online sample questions diligently so that you will have the "KEY" to achieving a successful score.

3. You don't have to be the most intelligent or educated person to be the highest scorer.

To prepare for the test, do the following:

1. Read carefully the descriptions of the different sections of the test.

2. Study carefully the HINTS in the sections and also for the test-taking section.

3. Do the exercises for each of the sections.

4. When you think you arc ready, take all of the 7 Practice Tests and review the online test questions samples (See page 83 for PostelTest.com Access Code).

You will be surprised at how much better you will do!

If you find that you need motivation, consider the following quote:

"Always bear in mind that your resolution to succeed is more important than any (other) thing."
- Abraham Lincoln

ADDRESS CHECKING

Comparing two addresses (Street number, City, State, and Zip) should be easy, but it is not as easy as it first appears. The reason is that this section of the test measures your ability to work BOTH QUICKLY AND ACCURATELY.

You are provided with 60 pairs of addresses which you must compare and decide whether:

A. There are no errors (differences) in the addresses: "NO ERRORS"

B. There is an error (difference) in the address only: "ADDRESS ONLY"

C. There is an error (difference) in the ZIP code only: "ZIP CODE ONLY"

D. There are errors (differences) in both the address and ZIP: "BOTH"

To accomplish this, you are allotted a maximum of 11 minutes (5-6 addresses per minute).

This is a reasonable amount of time. Even if at first you find the time limit difficult, with practice you should be able to comfortably complete the 60 comparisons within the allotted time.

7 HINTS for Success

Addresses are composed of numbers and letters. Therefore, for an address to be different from another address it must be different because of one or more of the following reasons:

1. Numbers(s) different

2. Number(s) omitted

3. Numbers(s) added

4. Letters(s) different

5. Letter(s) omitted

6. Letter(s) added

EXAMPLES:

1. Number(s) different:

2617 West Belmont Drive   2671 West Belmont Drive

The "17" in the left address is transposed to "71" in the right address.

2. Number(s) omitted:

2617 West Belmont Drive   261 West Belmont Drive

The "7" in the left address has been omitted in the right address.

3. Number(s) added:

2617 West Belmont Drive   26171 West Belmont Drive

An additional digit "1" has been added to the right column address.

4. Letter(s) different:

2617 West Belmont Drive   2617 West Bedmont Drive

The "l" in Belmont is changed to "d" in Bedmont.

5. Letter(s) omitted:

2617 West Belmont Drive   2617 West Bemont Drive

The "l" in Belmont is omitted in Bemont.

6. Letter(s) added:

2617 West Belmont Drive   2617 West Belmont Scenic Drive

The word "Scenic" is added to the right side address.

———————

HINT #1:

In the ADDRESS CHECKING section of the test you probably will be instructed to mark the answer space:

"A" if there are no errors (differences) in the two addresses

"B" if there is an error (difference) in the address only

"C" if there is an error (difference) in the ZIP code only

"D" if there is an error (difference) in both the address and ZIP code

Try to have these simple instructions clear in your mind. It will prevent you from losing points from selecting incorrect answers. Also, be aware that the instructions can change and you may be asked to mark different letters than the ones listed above.

HINT #2:

To increase speed, try comparing groups of letters or numbers instead of comparing single digits and letters. For example, comparing 3546 to 3564 is much faster than comparing the 3 in the first address to the 3 in the second address, then the 5 in the first address to the 5 in the second address, then the 4 in the first address to the 6 in the second address.... (get the point?). The greater the number of digits and letters that you can compare well at one glance, the faster your speed will be.

HOWEVER: do NOT compare the two addresses with just one sweep of the eyes. For example:

2478 Roget Ave SW   and   2478 Roget Ave WS

Compare 2478 and 2478 (Same)

Compare Roget Ave and Roget Ave (Same)

Compare SW and WS (Different)

                Or

Compare 2478 and 2478 (Same)

Compare Roget Ave SW and Roget Ave WS   (Different)

Remember that it is NOT crucial which segments you compare as long as they are not too short or too long. Short segments, such as individual letters and digits, will slow you down and prevent you from maximizing your score. Segments which are too long for you to quickly and accurately compare might cause you to make mistakes and lose precious points.

HINT #3:

"Practice makes perfect."

Practice address checking exercises every day from now until the test. You will be amazed at how much you will improve.

HINT #4:

Work quickly and accurately.

You are allowed approximately 10 seconds for each address comparison.

TRY NOT TO LET YOUR MIND WANDER - even for a second.

Do not let unusual or interesting words distract you.

Consider the following:

47 Snow White St.   47 Snow White Ave.

If upon reading the above addresses you entertain visions of Snow White and the Seven Dwarfs or visions of snow white mountains or visions of brilliant teeth, you may lose a valuable second or two - and even worse become distracted from the difference in the two addresses (St. and Ave.).

HINT #5:

Because the score is calculated by taking the number of correct answers and deducting from it 1/3 of the number of incorrect answers, it is **not** wise to guess blindly on this part of the test. However, you should not focus on an address pair until you are 200 per cent sure you have the correct answer. A second wasted is a second you could be working on the next address.

HINT #6:

When comparing addresses, do not whisper or read out loud. The mind works much faster than vocal muscles. In other words, do NOT sound out the addresses.

HINT #7:

Make sure your mind sees what is actually there and not what it thinks should be there. Do not read so fast that you skip words. During your school years your mind might have developed shortcuts that you might not be fully aware of.

Address Checking Examples

On the following page there are 15 address checking examples. The answers and explanations are on the page after that.

1. Read the instructions at the top of the page, then place a sheet of paper on the page where the answers are.

2. Do the 15 examples. The aim is to get familiar with this type of question. At this point do not be concerned about the speed of answering the questions. That will come with practice.

3. Check your answers. How did you do? Chances are that no matter how well you did, you will improve with practice.

4. Following this exercise there are four more exercises with answer explanations. After you complete these additional four exercises, you will be ready for the five exercises with 30 questions, and later on for the seven practice tests, each with 60 address checking questions. Whenever there is a time limit specified for that section, stop working at the end of that time limit. This will give you a sense of how quickly you are answering the questions.

(Please note: All the addresses and ZIP codes are fictitious and for practice only.)

(The "A", "B", "C", "D" answer circles are to the right of each question. To indicate your answer, quickly darken the appropriate circle. The actual test will be on a computer and you will not need a pencil to indicate your answer. You will simply click on the correct answer.)

When you are ready, turn the page. Cover the answers on the page on the right and then answer the 15 address checking questions on the left page.

(These examples are intended to help you become used to this type of question and are therefore not timed.)

Address Checking Example 1: Below is a list of 15 pairs of addresses. Compare each pair of addresses for errors and mark the answer sheet to indicate errors found as follows:

A. No errors   **B.** Errors in address only

C. Errors in Zip Code only   **D.** Errors in both address and Zip Code

	Correct List of Addresses		**Address List to be Checked**		**Answer Grid**
	Address	**ZIP**	**Address**	**ZIP**	
1	283 Fairbiew Cir. Classon,PA	09112	283 Fairbiew Cir. Classon,PA	09121	Ⓐ Ⓑ Ⓒ Ⓓ
2	4869 Tarp Terrace Albany, NY	28403-4235	4869 Tarp Terrace Albany, NY	28403-4235	Ⓐ Ⓑ Ⓒ Ⓓ
3	1792 Wilford Ave. Vernell, VA	66093-0010	1729 Wilford Ave. Vernell, VA	66093-0010	Ⓐ Ⓑ Ⓒ Ⓓ
4	P.O. Box 2702 Justino, FL	10004-7129	P.O. Box 2720 Justino, FL	10004-7192	Ⓐ Ⓑ Ⓒ Ⓓ
5	5700 Wilford Ln. Foly, FL	88913	5700 Wilfurd Ln. Foly, FL	89813	Ⓐ Ⓑ Ⓒ Ⓓ
6	882 Milton Ave. Meteor, MN	24112-3443	882 Milfon Ave. Meteor, MN	24121-3443	Ⓐ Ⓑ Ⓒ Ⓓ
7	713 James Ct. Parton, IL	40201	731 James Ct. Parton, IL	40501	Ⓐ Ⓑ Ⓒ Ⓓ
8	2862 West 6 Street Freely, NJ	36202-8941	2862 East 6 Street Freely, NJ	36202-8941	Ⓐ Ⓑ Ⓒ Ⓓ
9	3724 Talbot Way Wantak, TX	27529	3724 Talbot Way Wantak, TX	27529	Ⓐ Ⓑ Ⓒ Ⓓ
10	6944 Arizona Lane Bekker, AR	72696	6944 Arizona Lane Bekker, AR	76296	Ⓐ Ⓑ Ⓒ Ⓓ
11	9431 Lionel St. Hurmon, OR	79041-1349	9431 Lionel St. Harmon, OR	79041-1349	Ⓐ Ⓑ Ⓒ Ⓓ
12	10 Arlington Rd. Tanning, KS	74899-6749	10 Arlington Rd. Tanning, KS	74899-6449	Ⓐ Ⓑ Ⓒ Ⓓ
13	4820 Zebra Road Alouda, MI	76262-2556	4820 Zedra Road Alouda, MI	76262-2556	Ⓐ Ⓑ Ⓒ Ⓓ
14	1724 Trapper St. Gaynor, AK	78240	1724 Trapper St. Gaynor, AK	78240	Ⓐ Ⓑ Ⓒ Ⓓ
15	6735 Vestor Pkwy. Niles, RI	29220-3189	6735 Westor Pkwy. Niles, RI	29220-3189	Ⓐ Ⓑ Ⓒ Ⓓ

Address Checking Example 1

	Answers
1	**C.** Errors in Zip Code only: 09112 and 09121
2	**A.** No errors
3	**B.** Errors in address only: 1792 and 1729
4	**D.** Errors in both address and Zip Code: 2702 and 2720, 10004-7129 and 10004-7192
5	**D.** Errors in both address and Zip Code: Wilford and Wilfurd, 88913 and 89813
6	**D.** Errors in both address and Zip Code: Milton and Milfon, 24112-3443 and 24121-3443
7	**D.** Errors in both address and Zip Code: 713 and 731, 40201 and 40501
8	**B.** Errors in address only: West and East
9	**A.** No errors
10	**C.** Errors in Zip Code only: 72696 and 76296
11	**B.** Errors in address only: Hurmon and Harmon
12	**C.** Errors in Zip Code only: 74899-6749 and 74899-6449
13	**D.** Errors in both address and Zip Code: Zebra and Zedra, 76262-2556 and 76262-2256
14	**A.** No errors
15	**B.** Errors in address only: Vestor and Westor

Address Checking Example 2: Below is a list of 15 pairs of addresses. Compare each pair of addresses for errors and mark the answer sheet to indicate errors found as follows:

A. No Errors   **B.** Address Only   **C.** Zip Code Only   **D.** Both Address and ZIP Code

	Correct List of Addresses		Address List to be Checked		
	Address	**ZIP**	**Address**	**ZIP**	**Answer Grid**
1	1832 Easy Road Tropper, MA	44562	1832 Easy Road Tropper, MA	44562	Ⓐ Ⓑ Ⓒ Ⓓ
2	8842 Fern Pkwy. Corville, OH	13101-6261	8842 Furn Pkwy. Corville, OH	13701-6261	Ⓐ Ⓑ Ⓒ Ⓓ
3	6324 Custard Rd. Sackett, AR	84755	6324 Custurd Rd. Sackett, AR	84755	Ⓐ Ⓑ Ⓒ Ⓓ
4	3517 York St. Nantucket, CA	59321	3577 York St. Nantucket, CA	59821	Ⓐ Ⓑ Ⓒ Ⓓ
5	1618 Foley Street Deloitte, MO	22789-2211	1618 Foley Street Deloitte, MO	22789-2211	Ⓐ Ⓑ Ⓒ Ⓓ
6	5163 Clark Way Balliard, WA	35405	5163 Clark Way Balliard, WA	35505	Ⓐ Ⓑ Ⓒ Ⓓ
7	P.O. Box 971 Kensington, ME	43338-0002	P.O. Box 971 Kensington, ME	43338-0002	Ⓐ Ⓑ Ⓒ Ⓓ
8	48 Harrison Ln. Poplar, SC	26805-2783	48 Harison Ln. Poplar, SC	26805-2783	Ⓐ Ⓑ Ⓒ Ⓓ
9	793 Union Street Bedington, MS	04415-2174	793 Onion Street Bedington, MS	04415-2774	Ⓐ Ⓑ Ⓒ Ⓓ
10	262 Warington Ln. Waters, MI	55748	262 Warington Ln. Waters, MI	55748	Ⓐ Ⓑ Ⓒ Ⓓ
11	184 Vander Ct. Tourmont, AK	58346	184 Vander Ct. Tourmont, AK	58349	Ⓐ Ⓑ Ⓒ Ⓓ
12	1816 Isle Terrace Walket, CT	10007-3614	1816 Isle Terrace Walket, CT	10007-3914	Ⓐ Ⓑ Ⓒ Ⓓ
13	3984 Dyker St. Riccard, MD	03764	3984 Diker St. Riccard, MD	03764	Ⓐ Ⓑ Ⓒ Ⓓ
14	672 Broad Cir. Bluepath, MS	03017-4644	672 Broad St. Bluepath, MS	03017-4644	Ⓐ Ⓑ Ⓒ Ⓓ
15	672 Broad Cir. Cascade, GA	05392	672 Brad Cir. Cascade, GA	05392	Ⓐ Ⓑ Ⓒ Ⓓ

Address Checking Example 2

	Answers
1	**A.** No Errors
2	**D.** Both Address and ZIP Code: Fern and Furn, 13101-6261 and 13701-6261
3	**B.** Address Only: Custard and Custurd
4	**D.** Both Address and ZIP Code: 3517 and 3577, 59321 and 59821
5	**A.** No Errors
6	**C.** Zip Code Only: 35405 and 35505
7	**A.** No Errors
8	**B.** Address Only: Harrison and Harison
9	**D.** Both Address and ZIP Code: Union and Onion, 04415-2174 and 04415-2774
10	**A.** No Errors
11	**C.** Zip Code Only: 58346 and 58349
12	**C.** Zip Code Only: 10007-3614 and 10007-3914
13	**B.** Dyker and Diker
14	**D.** Both Address and ZIP Code: Cir. and St., 03017-4644
15	**B.** Address Only: Broad and Brad

Address Checking Example 3: Below is a list of 15 pairs of addresses. Compare each pair of addresses for errors and mark the answer sheet to indicate errors found as follows:

A. No Errors   **B.** Address Only   **C.** Zip Code Only   **D.** Both Address and ZIP Code

	Correct List of Addresses		Address List to be Checked		
	Address	**ZIP**	**Address**	**ZIP**	**Answer Grid**
1	6713 Clifford Road Boyd, NJ	33221-2434	6713 Clifford Road Boyd, NJ	33221-2434	Ⓐ Ⓑ Ⓒ Ⓓ
2	9234 Kings Ave. Bramen, PA	04201	9234 Kings Ave. Bramen, PA	04210	Ⓐ Ⓑ Ⓒ Ⓓ
3	4801 Tiger St. Tracker, GA	63022-9814	4801 Tigger St. Tracker, GA	63022-9814	Ⓐ Ⓑ Ⓒ Ⓓ
4	8713 Holiday Road Aden, NY	72925	8713 Holliday Road Aden, NY	79225	Ⓐ Ⓑ Ⓒ Ⓓ
5	24 Headley Cir. Bellor, WA	26594	24 Hadley Cir. Bellor, WA	26594	Ⓐ Ⓑ Ⓒ Ⓓ
6	3316 Divine Street Smallville, RI	65041-3194	3316 Divine Street Smallville, RI	65041-3194	Ⓐ Ⓑ Ⓒ Ⓓ
7	5751 Crator Way Wooster, MS	47989-7694	5751 Crator Way Wooster, MS	47989-7694	Ⓐ Ⓑ Ⓒ Ⓓ
8	P.O. Box 7650 Arcadia, MO	66161-5265	P.O. Box 7650 Arcadia, MO	66161-5565	Ⓐ Ⓑ Ⓒ Ⓓ
9	442 Remote Rd. Stenton, MO	86139	424 Remote Rd. Stenton, MO	86139	Ⓐ Ⓑ Ⓒ Ⓓ
10	8216 Quaker St. Surry, OH	18120-1398	8216 Quakker St. Surry, OH	18720-1398	Ⓐ Ⓑ Ⓒ Ⓓ
11	3371 Pearl Terrace Canton, MN	45561	3371 Pearl Terrace Canton, MN	45561	Ⓐ Ⓑ Ⓒ Ⓓ
12	7342 Contour Ln. Springfield, MI	12202-1619	7342 Contour Ln. Springfield, MI	12202-1919	Ⓐ Ⓑ Ⓒ Ⓓ
13	6937 Dairy Pkwy. Singer, RI	47654	6937 Dary Pkwy. Singer, RI	47624	Ⓐ Ⓑ Ⓒ Ⓓ
14	2872 Dean Ct. Brookville, CT	58235	2872 Dean Cir. Brookville, CT	58236	Ⓐ Ⓑ Ⓒ Ⓓ
15	8132 Florida Ln. Eastville, FL	21789-4524	8132 Florida Ln. Eastville, FL	21189-4524	Ⓐ Ⓑ Ⓒ Ⓓ

Address Checking Example 3

	Answers
1	**A.** No Errors
2	**C.** Zip Code Only: 04201 and 04210
3	**B.** Address Only: Tiger and Tigger
4	**D.** Both Address and ZIP Code: Holiday and Holliday, 72925 and 79225
5	**B.** Address Only: Headley and Hadley
6	**A.** No Errors
7	**A.** No Errors
8	**C.** Zip Code Only: 66161-5265 and 66161-5565
9	**B.** Address Only: 442 and 424
10	**D.** Both Address and ZIP Code: Quaker and Quakker, 18120-1398 and 18720-1398
11	**A.** No Errors
12	**C.** Zip Code Only: 12202-1619 and 12202-1919
13	**D.** Both Address and ZIP Code: Dairy and Dary, 47654 and 47624
14	**B.** Address Only: Ct. and Cir.
15	**C.** Zip Code Only: 21789-4524 and 21189-4524

Address Checking Example 4: Below is a list of 15 pairs of addresses. Compare each pair of addresses for errors and mark the answer sheet to indicate errors found as follows:

A. No Errors   **B.** Address Only   **C.** Zip Code Only   **D.** Both Address and ZIP Code

	Correct List of Addresses		Address List to be Checked		
	Address	**ZIP**	**Address**	**ZIP**	**Answer Grid**
1	3614 Ebony Ave. Wilkes, PA	52306	3614 Ebbony Ave. Wilkes, PA	52806	Ⓐ Ⓑ Ⓒ Ⓓ
2	7657 Yeager Pkwy. Bundy, SC	42328-0013	7657 Yaeger Pkwy. Bundy, SC	42328-0013	Ⓐ Ⓑ Ⓒ Ⓓ
3	2455 Clement Rd. Carnac, AK	15705-1731	2455 Clement Rd. Carnac, AK	15705-1131	Ⓐ Ⓑ Ⓒ Ⓓ
4	P.O. Box 4480 Coalville, PA	03414-2641	P.O. Box 4480 Coalville, PA	03414-2641	Ⓐ Ⓑ Ⓒ Ⓓ
5	1831 Charles Ct. Mentoray, IL	53637	1831 Charles Ct. Mantoray, IL	53631	Ⓐ Ⓑ Ⓒ Ⓓ
6	3924 Surf Way Blouton, MA	51436	3924 Surf Way Bluoton, MA	51436	Ⓐ Ⓑ Ⓒ Ⓓ
7	777 Flamingo Road Fallville, AR	10005-2542	777 Flamingo Road Fallville, AR	10005-2542	Ⓐ Ⓑ Ⓒ Ⓓ
8	56 Lakeview Road Mandiville, AR	07643	56 Lakerview Road Mandiville, AR	07648	Ⓐ Ⓑ Ⓒ Ⓓ
9	6816 Pacific Street South Town, NY	03915	6816 Pacific Street South Town, NY	03915	Ⓐ Ⓑ Ⓒ Ⓓ
10	8462 Park Terrace Loadington, OR	09018-3644	8462 Park Terrace Loadington, OR	09108-3644	Ⓐ Ⓑ Ⓒ Ⓓ
11	3411 Cactus St. Marmac, TX	08214	3411 Cactus St. Tarmac, TX	08214	Ⓐ Ⓑ Ⓒ Ⓓ
12	9872 Leggert Cir. Gaynor, NJ	17305-2627	9872 Legert Cir. Gaynor, NJ	17302-2627	Ⓐ Ⓑ Ⓒ Ⓓ
13	5761 Attica Lane Volker, FL	55194-0180	5761 Attica Lane Volker, FL	52194-0180	Ⓐ Ⓑ Ⓒ Ⓓ
14	6213 Rome Ave. Sunnyside, KS	21104-1029	6213 Rome Ave. Sunnyside, KS	21104 1029	Ⓐ Ⓑ Ⓒ Ⓓ
15	4827 Powers Ln. Plimpton, CA	44835	4827 Powders Ln. Plimpton, CA	44835	Ⓐ Ⓑ Ⓒ Ⓓ

Address Checking Example 4

	Answers
1	**D.** Both Address and ZIP Code: Ebony and Ebbony, 52306 and 52806
2	**B.** Address Only: Yeager and Yaeger
3	**C.** Zip Code Only: 15705-1731 and 15705-1131
4	**A.** No Errors
5	**D.** Both Address and ZIP Code: Mentoray and Mantorey, 53637 and 53631
6	**B.** Address Only: Blouton and Bluoton
7	**A.** No Errors
8	**D.** Both Address and ZIP Code: Lakeview and Lakerview, 07643 and 07648
9	**A.** No Errors
10	**C.** Zip Code Only: 09018-3644 and 09108-3644
11	**B.** Address Only: Marmac and Tarmac
12	**D.** Both Address and ZIP Code: Leggert and Legert, 17305-2627 and 17302-2627
13	**C.** Zip Code Only: 55194-0180 and 52194-0180
14	**A.** No Errors
15	**B.** Address Only: Powers and Powders

Address Checking Example 5: Below is a list of 15 pairs of addresses. Compare each pair of addresses for errors and mark the answer sheet to indicate errors found as follows:

A. No Errors   **B.** Address Only   **C.** Zip Code Only   **D.** Both Address and ZIP Code

	Correct List of Addresses		Address List to be Checked		Answer Grid
	Address	ZIP	Address	ZIP	
1	3115 Farms Ave. Adam, MD	07013-2277	3115 Farms Ave. Adam, MD	07073-2277	Ⓐ Ⓑ Ⓒ Ⓓ
2	2116 Fairfield Ct. St. John's, MD	08173	2116 Fairfield Ct. St. John's, MD	08173	Ⓐ Ⓑ Ⓒ Ⓓ
3	7453 Glasser St. Stepford, MA	37150-6219	7453 Glasser St. Stepford, MA	37150-6216	Ⓐ Ⓑ Ⓒ Ⓓ
4	5128 Princess Ln. Warrant, TX	33283-1079	5128 Princess Ln. Warant, TX	33283-1079	Ⓐ Ⓑ Ⓒ Ⓓ
5	6918 Grace Street Culler, PA	44131-6761	6918 Grace Street Culler, PA	44131-6761	Ⓐ Ⓑ Ⓒ Ⓓ
6	4146 Dawn Way Diamond, OR	22746	4146 Daun Way Diamond, OR	22146	Ⓐ Ⓑ Ⓒ Ⓓ
7	3417 Baker Street Crossbay, NJ	61221-3243	3417 Bakker Street Crossbay, NJ	61221-3243	Ⓐ Ⓑ Ⓒ Ⓓ
8	6842 Forest Pkwy. Greenfield, NY	05321	6842 Forest Pkwy. Greenfield, NY	05231	Ⓐ Ⓑ Ⓒ Ⓓ
9	9114 King Cir. Clinton, AR	73023-8941	9114 Kling Cir. Clinton, AR	73023-8947	Ⓐ Ⓑ Ⓒ Ⓓ
10	3117 Boulder Lane White Forest, AR	27295	3117 Boulder Lane White Forest, AR	27595	Ⓐ Ⓑ Ⓒ Ⓓ
11	92 Realty Terrace Condor, IL	62945	92 Realty Terrace Condor, IL	62945	Ⓐ Ⓑ Ⓒ Ⓓ
12	P.O. Box 3771 Croton, WA	57142-4249	P.O. Box 3771 Cruton, WA	57142-4249	Ⓐ Ⓑ Ⓒ Ⓓ
13	9702 Strommer Rd. Ganning, NJ	38876-6593	9702 Stromer Rd. Ganning, NJ	38879-6593	Ⓐ Ⓑ Ⓒ Ⓓ
14	8924 Buster Road Magee, FL	09201-4104	8924 Buster Road Magee, FL	00201 4104	Ⓐ Ⓑ Ⓒ Ⓓ
15	3393 Market Ave. Sayville, OH	75248	3893 Market Ave. Sayville, OH	75248	Ⓐ Ⓑ Ⓒ Ⓓ

Address Checking Example 5

	Answers
1	**C.** Zip Code Only: 07013-2277 and 07073-2277
2	**A.** No Errors
3	**C.** Zip Code Only: 37150-6219 and 37150-6216
4	**B.** Address Only: Warrant and Warant
5	**A.** No Errors
6	**D.** Both Address and ZIP Code: Dawn and Daun, 22746 and 22146
7	**B.** Address Only: Baker and Bakker
8	**C.** Zip Code Only: 05321 and 05231
9	**D.** Both Address and ZIP Code: King and Kling, 73023-8941 and 73023-8947
10	**C.** Zip Code Only: 27295 and 27595
11	**A.** No Errors
12	**B.** Address Only: Croton and Cruton
13	**D.** Both Address and ZIP Code: Strommer and Stromer, 38876-6593 and 38879-6593
14	**A.** No Errors
15	**B.** Address Only: 3393 and 3893

Address Checking Exercise 1: (Time limit 6 min.) Below is a list of 30 pairs of addresses. Compare each pair of addresses for errors and mark the answer sheet as follows:

A. No Errors   **B.** Address Only   **C.** Zip Code Only   **D.** Both Address and ZIP Code

	Correct List of Addresses		Address List to be Checked		
	Address	**ZIP**	**Address**	**ZIP**	**Answer Grid**
1	3283 Summer Ln. Trapper, FL	27210-3186	3283 Sumner Ln. Trapper, FL	27210-3186	Ⓐ Ⓑ Ⓒ Ⓓ
2	6711 Hector Road Willis, CT	74516	6711 Hektor Road Willis, CT	74516	Ⓐ Ⓑ Ⓒ Ⓓ
3	P.O. Box 9113 Chorale, MD	21101-1691	P.O. Box 9113 Chorale, MD	21101-1691	Ⓐ Ⓑ Ⓒ Ⓓ
4	241 Harrison Ave. Savin, MS	69146	241 Harrison Ave. Savin, MS	69746	Ⓐ Ⓑ Ⓒ Ⓓ
5	241 Lumber Cir. Aruba, CA	76454	241 Lumber St. Aruba, CA	79454	Ⓐ Ⓑ Ⓒ Ⓓ
6	6377 Contract Ln. Kayton, AK	32678-3642	6377 Contract Ln. Kayton, AK	32678-3645	Ⓐ Ⓑ Ⓒ Ⓓ
7	672 Bravo Street Greenville, SC	63405	672 Bravo Street Greenview, SC	63402	Ⓐ Ⓑ Ⓒ Ⓓ
8	7714 Clifford Rd. Irving, VA	45238-0130	7114 Clifford Rd. Irving, VA	45238-0130	Ⓐ Ⓑ Ⓒ Ⓓ
9	4321 Irvington Ave. Sycamore, MI	03565-6192	4327 Irvington Ave. Sycamore, MI	03565-6195	Ⓐ Ⓑ Ⓒ Ⓓ
10	5226 Ray Way Pounder, RI	16057-7121	5226 Ray Way Pounder, RI	16057-7121	Ⓐ Ⓑ Ⓒ Ⓓ
11	7618 Waret St. Enderton, KS	36371	7618 Waret St. Enderton, KS	36871	Ⓐ Ⓑ Ⓒ Ⓓ
12	9641 Gator St. Endville, MO	45163	9641 Gator St. Endville, MO	45763	Ⓐ Ⓑ Ⓒ Ⓓ
13	8112 Quarter Ave. Bath Beach, CA	06432	8112 Quarter Ave. Bath Beach, CA	06432	Ⓐ Ⓑ Ⓒ Ⓓ
14	5734 People Lane Benson, CA	00432	5734 People Lane Benton, CA	06482	Ⓐ Ⓑ Ⓒ Ⓓ
15	672 Lifton Ct. Menington, CT	09513	672 Lifton Ct. Meninton, CT	09513	Ⓐ Ⓑ Ⓒ Ⓓ

Address Checking Exercise 1 (cont'd): Continue to compare each pair of addresses for errors and mark the answer sheet as follows:

A. No Errors   **B.** Address Only   **C.** Zip Code Only   **D.** Both Address and ZIP Code

	Correct List of Addresses		Address List to be Checked		
	Address	**ZIP**	**Address**	**ZIP**	**Answer Grid**
16	3397 Eastern Rd. Nippon, CA	02182-4634	3379 Eastern Rd. Nippon, CA	02182-4634	Ⓐ Ⓑ Ⓒ Ⓓ
17	5519 Silver Ln. Strummer, AK	07317	5519 Silver Ln. Strumner, AK	07317	Ⓐ Ⓑ Ⓒ Ⓓ
18	6615 Jasper Ave. Shephard, NY	26204-1518	6615 Jasper Ave. Shepard, NY	26204-7518	Ⓐ Ⓑ Ⓒ Ⓓ
19	8114 South Way East Port, MD	33291-0379	8114 South Way East Port, MD	33291-0376	Ⓐ Ⓑ Ⓒ Ⓓ
20	7237 Kramer St. Salem, MO	39213-7718	7237 Kramer St. Salem, MO	39213-7718	Ⓐ Ⓑ Ⓒ Ⓓ
21	4933 Media Pkwy. Arlo, WA	21726	4933 Media Pkwy. Arlo, WA	27726	Ⓐ Ⓑ Ⓒ Ⓓ
22	2482 Candle St. Seneca, NJ	05113-2168	2482 Candle St. Seneka, NJ	05113-2163	Ⓐ Ⓑ Ⓒ Ⓓ
23	7119 Luke Ct. Waverly, MI	04772	7119 Luke Ct. Waverly, MI	04772	Ⓐ Ⓑ Ⓒ Ⓓ
24	2124 Spring Cir. Davenville, CT	38151-7220	2124 Spring Cir. Davenvile, CT	38151-7250	Ⓐ Ⓑ Ⓒ Ⓓ
25	3436 West Ave. Bunsky, KS	34824-1080	3436 West Ave. Bundy, KS	34824-1080	Ⓐ Ⓑ Ⓒ Ⓓ
26	5813 Clover St. Mastic, OH	45132-6762	5818 Clover St. Mastic, OH	45132-6162	Ⓐ Ⓑ Ⓒ Ⓓ
27	92 Main Road Lepper, RI	32747	92 Main Road Lemper, RI	35747	Ⓐ Ⓑ Ⓒ Ⓓ
28	P.O. Box 3731 Brassford, ME	71222-4244	P.O. Box 3731 Brassford, ME	71222-4244	Ⓐ Ⓑ Ⓒ Ⓓ
29	68 Canary St. Tucker, CA	06322	63 Canary St. Tucker, CA	06322	Ⓐ Ⓑ Ⓒ Ⓓ
30	9746 Corner Lane Ford, FL	83024-8941	9746 Corner Lane Fords, FL	83024-8941	Ⓐ Ⓑ Ⓒ Ⓓ

Address Checking Exercise 2: (Time limit 6 min.) Below is a list of 30 pairs of addresses. Compare each pair of addresses for errors and mark the answer sheet as follows:

A. No Errors   **B.** Address Only   **C.** Zip Code Only   **D.** Both Address and ZIP Code

	Correct List of Addresses		Address List to be Checked		Answer Grid
	Address	**ZIP**	**Address**	**ZIP**	
1	5512 Norway Ct. Appler, MS	37286	5512 Norway Ct. Appler, MS	37209	A B C D
2	3837 Norman Ave. Bay View, CT	73946	3837 Normen Ave. Bay View, CT	73946	A B C D
3	1924 Bush St. Miller, IL	67412-5250	1924 Bush St. Miner, IL	67472-5250	A B C D
4	72 Constitution Ln. Tarkadered, OR	70282-5263	72 Constitution Ln. Tarkadered, OR	70282-5263	A B C D
5	P.O. Box 813 Olsen, OR	48877-7594	P.O. Box 8133 Olsen, OR	48877-7594	A B C D
6	7337 Maloney Rd. Carroway, VA	37221-4285	7337 Maloney Rd. Caroway, VA	37251-4285	A B C D
7	4684 Optimum St. Corvette, TX	85347	4684 Optimum St. Corvelle, TX	85357	A B C D
8	3731 Military Way North King, NY	85417	3731 Military Way North King, NY	85471	A B C D
9	6118 Evelyn Street South Bay, PA	32110-2792	6118 Evlyn Street South Bay, PA	32110-2792	A B C D
10	8156 Mexican Ave. Parish, FL	69461	8156 Mexican Ave. Parish, FL	69491	A B C D
11	6713 Fern Terrace Oakville, MN	76543	6713 Fern Terrace Oakville, MN	76548	A B C D
12	7548 Proper Lane Homer, AR	33766-1643	7548 Prosper Lane Homer, AR	33766-1643	A B C D
13	172 Beach Cir. Herkimer, NJ	73406	172 Beach Cir. Herkimur, NJ	73409	A B C D
14	4713 Miranda Road Quiet Bay, MA	55237-2104	4713 Miranda Road Quiet Bay, MA	55237-2104	A B C D
15	3273 Busy Pkwy. Lakeview, SC	17175-7079	3273 Buzy Pkwy. Lakeview, SC	17175-7079	A B C D

Address Checking Exercise 2 (cont'd): Continue to compare each pair of addresses for errors and mark the answer sheet as follows:

A. No Errors   **B.** Address Only   **C.** Zip Code Only   **D.** Both Address and ZIP Code

	Correct List of Addresses		Address List to be Checked		
	Address	**ZIP**	**Address**	**ZIP**	**Answer Grid**
16	6347 Classic Rd. S. Monica, CA	14433-7293	6347 Classic Rd. S. Monica, CA	14438-7293	A B C D
17	1876 Gate Ln. Ryder, NY	47462	1876 Gate Ln. Ryder, NY	47462	A B C D
18	1072 Ellenby St. Collier, PA	55274	1072 Ellendy St. Collier, PA	55274	A B C D
19	681 Dickens Way Harvey, CA	10004-0468	681 Dikkens Way Harvey, CA	10004-0498	A B C D
20	P.O.Box 2184 Pinnacle, VA	08543	P.O.Box 2184 Pinnacle, VA	08243	A B C D
21	2816 Wayly Road Montview, MN	87531	2816 Wayly Road Montview, MN	87581	A B C D
22	3492 Monaor Ct. Steiner, SC	21083-6735	3492 Monor Ct. Steiner, SC	21083-6735	A B C D
23	746 Vetran Pkwy. South End, NY	37103-2692	746 Vetran Pkwy. South End, NJ	37103-2629	A B C D
24	593 Forest Ter. Dinkens, IL	43390-1396	593 Forest Ter. Dinkens, IL	43390-1396	A B C D
25	4252 Mexico Ave. Fuller, MA	38414-6617	4225 Mexico Ave. Fuller, MA	38414-6617	A B C D
26	7189 Darby Street Molly, AR	32625	7189 Darcy Street Molly, AR	32622	A B C D
27	632 Boxer Cir. Rangoon, NJ	15321-6182	632 Boxers Cir. Rangoon, NJ	15321-6182	A B C D
28	9726 Bradford Rd. Martin, TX	05681	9726 Bradford Rd. Martin, TX	05981	A B C D
29	3582 Zebra Lane Pacific, FL	47252-8331	3582 Zebra Lane Pacific, FL	47255-8331	A B C D
30	3746 Candle St. Brooklyn, NY	11285	3746 Candle St. Brooklyn, NY	11285	A B C D

Address Checking Exercise 3: (Time limit 6 min.) Below is a list of 30 pairs of addresses. Compare each pair of addresses for errors and mark the answer sheet as follows:

A. No Errors   **B.** Address Only   **C.** Zip Code Only   **D.** Both Address and ZIP Code

	Correct List of Addresses		Address List to be Checked		
	Address	**ZIP**	**Address**	**ZIP**	**Answer Grid**
1	5062 Flower St. Culty, MO	35383-2181	5062 Flower St. Culty, MO	35383-2187	Ⓐ Ⓑ Ⓒ Ⓓ
2	183 Eastern Pkwy. Puller, ME	46133-6863	183 Eastern Pkwy. Pulter, ME	46733-6863	Ⓐ Ⓑ Ⓒ Ⓓ
3	7002 Marlow Ln. Commons, MD	43849	7002 Marlow Ln. Commons, MD	43849	Ⓐ Ⓑ Ⓒ Ⓓ
4	1791 Ferndale Cir. Century, MS	82113-5145	1791 Ferndale Cir. Century, MS	85113-5145	Ⓐ Ⓑ Ⓒ Ⓓ
5	4447 Welford Way Exeter, OH	07433	4447 Wellford Way Exeter, OH	07433	Ⓐ Ⓑ Ⓒ Ⓓ
6	3912 Redford Road Long Falls, KS	92113-7852	3912 Redford Road Lang Falls, KS	92173-7852	Ⓐ Ⓑ Ⓒ Ⓓ
7	P.O. Box 5937 Hamlet, WA	48397	P.O. Box 5937 Hamlet, WA	48397	Ⓐ Ⓑ Ⓒ Ⓓ
8	98 Hemingway Rd. Booker, CT	84057	98 Hemingway Rd. Bocker, CT	84057	Ⓐ Ⓑ Ⓒ Ⓓ
9	6394 Finn Pkwy. Foulder, MI	78124-5358	6894 Finn Pkwy. Foulder, MI	78124-5358	Ⓐ Ⓑ Ⓒ Ⓓ
10	9283 Pumpkin St. Bemington, MI	49776-7605	9283 Pumpkin St. Bemington, MI	49776-7905	Ⓐ Ⓑ Ⓒ Ⓓ
11	2426 Flavos St. Puller, AK	81384-5367	2426 Flavor St. Puller, AK	81384-5367	Ⓐ Ⓑ Ⓒ Ⓓ
12	3912 Hudson Ave. Atlantic, RI	96458	3912 Hadson Ave. Atlantic, RI	96458	Ⓐ Ⓑ Ⓒ Ⓓ
13	5782 Tibet Lane Mirage, AR	38321-5394	5782 Tibet Lane Mirage, AR	38321-5894	Ⓐ Ⓑ Ⓒ Ⓓ
14	661 Martin Ct. Bayshore, PA	94318	001 Martin Ct. Bayshore, PA	94318	Ⓐ Ⓑ Ⓒ Ⓓ
15	7664 Govern Lane West Lake, CA	43221-2894	7694 Govern Lane West Lake, CA	43221-5894	Ⓐ Ⓑ Ⓒ Ⓓ

Address Checking Exercise 3 (cont'd): Continue to compare each pair of addresses for errors and mark the answer sheet as follows:

A. No Errors   **B.** Address Only   **C.** Zip Code Only   **D.** Both Address and ZIP Code

	Correct List of Addresses		Address List to be Checked		
	Address	**ZIP**	**Address**	**ZIP**	**Answer Grid**
16	940 Albany Pkwy. Albany, CA	87644	640 Albany Pkwy. Albany, CA	37644	A B C D
17	2872 Brendan St. King City, SC	70562	2872 Brendan St. King City, SC	70562	A B C D
18	2105 Napper Ave. Huron, KS	44867-2741	2105 Napper Ave. Huron, KS	44867-2741	A B C D
19	158 Lorraine Ct. Perris, MO	84315	158 Lorraine Ct. Perris, MO	84375	A B C D
20	7328 Monk Street Huron, MD	45326-3214	7828 Monk Street Huron, MD	45325-3214	A B C D
21	7625 Back Ter. Hemet, OH	28271-8197	7625 Back Ter. Hemet, OH	28271-8197	A B C D
22	1193 Avelon St. Pomona, MS	43541-2937	1193 Avellon St. Pomona, MS	43541-2931	A B C D
23	4182 Navy Way Gustine, NY	74624	4182 Navy Way Gustine, NY	74924	A B C D
24	2446 Spring Lane Rialto, TX	52745	2446 Spring Lake Rialto, TX	52742	A B C D
25	776 Statler Cir. Bishop, MI	01004-4680	776 Statler Cir. Bishop, MI	01004-4680	A B C D
26	6899 Reserve Ln. Marina, WA	85430	6896 Reserve Ln. Marina, WA	85430	A B C D
27	P.O. Box 1821 Brea, PA	78531	P.O. Box 1851 Brea, PA	78231	A B C D
28	8246 Stepford Rd. Tracy, ME	12083-7355	8246 Stepford Rd. Tracy, ME	12083-7355	A B C D
29	5326 India Road Malibu, RI	74281	5326 India Road Malibu, RI	74581	A B C D
30	3424 District Ave. Montclair, NJ	31730-6291	3454 District Ave. Montclair, NJ	31730-6291	A B C D

Address Checking Exercise 4: (Time limit 6 min.) Below is a list of 30 pairs of addresses. Compare each pair of addresses for errors and mark the answer sheet as follows:

A. No Errors   **B.** Address Only   **C.** Zip Code Only   **D.** Both Address and ZIP Code

	Correct List of Addresses		Address List to be Checked		
	Address	**ZIP**	**Address**	**ZIP**	**Answer Grid**
1	9400 Circle Ln. Hughson, CT	33490-3916	9400 Circle Ln. Hugson, CT	33490-3916	Ⓐ Ⓑ Ⓒ Ⓓ
2	P.O. Box 6259 Etna, MN	84314-6176	P.O. Box 6259 Etna, MN	84314-6179	Ⓐ Ⓑ Ⓒ Ⓓ
3	4569 Jenkins Road Fortuna, CA	26253	4569 Jenkin Road Fortuna, CA	26553	Ⓐ Ⓑ Ⓒ Ⓓ
4	3742 Wronsky Way Altura, TX	53121-1826	3742 Wronsky Way Altura, TX	53121-1826	Ⓐ Ⓑ Ⓒ Ⓓ
5	9172 Crawford St. Lakeport, NY	56890	9172 Cramford St. Lakeport, NY	56890	Ⓐ Ⓑ Ⓒ Ⓓ
6	671 Writers Ln. Redding, FL	72531-3183	671 Writer Ln. Redding, FL	72531-3983	Ⓐ Ⓑ Ⓒ Ⓓ
7	2239 Parsons Ct. Selma, MA	53812-1824	2239 Parson Ct. Selma, MA	53812-1824	Ⓐ Ⓑ Ⓒ Ⓓ
8	7925 Jersey Pkwy. Lafayette, NJ	61335-8635	7925 Jersey Pkwy. Lafayette, NJ	61335-8685	Ⓐ Ⓑ Ⓒ Ⓓ
9	4471 Tenent Street Shafter, VA	38495	4471 Tenent Street Shafter, VA	38495	Ⓐ Ⓑ Ⓒ Ⓓ
10	88 Revenue Rd. Arvin, AR	28113-1452	88 Revenue Rd. Alvin, AR	28113-1452	Ⓐ Ⓑ Ⓒ Ⓓ
11	5632 Trade Ave. Napa, IL	74034	5632 Trade Ave. Napa, IL	74034	Ⓐ Ⓑ Ⓒ Ⓓ
12	4263 Region Lane Chico, OR	93225-4651	4263 Region Lake Chico, OR	93225-4621	Ⓐ Ⓑ Ⓒ Ⓓ
13	8563 Newman St. Orange, NY	48166	8563 Newman St. Orange, NY	48166	Ⓐ Ⓑ Ⓒ Ⓓ
14	1472 Jamaica Cir. Sonora, AK	83974	1472 Jamaica Cir. Sonora, AK	83974	Ⓐ Ⓑ Ⓒ Ⓓ
15	6368 Hill Terrace Paramount, OH	68241-4179	6368 Hill Terrace Paramount, OH	68241-4179	Ⓐ Ⓑ Ⓒ Ⓓ

Address Checking Exercise 4 (cont'd): Continue to compare each pair of addresses for errors and mark the answer sheet as follows:

A. No Errors   **B.** Address Only   **C.** Zip Code Only   **D.** Both Address and ZIP Code

	Correct List of Addresses		**Address List to be Checked**		**Answer Grid**
	Address	**ZIP**	**Address**	**ZIP**	
16	8819 Terrace Ct. Varian, PA	71030-4464	889 Terrace Ct. Varian, PA	77030-4464	A B C D
17	410 Peach Road Dunking, MN	29350	410 Parch Road Dunking, MN	29350	A B C D
18	6740 Venetian Ln. Celia, FL	46730	6740 Venetian Ln. Celia, FL	49730	A B C D
19	3217 Johnson St. Quincy, TX	71021-4163	327 Johnson St. Quincy, TX	71021-4193	A B C D
20	1599 Juniper Rd. Reily, NY	64385	1599 Juniper Rd. Reily, NY	64385	A B C D
21	46 Clifford Rd. Flatly, VA	84754	46 Clifford Rd. Flatly, VA	84254	A B C D
22	2632 Prince St. Selma, FL	51540-4712	2632 Prince St. Selma, FL	51540-4712	A B C D
23	5516 Bangor Way Evers, AK	50862-3872	5516 Bangor Way Evers, AK	50862-3372	A B C D
24	982 Warrior Pkwy. Topper, CT	83324-2012	985 Warior Pkwy. Topper, CT	83324-2015	A B C D
25	5361 Bradley Ave. Delta, PA	50454	5361 Bradley Ave. Delta, PA	50454	A B C D
26	7125 Florinda Cir. Norman, CT	89722-1221	7125 Florida Cir. Norman, CT	89725-1221	A B C D
27	3884 Place Ave. Iberia, OR	12395	3834 Place Ave. Iberia, OR	12395	A B C D
28	1341 Porter Lane Unger, MA	54757	1341 Porter Lane Unger, MA	54757	A B C D
29	4637 Lion Terrace Valmont, NY	62547	4637 Lion Terrace Valmont, NY	62547	A B C D
30	P.O. Box 8739 Keller, IL	11231-1625	P.O. Box 8739 Keller, IL	11231-7625	A B C D

Address Checking Exercise 5: (Time limit 6 min.) Below is a list of 30 pairs of addresses. Compare each pair of addresses for errors and mark the answer sheet as follows:

A. No Errors   **B.** Address Only   **C.** Zip Code Only   **D.** Both Address and ZIP Code

	Correct List of Addresses		Address List to be Checked		
	Address	ZIP	Address	ZIP	Answer Grid
1	5921 Quaker St. Broom, MO	25645	592 Quaker St. Broom, MO	25645	A B C D
2	4293 Tipper Ave. Parsons, NJ	12132-1625	4293 Tipper Ave. Parsons, NJ	12132-1655	A B C D
3	6788 Parker Ln. Grace, SC	54847	6788 Parker Ln. Grace, SC	54847	A B C D
4	1516 Minor Ct. Odeon, RI	12386	1516 Minors Ct. Odeon, RI	12336	A B C D
5	882 Reagan St. Fogel, CA	98724-1273	882 Raegan St. Fogel, CA	98724-1273	A B C D
6	P.O. Box 7405 Absicon, AR	50453	P.O. Box 7402 Absicon, AR	50458	A B C D
7	7489 Granger Way Nolly, MD	82224-2012	7489 Granger Way Nolly, MD	82242-2012	A B C D
8	2273 Cooper Lane Manor, MS	50751-3873	2273 Cooper Lane Manor, MS	50751-3873	A B C D
9	3825 Kronos Road Hilton, PA	51340-4721	3825 Kronos Road Hilter, PA	51340-4721	A B C D
10	98 Simford Rd. Campers, WA	93654	98 Simford St. Campers, WA	93624	A B C D
11	6204 Telco Ln. Granary, MI	64485	6204 Telco Ln. Granary, MI	64485	A B C D
12	5657 Hartford Ave. Love, ME	70142-4136	5627 Hartford Ave. Love, ME	70142-4136	A B C D
13	8119 Trans Pkwy. Younkins, KS	46730	819 Trans Pkwy. Younkins, KS	46736	A B C D
14	4213 Downy Cir. Jenkins, NJ	29351	4213 Downy Cir. Jenkins, NJ	29351	A B C D
15	37 Square Terrace Waring, OH	71016-5245	37 Square Terrace Waring, OH	71019-5245	A B C D

Address Checking Exercise 5 (cont'd): Continue to compare each pair of addresses for errors and mark the answer sheet as follows:

A. No Errors   **B.** Address Only   **C.** Zip Code Only   **D.** Both Address and ZIP Code

	Correct List of Addresses		Address List to be Checked		
	Address	**ZIP**	**Address**	**ZIP**	**Answer Grid**
16	P.O Box 2119 Absalom, NJ	11050-6238	P.O Box 2119 Absalom, NJ	11050-6288	A B C D
17	2257 Fuller St. Crawford, AK	78824	2257 Fuller St. Crawford, AK	78824	A B C D
18	6744 Farm Way Ripley, MD	33221-4344	6744 Farm West Ripley, MD	33221-4344	A B C D
19	4283 Justice St. Arrow, CA	04302	4288 Justice St. Arrow, CA	04305	A B C D
20	3914 Olmert Road Kensy, RI	48101-7732	3914 Olmert Road Kensy, RI	48101-7732	A B C D
21	181 Shopping Cir. Juniper, MO	46438	181 Shopping Cir. Juniper, MO	49438	A B C D
22	8338 Queen St. Brinkley, ME	51695	8338 Queen St. Brinkley, ME	51695	A B C D
23	5467 Market Ln. Hollis, CA	68141-4913	5467 Market St. Hollis, CA	68141-4973	A B C D
24	7392 Sailor Lane Dupry, AR	89974-4976	7392 Salor Lane Dupry, AR	89974-4976	A B C D
25	4668 Talley Pkwy. Gaston, PA	26276-5652	4668 Talley Pkwy. Gaston, PA	26276-5655	A B C D
26	667 Woodley Ct. Courtly, KS	24078	667 Wodley Ct. Courtly, KS	24073	A B C D
27	3746 Wolf Ave. Mineola, NJ	21092-1893	3749 Wolf Ave. Mineola, NJ	21092-1893	A B C D
28	822 Vermont St. Smith, SC	56243	822 Vermont St. Smith, SC	56243	A B C D
29	4080 Mirror Road Artford, OH	10131-6162	4080 Mirror Road Artford, OH	10113-6162	A B C D
30	62 Church St. Melvin, MS	75548	26 Church St. Melvin, MS	75548	A B C D

Address Checking Exercise #1 Answers

1	B	6	C	11	C	16	B	21	C	26	D
2	B	7	D	12	C	17	B	22	D	27	D
3	A	8	B	13	A	18	D	23	A	28	A
4	C	9	D	14	D	19	C	24	D	29	B
5	D	10	A	15	B	20	A	25	B	30	B

Address Checking Exercise #2 Answers

1	C	6	D	11	C	16	C	21	C	26	D
2	B	7	D	12	B	17	A	22	B	27	B
3	D	8	C	13	D	18	B	23	D	28	C
4	A	9	B	14	A	19	D	24	A	29	C
5	B	10	C	15	B	20	C	25	B	30	A

Address Checking Exercise #3 Answers

1	C	6	D	11	B	16	D	21	A	26	B
2	D	7	A	12	B	17	A	22	D	27	D
3	A	8	B	13	C	18	A	23	C	28	A
4	C	9	B	14	A	19	C	24	D	29	C
5	B	10	C	15	D	20	D	25	B	30	B

Address Checking Exercise #4 Answers

1	B	6	D	11	A	16	D	21	C	26	D
2	C	7	B	12	D	17	B	22	A	27	B
3	D	8	C	13	A	18	C	23	C	28	A
4	A	9	A	14	A	19	D	24	D	29	A
5	B	10	B	15	A	20	A	25	A	30	C

Address Checking Exercise #5 Answers

1	B	6	D	11	A	16	C	21	C	26	D
2	C	7	C	12	B	17	A	22	A	27	B
3	A	8	A	13	D	18	B	23	D	28	A
4	D	9	R	14	A	19	D	24	B	29	C
5	B	10	D	15	C	20	A	25	C	30	B

FORMS COMPLETION 2

Postal employees come in contact with postal forms every day. Sometimes postal employees have to complete forms. Sometimes they must review them for accuracy. To work efficiently and with minimal errors, a postal employee must understand forms and be comfortable with their use.

Part	Time Allowed	Number of Ques.	Description of Question
2. Forms Completion	15 minutes	30	Correctly complete forms.

The forms completion section of the postal test presents you with sample forms which you must use to answer 30 questions within the allotted 15 minutes. The forms used in this book are not USPS forms. If you wish to review official USPS forms, please visit: www.USPS.com

IMPORTANT!	On this forms completion part of the test there is **NO** penalty for guessing.
	You **will** receive credit if you guess correctly.
	You will **NOT** be penalized if you guess incorrectly.
	Therefore, you should answer all 30 questions, even if you have to guess on some of them.

Hint #1:

Look at the form carefully.

1. Title of form (What is the purpose of the form?)
2. Titles of sections (Who is responsible for filling out each section?)
3. What information is asked for in each section?

   (Address, description of contents of package, postage, other fees, etc.)

Hint #2:

Answer **ALL** the questions. If you don't know the answer, **GUESS.** In this section there is NO penalty for guessing wrong.

Hint #3:

Keep in mind that this section is timed (30 questions in 15 minutes). Try to work as quickly and accurately as you can. Do **NOT** linger on a question until you are 200% certain that you answered correctly.

Hint #4:

Try to look at as many official USPS forms as you can. USPS forms may be found online at www.USPS.com. The more familiar and comfortable you become with these forms, the greater the likelihood that you will attain a high score.

———————

The following pages contain 5 practice forms

These forms, like all other forms in this book, are for practice and are not USPS forms.

Examine each form. Take as long as you wish. These 5 examples are not timed. The purpose of these forms and questions relating to them is to provide you with brief exercises to help you develop an approach to tackling this type of question. Later, in the seven simulated postal exams, you will have timed practice.

Good luck!

FORMS COMPLETION EXAMPLE #1

Study the following form, then answer the following 10 questions about the form.

(This practice example is not timed.)

1. RECEIPT FOR INSURED MAIL		
15.	2. Postage	6. ☐ Fragile 7. ☐ Perishable
		8. ☐ Liquid 9. ☐ Hazardous
	3. Insurance Fee	10.
		11. Stamp Postmark Here
	4. Handling Fee	
	5. Total (Postage plus Fees) $_____	
12. Addressee (Sent to):		
13. Street, Apt. Number; or PO Box Number		
14. City, State and ZIP		

	Question	Answer Grid
1	The name of the person or company to whom the article is sent to should be entered in box : A. 13 B. 12 C. 14 D. 10	Ⓐ Ⓑ Ⓒ Ⓓ
2	The postmark should be properly stamped in area: A. 15 B. 2 C. 5 D. 11	Ⓐ Ⓑ Ⓒ Ⓓ

3	Where on this form should the ZIP number of the addressee be entered? A. 11 B. 12 C. 13 D. 14	Ⓐ Ⓑ Ⓒ Ⓓ
4	Which of the following is a correct entry for box 4? A. 6/12/10 B. NYC C. $6.50 D. Fragile	Ⓐ Ⓑ Ⓒ Ⓓ
5	The contents of the article include fresh New York State apples. Because of this, which of the following boxes should be checked? A. 9 B. 7 C. 14 D. 10	Ⓐ Ⓑ Ⓒ Ⓓ
6	A $25.00 insurance fee was paid. In which box should this be indicated? A. 2 B. 12 C. 3 D. 10	Ⓐ Ⓑ Ⓒ Ⓓ
7	Total paid for postage was $10.00. The total paid for other fees was $6.00 ($3.00 insurance fee plus $3.00 handling fee). The amount that should be entered in box 5 is: A. $10.00 B. $6.00 C. $16.00 D. $13.00	Ⓐ Ⓑ Ⓒ Ⓓ
8	In which box would you indicate that the item is dangerous and should be handled carefully? A. 6 B. 7 C. 8 D. 9	Ⓐ Ⓑ Ⓒ Ⓓ
9	Which of the following is a correct entry in box 13? A. Fragile B. $3.95 C. 14 Hale St. D. New York City	Ⓐ Ⓑ Ⓒ Ⓓ
10	A money amount is a correct entry for each of the following boxes, except: A. 11 B. 4 C. 3 D. 2	Ⓐ Ⓑ Ⓒ Ⓓ

FORMS COMPLETION EXAMPLE #2

Study the following form, then answer the following 9 questions about the form.

(This practice example is not timed.)

1. RETURN RECEIPT FOR DOMESTIC MAIL	
THIS SECTION IS TO BE COMPLETED BY THE SENDER	**THIS SECTION IS TO BE COMPLETED UPON DELIVERY OF THE ITEM**
2. ▶Sender must complete items 5, 6, (and 12, 13, 14, 15, 16, 17, 18, if applicable.) 3. ▶Sender must print sender's name and address on the reverse side of this card so that card can be returned to sender. 4. ▶Peel off glue protector strips on opposite side and attach to the back of the mail, or on the front if there is enough space.	7. Signature ▶ □ Addressee □ Agent 8. Received by (PRINT) 9. Delivery Date 10. Is delivery address same or different from item 5? □ Same □ Different (If different, write delivery address below:
5. Article addressed to:	Type of mail service: 12. □ Registered 15. □ C.O.D. 13. □ Insured 16. □ Express 14. □ Certified 17. □ Merchandise Return receipt 18. Restricted delivery (Additional fee) $_____ □ Yes
6. Article number (from service label)	

	Question	Answer Grid
1	Which of the following items is never completed by the sender? A. 15 B. 18 C. 14 D. 7	Ⓐ Ⓑ Ⓒ Ⓓ

2	The address of the addressee is entered in box: A. 6 B. 12 C. 5 D. 9	Ⓐ Ⓑ Ⓒ Ⓓ
3	Where does one get the "article number"? A. bulletin board B. newspaper C. service label D. None of the above	Ⓐ Ⓑ Ⓒ Ⓓ
4	Which of the following is a correct entry for box 8? A. 6/12/10 B. John Kern C. $6.50 D. Fragile	Ⓐ Ⓑ Ⓒ Ⓓ
5	If the article is to be mailed by express mail, which box must be checked off? A. 5 B. 16 C. 6 D. 14	Ⓐ Ⓑ Ⓒ Ⓓ
6	If an agent of the addressee receives the mail, the addressee's agent must print his name in box: A. 7 B. 8 C. 6 D. 10	Ⓐ Ⓑ Ⓒ Ⓓ
7	The darkened section of this form must be completed by: A. sender B. postal employee only C. postal supervisor D. None of the above	Ⓐ Ⓑ Ⓒ Ⓓ
8	In which box would you indicate that the type of mail service is "Certified"? A. 14 B. 15 C. 18 D. 10	Ⓐ Ⓑ Ⓒ Ⓓ
9	Which of the following is a correct entry in box 9? A. 3:00 p.m. B. 12/10 C. 7/14/10 D. 24:02	Ⓐ Ⓑ Ⓒ Ⓓ

FORMS COMPLETION EXAMPLE #3

Study the following form, then answer the following 7 questions about the form.

(This practice example is not timed.)

RECEIPT FOR REGISTERED MAIL				
:	2.Registered Number	4. Date Stamp		
1.This section is to be completed by the post office.	3. Registration Fee $ _____	5. Charge for Handling	8. Fee for Return Receipt	
		6. Postage Amount	9. Fee for Restricted Delivery	
		7. Received by		
10. This section is to be completed by the postal customer. Please PRINT with ballpoint pen, or TYPE.	11. TO:			
	12. FROM:			

FORM # 7477 (Copy 1 – Customer) (Copy 2 – Post Office)

(See information on reverse side of this form.)

Question	Answer Grid
1	The name of the person or company to whom the article is sent to should be entered in box : A. 12 B. 11 C. 10 D. 1	Ⓐ Ⓑ Ⓒ Ⓓ
2	The date should be stamped by the post office in box: A. 1 B. 10 C. 4 D. 11	Ⓐ Ⓑ Ⓒ Ⓓ
3	Where on this form should the ZIP number of the addressee be entered? A. 11 B. 12 C. 2 D. 4	Ⓐ Ⓑ Ⓒ Ⓓ
4	Which of the following is a correct entry for box 3? A. insured B. 12/11/10 C. 7.50 D. #3	Ⓐ Ⓑ Ⓒ Ⓓ
5	Which of the following boxes should not be completed by the post office? A. 4 B. 8 C. 6 D. 12	Ⓐ Ⓑ Ⓒ Ⓓ
6	A $4.75 fee for return receipt was paid. In which box should this be indicated? A. 8 B. 5 C. 9 D. 4	Ⓐ Ⓑ Ⓒ Ⓓ
7	Total paid for postage was $12.00. This amount that should be entered in box: A. 5 B. 6 C. 9 D. 8	Ⓐ Ⓑ Ⓒ Ⓓ

FORMS COMPLETION EXAMPLE #4

Study the following form, then answer the following 9 questions about the form.

(This practice example is not timed.)

STATEMENT FOR PICKUP SERVICE		
1. Information (Product)		**2. Information (Customer)**
Type of pickup service	**Quantity**	13. First and Last Name
3. Priority Mail	8.	14. Company Name
4. Express Mail	9.	15. Address 1
5. Parcel Post	10.	16. Address 2
6. Global Express Guaranteed	11.	17. City
		18. State
7. Estimated weight (total) of all packages (in pounds)	12.	19. Zip + 4

20. Affix stamps or Meter Strip in this space	**Method of Payment**
	21. ☐ Metered Postage or Stamps
	22. ☐ Postage Due Account
	23. ☐ Express Mail Corporate Account Number
	24. ☐ Check (Payable to Postmaster)
	25. ☐ Label For Merchandise Return

26. Signature of Customer	27. Signature of USPS employee	28. Pickup Date and Time

	Question	Answer Grid
1	The first and last name of the customer should be entered in box: A. 14 B. 13 C. 9 D. 2	Ⓐ Ⓑ Ⓒ Ⓓ

2	The stamps should be affixed in box: A. 8 B. 9 C. 5 D. 20	Ⓐ Ⓑ Ⓒ Ⓓ
3	Where on this form should the customer sign? A. 27 B. 28 C. 13 D. 26	Ⓐ Ⓑ Ⓒ Ⓓ
4	Which of the following is a correct entry for box 28? A. done B. 9/12/10, 10:15 a.m. C. $6.50 D. None	Ⓐ Ⓑ Ⓒ Ⓓ
5	The customer paid $16.00 in the form of a check payable to the Postmaster. Which box should be checked? A. 21 B. 7 C. 24 D. 22	Ⓐ Ⓑ Ⓒ Ⓓ
6	The pickup consists of 18 pieces of express mail. In what box should this be indicated? A. 8 B. 9 C. 10 D. 11	Ⓐ Ⓑ Ⓒ Ⓓ
7	What would be a correct entry for box 12? A. $10.00 B. 26 in. C. 4 ft. 2 in. D. 3 lbs.	Ⓐ Ⓑ Ⓒ Ⓓ
8	The customer is ABC Company. In which box would this information appear? A. 6 B. 14 C. 8 D. 9	Ⓐ Ⓑ Ⓒ Ⓓ
9	Which of the following is a correct entry in box 19? A. 39 B. 225 C. 718-456-3456 D. 11208-2546	Ⓐ Ⓑ Ⓒ Ⓓ

FORMS COMPLETION EXAMPLE #5

Study the following form, then answer the following 7 questions about the form.

(This practice example is not timed.)

HOLD MAIL (AUTHORIZATION)		
1. This form authorizes the USPS to hold mail for a minimum of 3 days but not more than 30 days for the following individual(s).		
2. Name(s)		
3. Address (including number and street, Apartment or suite number, city, state, ZIP)		
4. A. ☐ I shall pick up my mail upon my return. I understand that if I do not pick up my mail, then mail delivery will not be made until I pick up the mail. 4.B. ☐ I am authorizing the USPS to deliver all held mail and resume mail delivery on the ending date indicated below.		
5. Beginning Date To Hold Mail	6. Ending Date To Hold Mail (This date can only be changed by the customer – in writing)	7. Signature of Customer
Shaded section is for Post Office (USPS) use only.		
8. Date this form received:		
9. Carrier name and ID Number receiving this form:	10. Carrier Name	11. Carrier ID Number
12. Clerk name and ID Number receiving this form	13. Clerk Name	14. Clerk ID Number
15. If option B was selected, complete this section: 16. ☐ All mail has been picked up on (Date)_____ 17. ☐ Regular mail delivery to be resumed on (Date) _____		
Signature of: 18. USPS Employee: _____ 19. Date Signed: _____		

	Question	Answer Grid
1	The name(s) of the persons whose mail is to be held should be written in box: A. 1　　　　B. 2　　　　C. 10　　　　D. 18	Ⓐ Ⓑ Ⓒ Ⓓ
2	The customer should sign in box: A. 2　　　　B. 10　　　　C. 18　　　　D. 7	Ⓐ Ⓑ Ⓒ Ⓓ
3	Where on this form should the ZIP number of the person whose mail is to be held be entered? A. 2　　　　B. 4B　　　　C. 3　　　　D. 6	Ⓐ Ⓑ Ⓒ Ⓓ
4	The last (ending) date to hold mail is entered in box: A. 19　　　　B. 6　　　　C. 4B　　　　D. 16	Ⓐ Ⓑ Ⓒ Ⓓ
5	The postal service received the form on 9/25/10. This date should be recorded in box: A. 19　　　　B. 8　　　　C. 14　　　　D. 7	Ⓐ Ⓑ Ⓒ Ⓓ
6	Karen Goins, a Carrier, receives this form from the customer. She should write her ID number in box: A. 14　　　　B. 11　　　　C. 8　　　　D. 19	Ⓐ Ⓑ Ⓒ Ⓓ
7	The first date that mail should be held should be recorded in box: A. 6　　　　B. 5　　　　C. 19　　　　D. 15	Ⓐ Ⓑ Ⓒ Ⓓ

FORMS COMPLETION ANSWERS (EXAMPLES 1 – 5)

#1	#2	#3	#4	#5
1. B	1. D	1. B	1. B	1. B
2. D	2. C	2. C	2. D	2. D
3. D	3. C	3. A	3. D	3. C
4. C	4. B	4. C	4. B	4. B
5. B	5. B	5. D	5. C	5. B
6. C	6. B	6. A	6. B	6. B
7. C	7. D	7. B	7. D	7. B
8. D	8. A		8. B	
9. C	9. C		9. D	
10. A				

Part	Time Allowed	Number of Ques.	Description of Question
3. Coding	6 minutes	36	Find correct code for an address.

In the **CODING** part of the test you will be provided with a table (a Coding Guide). The format of the Coding Guide will probably be similar to the following coding guide:

Coding Guide

Range of Addresses	Delivery Route
1 - 99 Rochester Avenue 100 - 1000 Bleeker Street 20 - 90 S. 18th Road	A
100 - 300 Rochester Avenue 91 - 200 S. 18th Road	B
5000 - 15000 Jefferson Lane 1 - 100 Rural Route 12 1001 - 5000 Bleeker Street	C
All mail that does not fall in one of address ranges listed above	D

You will be given 36 addresses which fall into one of the listed "Delivery Routes" in the coding guide (Delivery routes A, B, C, D). Your job will be to determine into which "Delivery Route" each one of the addresses falls into.

For example, 24 Rochester Avenue falls into Delivery Route "A" because 24 Rochester Avenue falls between 1 Rochester Avenue and 99 Rochester Avenue (1 – 99 Rochester Avenue).

6900 Jefferson Lane belongs in Delivery Route "C" because 6900 Jefferson Lane falls between 5000 Jefferson Lane and 15000 Jefferson Lane (5000 – 15000 Jefferson Lane).

The next three addresses belong to Delivery Route "D" because they do not fall within the range of any of the addresses listed in the "Range of Addresses" column.

6000 Bleeker Street,   2856 Adams Street,   301 Rochester Avenue

The following are further examples of correct coding of addresses:

Address	Delivery Route
88 Rural Route 25	D
600 Rochester Avenue	D
25 Rochester Avenue	A
2000 Bleeker Street	C
95 S. 18th Road	B
50 Rural Route 12	C
6000 Jefferson Lane	C
150 Rural Route 12	D
28 Rochester Avenue	A
142 Bleeker Street	A
60 S. 18th Road	A
10000 Jefferson Lane	C

On the test you will be given 36 addresses to code in 6 minutes. In practicing for this part of the test, your aim should be to work quickly and accurately and finish all 36 addresses in the 6 allotted minutes.

Directions for the following 5 Coding Exercises

For each of the following 5 exercises a "Coding Guide" is provided, followed by 36 addresses. For each address, determine whether the address belongs to Delivery Route A, B, C or D, and mark your answer sheet accordingly. You have 6 minutes to complete each of the 5 coding exercises.

(Time limit on each exercise is 6 minutes for 36 questions).

Good Luck!

Coding Exercise #1:   Coding Guide

Range of Addresses	Delivery Route
1 - 99 Ferndale Avenue 100 - 1000 Hazel Street 20 - 90 S. 12th Road	A
100 - 300 Ferndale Avenue 91 - 200 S. 12th Road	B
5000 - 15000 Lincoln Lane 1 - 100 Rural Route 2 1001 - 5000 Hazel Street	C
All mail that does not fall in one of address ranges listed above	D

	Delivery Address	Delivery Route				Answer Grid
1	6000 Lincoln Lane	A	B	C	D	Ⓐ Ⓑ Ⓒ Ⓓ
2	20 S. 12th Road	A	B	C	D	Ⓐ Ⓑ Ⓒ Ⓓ
3	34 Rural Route 2	A	B	C	D	Ⓐ Ⓑ Ⓒ Ⓓ
4	45 Ferndale Avenue	A	B	C	D	Ⓐ Ⓑ Ⓒ Ⓓ
5	132 S. 12th Road	A	B	C	D	Ⓐ Ⓑ Ⓒ Ⓓ
6	2000 Hazel Street	A	B	C	D	Ⓐ Ⓑ Ⓒ Ⓓ
7	88 S. 12th Road	A	B	C	D	Ⓐ Ⓑ Ⓒ Ⓓ
8	6000 Hazel Street	A	B	C	D	Ⓐ Ⓑ Ⓒ Ⓓ
9	189 Ferndale Avenue	A	B	C	D	Ⓐ Ⓑ Ⓒ Ⓓ
10	55 Rural Route 2	A	B	C	D	Ⓐ Ⓑ Ⓒ Ⓓ
11	25 Ferndale Avenue	A	B	C	D	Ⓐ Ⓑ Ⓒ Ⓓ
12	12500 Lincoln Lane	A	B	C	D	Ⓐ Ⓑ Ⓒ Ⓓ
13	4000 Hazel Street	A	B	C	D	Ⓐ Ⓑ Ⓒ Ⓓ
14	160 Ferndale Avenue	A	B	C	D	Ⓐ Ⓑ Ⓒ Ⓓ

	Delivery Address	Delivery Route				Answer Grid
15	7800 Lincoln Lane	A	B	C	D	Ⓐ Ⓑ Ⓒ Ⓓ
16	5 Ferndale Avenue	A	B	C	D	Ⓐ Ⓑ Ⓒ Ⓓ
17	9000 Hazel Street	A	B	C	D	Ⓐ Ⓑ Ⓒ Ⓓ
18	400 S. 12th Road	A	B	C	D	Ⓐ Ⓑ Ⓒ Ⓓ
19	350 Hazel Street	A	B	C	D	Ⓐ Ⓑ Ⓒ Ⓓ
20	500 Ferndale Avenue	A	B	C	D	Ⓐ Ⓑ Ⓒ Ⓓ
21	50 S. 12th Road	A	B	C	D	Ⓐ Ⓑ Ⓒ Ⓓ
22	290 Ferndale Avenue	A	B	C	D	Ⓐ Ⓑ Ⓒ Ⓓ
23	95 S. 12th Road	A	B	C	D	Ⓐ Ⓑ Ⓒ Ⓓ
24	82 Ferndale Avenue	A	B	C	D	Ⓐ Ⓑ Ⓒ Ⓓ
25	90 Rural Route 2	A	B	C	D	Ⓐ Ⓑ Ⓒ Ⓓ
26	240 S. 12th Road	A	B	C	D	Ⓐ Ⓑ Ⓒ Ⓓ
27	105 Hazel Street	A	B	C	D	Ⓐ Ⓑ Ⓒ Ⓓ
28	147 S. 12th Road	A	B	C	D	Ⓐ Ⓑ Ⓒ Ⓓ
29	5500 Lincoln Lane	A	B	C	D	Ⓐ Ⓑ Ⓒ Ⓓ
30	3300 Hazel Street	A	B	C	D	Ⓐ Ⓑ Ⓒ Ⓓ
31	90 Ferndale Avenue	A	B	C	D	Ⓐ Ⓑ Ⓒ Ⓓ
32	75 S. 12th Road	A	B	C	D	Ⓐ Ⓑ Ⓒ Ⓓ
33	150 Ferndale Avenue	A	B	C	D	Ⓐ Ⓑ Ⓒ Ⓓ
34	16000 Lincoln Lane	A	B	C	D	Ⓐ Ⓑ Ⓒ Ⓓ
35	600 Hazel Street	A	B	C	D	Ⓐ Ⓑ Ⓒ Ⓓ
36	9000 Ferndale Avenue	A	B	C	D	Ⓐ Ⓑ Ⓒ Ⓓ

Coding Exercise #2: Coding Guide

Range of Addresses	Delivery Route
1 - 49 Western Lane 200 - 900 Jennings Street 25 - 75 North Circle	A
50 - 200 Western Lane 76 - 200 North Circle	B
100 - 1200 King Ave. 1 - 100 Furman Route 10 901 - 1000 Jennings Street	C
All mail that doesn't fall in one of the address ranges listed above	D

	Delivery Address	Delivery Route				Answer Grid
1	44 Western Lane	A	B	C	D	Ⓐ Ⓑ Ⓒ Ⓓ
2	1400 King Ave.	A	B	C	D	Ⓐ Ⓑ Ⓒ Ⓓ
3	300 Jennings Street	A	B	C	D	Ⓐ Ⓑ Ⓒ Ⓓ
4	300 Furman Route 10	A	B	C	D	Ⓐ Ⓑ Ⓒ Ⓓ
5	500 King Ave.	A	B	C	D	Ⓐ Ⓑ Ⓒ Ⓓ
6	30 North Circle	A	B	C	D	Ⓐ Ⓑ Ⓒ Ⓓ
7	30 Western Lane	A	B	C	D	Ⓐ Ⓑ Ⓒ Ⓓ
8	1300 North Circle	A	B	C	D	Ⓐ Ⓑ Ⓒ Ⓓ
9	90 Furman Route 10	A	B	C	D	Ⓐ Ⓑ Ⓒ Ⓓ
10	24 Western Lane	A	B	C	D	Ⓐ Ⓑ Ⓒ Ⓓ
11	1100 Jennings Street	A	B	C	D	Ⓐ Ⓑ Ⓒ Ⓓ
12	220 Furman Route 10	A	B	C	D	Ⓐ Ⓑ Ⓒ Ⓓ
13	50 North Circle	A	B	C	D	Ⓐ Ⓑ Ⓒ Ⓓ
14	850 Jennings Street	A	B	C	D	Ⓐ Ⓑ Ⓒ Ⓓ

	Delivery Address	Delivery Route				Answer Grid
15	240 Jennings Street	A	B	C	D	Ⓐ Ⓑ Ⓒ Ⓓ
16	80 North Circle	A	B	C	D	Ⓐ Ⓑ Ⓒ Ⓓ
17	1300 King Ave.	A	B	C	D	Ⓐ Ⓑ Ⓒ Ⓓ
18	55 Western Lane	A	B	C	D	Ⓐ Ⓑ Ⓒ Ⓓ
19	62 Western Lane	A	B	C	D	Ⓐ Ⓑ Ⓒ Ⓓ
20	150 Furman Route 10	A	B	C	D	Ⓐ Ⓑ Ⓒ Ⓓ
21	1220 Jennings Street	A	B	C	D	Ⓐ Ⓑ Ⓒ Ⓓ
22	100 Western Lane	A	B	C	D	Ⓐ Ⓑ Ⓒ Ⓓ
23	600 King Ave.	A	B	C	D	Ⓐ Ⓑ Ⓒ Ⓓ
24	89 North Circle	A	B	C	D	Ⓐ Ⓑ Ⓒ Ⓓ
25	400 Jennings Street	A	B	C	D	Ⓐ Ⓑ Ⓒ Ⓓ
26	85 Furman Route 10	A	B	C	D	Ⓐ Ⓑ Ⓒ Ⓓ
27	60 North Circle	A	B	C	D	Ⓐ Ⓑ Ⓒ Ⓓ
28	950 Jennings Street	A	B	C	D	Ⓐ Ⓑ Ⓒ Ⓓ
29	189 North Circle	A	B	C	D	Ⓐ Ⓑ Ⓒ Ⓓ
30	175 Western Lane	A	B	C	D	Ⓐ Ⓑ Ⓒ Ⓓ
31	1010 Jennings Street	A	B	C	D	Ⓐ Ⓑ Ⓒ Ⓓ
32	92 North Circle	A	B	C	D	Ⓐ Ⓑ Ⓒ Ⓓ
33	700 Jennings Street	A	B	C	D	Ⓐ Ⓑ Ⓒ Ⓓ
34	153 Western Lane	A	B	C	D	Ⓐ Ⓑ Ⓒ Ⓓ
35	140 King Ave.	A	B	C	D	Ⓐ Ⓑ Ⓒ Ⓓ
36	200 Western Lane	A	B	C	D	Ⓐ Ⓑ Ⓒ Ⓓ

Coding Exercise #3:   Coding Guide

Range of Addresses	Delivery Route
1000 - 9900 Solomon Lane 1- 500 Walker Road 50 -100 Western Street	A
9901 - 10000 Solomon Lane 101 - 500 Western Street	B
25 - 400 Crawley Ave. 1 - 200 Vernell Route 1 501 - 1000 Walker Road	C
All mail that doesn't fall in one of the address ranges listed above	D

	Delivery Address	Delivery Route				Answer Grid
1	1800 Solomon Lane	A	B	C	D	Ⓐ Ⓑ Ⓒ Ⓓ
2	345 Western Street	A	B	C	D	Ⓐ Ⓑ Ⓒ Ⓓ
3	400 Walker Road	A	B	C	D	Ⓐ Ⓑ Ⓒ Ⓓ
4	145 Vernell Route 1	A	B	C	D	Ⓐ Ⓑ Ⓒ Ⓓ
5	604 Walker Road	A	B	C	D	Ⓐ Ⓑ Ⓒ Ⓓ
6	68 Western Street	A	B	C	D	Ⓐ Ⓑ Ⓒ Ⓓ
7	9543 Solomon Lane	A	B	C	D	Ⓐ Ⓑ Ⓒ Ⓓ
8	1245 Walker Road	A	B	C	D	Ⓐ Ⓑ Ⓒ Ⓓ
9	178 Vernell Route 1	A	B	C	D	Ⓐ Ⓑ Ⓒ Ⓓ
10	498 Western Street	A	B	C	D	Ⓐ Ⓑ Ⓒ Ⓓ
11	470 Crawley Ave.	A	B	C	D	Ⓐ Ⓑ Ⓒ Ⓓ
12	398 Walker Road	A	B	C	D	Ⓐ Ⓑ Ⓒ Ⓓ
13	348 Vernell Route 1	A	B	C	D	Ⓐ Ⓑ Ⓒ Ⓓ
14	157 Crawley Ave.	A	B	C	D	Ⓐ Ⓑ Ⓒ Ⓓ

	Delivery Address	Delivery Route				Answer Grid
15	9860 Solomon Lane	A	B	C	D	Ⓐ Ⓑ Ⓒ Ⓓ
16	659 Walker Road	A	B	C	D	Ⓐ Ⓑ Ⓒ Ⓓ
17	1200 Solomon Lane	A	B	C	D	Ⓐ Ⓑ Ⓒ Ⓓ
18	56 Crawley Ave.	A	B	C	D	Ⓐ Ⓑ Ⓒ Ⓓ
19	34 Vernell Route 1	A	B	C	D	Ⓐ Ⓑ Ⓒ Ⓓ
20	345 Crawley Ave.	A	B	C	D	Ⓐ Ⓑ Ⓒ Ⓓ
21	224 Vernell Route 1	A	B	C	D	Ⓐ Ⓑ Ⓒ Ⓓ
22	95 Western Street	A	B	C	D	Ⓐ Ⓑ Ⓒ Ⓓ
23	9450 Solomon Lane	A	B	C	D	Ⓐ Ⓑ Ⓒ Ⓓ
24	895 Walker Road	A	B	C	D	Ⓐ Ⓑ Ⓒ Ⓓ
25	10901 Solomon Lane	A	B	C	D	Ⓐ Ⓑ Ⓒ Ⓓ
26	360 Western Street	A	B	C	D	Ⓐ Ⓑ Ⓒ Ⓓ
27	876 Crawley Ave.	A	B	C	D	Ⓐ Ⓑ Ⓒ Ⓓ
28	9000 Solomon Lane	A	B	C	D	Ⓐ Ⓑ Ⓒ Ⓓ
29	890 Walker Road	A	B	C	D	Ⓐ Ⓑ Ⓒ Ⓓ
30	30 Crawley Ave.	A	B	C	D	Ⓐ Ⓑ Ⓒ Ⓓ
31	2000 Walker Road	A	B	C	D	Ⓐ Ⓑ Ⓒ Ⓓ
32	67 Western Street	A	B	C	D	Ⓐ Ⓑ Ⓒ Ⓓ
33	67 Vernell Route 1	A	B	C	D	Ⓐ Ⓑ Ⓒ Ⓓ
34	505 Western Street	A	B	C	D	Ⓐ Ⓑ Ⓒ Ⓓ
35	256 Walker Road	A	B	C	D	Ⓐ Ⓑ Ⓒ Ⓓ
36	9750 Solomon Lane	A	B	C	D	Ⓐ Ⓑ Ⓒ Ⓓ

Coding Exercise #4: Coding Guide

Range of Addresses	Delivery Route
10 - 200 Hudson Drive 50 - 300 Postal Ave. 5 - 25 N. 38th Street	A
201 - 300 Hudson Drive 26 - 90 N 38th Street	B
300 - 700 Cohen Ave. 1 - 99 Vander Route 1 301 - 900 Postal Ave.	C
All mail that doesn't fall in one of the address ranges listed above	D

	Delivery Address	Delivery Route				Answer Grid
1	62 Postal Ave.	A	B	C	D	Ⓐ Ⓑ Ⓒ Ⓓ
2	16 N. 38th Street	A	B	C	D	Ⓐ Ⓑ Ⓒ Ⓓ
3	492 Cohen Ave.	A	B	C	D	Ⓐ Ⓑ Ⓒ Ⓓ
4	33 N 38th Street	A	B	C	D	Ⓐ Ⓑ Ⓒ Ⓓ
5	279 Hudson Drive	A	B	C	D	Ⓐ Ⓑ Ⓒ Ⓓ
6	453 Postal Ave.	A	B	C	D	Ⓐ Ⓑ Ⓒ Ⓓ
7	89 Vander Route 1	A	B	C	D	Ⓐ Ⓑ Ⓒ Ⓓ
8	400 Hudson Drive	A	B	C	D	Ⓐ Ⓑ Ⓒ Ⓓ
9	192 Hudson Drive	A	B	C	D	Ⓐ Ⓑ Ⓒ Ⓓ
10	322 Postal Ave.	A	B	C	D	Ⓐ Ⓑ Ⓒ Ⓓ
11	688 Cohen Ave.	A	B	C	D	Ⓐ Ⓑ Ⓒ Ⓓ
12	21 N. 38th Street	A	B	C	D	Ⓐ Ⓑ Ⓒ Ⓓ
13	717 Cohen Ave.	A	B	C	D	Ⓐ Ⓑ Ⓒ Ⓓ
14	299 Hudson Drive	A	B	C	D	Ⓐ Ⓑ Ⓒ Ⓓ

	Delivery Address	Delivery Route				Answer Grid
15	667 Cohen Ave.	A	B	C	D	Ⓐ Ⓑ Ⓒ Ⓓ
16	15 Hudson Drive	A	B	C	D	Ⓐ Ⓑ Ⓒ Ⓓ
17	84 Vander Route 1	A	B	C	D	Ⓐ Ⓑ Ⓒ Ⓓ
18	891 Postal Ave.	A	B	C	D	Ⓐ Ⓑ Ⓒ Ⓓ
19	75 Postal Ave.	A	B	C	D	Ⓐ Ⓑ Ⓒ Ⓓ
20	72 Lake Street	A	B	C	D	Ⓐ Ⓑ Ⓒ Ⓓ
21	33 Vander Route 1	A	B	C	D	Ⓐ Ⓑ Ⓒ Ⓓ
22	224 Hudson Drive	A	B	C	D	Ⓐ Ⓑ Ⓒ Ⓓ
23	347 Cohen Ave.	A	B	C	D	Ⓐ Ⓑ Ⓒ Ⓓ
24	58 N 38th Street	A	B	C	D	Ⓐ Ⓑ Ⓒ Ⓓ
25	99 Herkimer Place	A	B	C	D	Ⓐ Ⓑ Ⓒ Ⓓ
26	222 Postal Ave.	A	B	C	D	Ⓐ Ⓑ Ⓒ Ⓓ
27	22 Williams Street	A	B	C	D	Ⓐ Ⓑ Ⓒ Ⓓ
28	270 Hudson Drive	A	B	C	D	Ⓐ Ⓑ Ⓒ Ⓓ
29	679 Cohen Ave.	A	B	C	D	Ⓐ Ⓑ Ⓒ Ⓓ
30	20 N. 38th Street	A	B	C	D	Ⓐ Ⓑ Ⓒ Ⓓ
31	742 Postal Ave.	A	B	C	D	Ⓐ Ⓑ Ⓒ Ⓓ
32	77 N 38th Street	A	B	C	D	Ⓐ Ⓑ Ⓒ Ⓓ
33	454 Hudson Drive	A	B	C	D	Ⓐ Ⓑ Ⓒ Ⓓ
34	54 Hudson Drive	A	B	C	D	Ⓐ Ⓑ Ⓒ Ⓓ
35	55 Vander Route 1	A	B	C	D	Ⓐ Ⓑ Ⓒ Ⓓ
36	45 N 38th Street	A	B	C	D	Ⓐ Ⓑ Ⓒ Ⓓ

Coding Exercise #5:   Coding Guide

Range of Addresses	Delivery Route
1 - 49 Manor Lane 10 - 300 Zebra Ave. 50 - 100 E. 8th Street	A
50 - 200 Manor Lane 101 - 150 E. 8th Street	B
1 - 2000 Belmont Road 200 - 800 Vegas Circle 301 - 1500 Zebra Ave.	C
All mail that doesn't fall in one of the address ranges listed above	D

	Delivery Address	Delivery Route	Answer Grid
1	50 Manor Lane	A B C D	Ⓐ Ⓑ Ⓒ Ⓓ
2	2 Manor Lane	A B C D	Ⓐ Ⓑ Ⓒ Ⓓ
3	18 E. 8th Street	A B C D	Ⓐ Ⓑ Ⓒ Ⓓ
4	288 Vegas Circle	A B C D	Ⓐ Ⓑ Ⓒ Ⓓ
5	258 Zebra Ave.	A B C D	Ⓐ Ⓑ Ⓒ Ⓓ
6	344 Zebra Ave.	A B C D	Ⓐ Ⓑ Ⓒ Ⓓ
7	455 Vegas Circle	A B C D	Ⓐ Ⓑ Ⓒ Ⓓ
8	77 Manor Lane	A B C D	Ⓐ Ⓑ Ⓒ Ⓓ
9	19 Forster Ave.	A B C D	Ⓐ Ⓑ Ⓒ Ⓓ
10	777 Vegas Circle	A B C D	Ⓐ Ⓑ Ⓒ Ⓓ
11	55 E. 8th Street	A B C D	Ⓐ Ⓑ Ⓒ Ⓓ
12	205 Manor Lane	A B C D	Ⓐ Ⓑ Ⓒ Ⓓ
13	122 E. 8th Street	A B C D	Ⓐ Ⓑ Ⓒ Ⓓ
14	1028 Belmont Road	A B C D	Ⓐ Ⓑ Ⓒ Ⓓ

	Delivery Address	Delivery Route				Answer Grid
15	22 Manor Lane	A	B	C	D	Ⓐ Ⓑ Ⓒ Ⓓ
16	2000 Belmont Road	A	B	C	D	Ⓐ Ⓑ Ⓒ Ⓓ
17	1600 Zebra Ave.	A	B	C	D	Ⓐ Ⓑ Ⓒ Ⓓ
18	137 E. 8th Street	A	B	C	D	Ⓐ Ⓑ Ⓒ Ⓓ
19	222 Zebra Ave.	A	B	C	D	Ⓐ Ⓑ Ⓒ Ⓓ
20	12 Zebra Ave.	A	B	C	D	Ⓐ Ⓑ Ⓒ Ⓓ
21	456 King Road	A	B	C	D	Ⓐ Ⓑ Ⓒ Ⓓ
22	101 Manor Lane	A	B	C	D	Ⓐ Ⓑ Ⓒ Ⓓ
23	15 Belmont Road	A	B	C	D	Ⓐ Ⓑ Ⓒ Ⓓ
24	390 Manor Lane	A	B	C	D	Ⓐ Ⓑ Ⓒ Ⓓ
25	51 Zebra Ave.	A	B	C	D	Ⓐ Ⓑ Ⓒ Ⓓ
26	1343 Zebra Ave.	A	B	C	D	Ⓐ Ⓑ Ⓒ Ⓓ
27	1941 Belmont Road	A	B	C	D	Ⓐ Ⓑ Ⓒ Ⓓ
28	157 Manor Lane	A	B	C	D	Ⓐ Ⓑ Ⓒ Ⓓ
29	556 Vegas Circle	A	B	C	D	Ⓐ Ⓑ Ⓒ Ⓓ
30	15 Zebra Ave.	A	B	C	D	Ⓐ Ⓑ Ⓒ Ⓓ
31	54 Manor Lane	A	B	C	D	Ⓐ Ⓑ Ⓒ Ⓓ
32	667 Vegas Circle	A	B	C	D	Ⓐ Ⓑ Ⓒ Ⓓ
33	127 E. 8th Street	A	B	C	D	Ⓐ Ⓑ Ⓒ Ⓓ
34	290 Belmont Road	A	B	C	D	Ⓐ Ⓑ Ⓒ Ⓓ
35	131 E. 8th Street	A	B	C	D	Ⓐ Ⓑ Ⓒ Ⓓ
36	367 Zebra Ave.	A	B	C	D	Ⓐ Ⓑ Ⓒ Ⓓ

ANSWERS TO CODING EXERCISES

Coding Exercise #1

1. C	5. B	9. B	13. C	17. D	21. A	25. C	29. C	33. B
2. A	6. C	10. C	14. B	18. D	22. B	26. D	30. C	34. D
3. C	7. A	11. A	15. C	19. A	23. B	27. A	31. A	35. A
4. A	8. D	12. C	16. A	20. D	24. A	28. B	32. A	36. D

Coding Exercise #2

1. A	5. C	9. C	13. A	17. D	21. D	25. A	29. B	33. A
2. D	6. A	10. A	14. A	18. B	22. B	26. C	30. B	34. B
3. A	7. A	11. D	15. A	19. B	23. C	27. A	31. D	35. C
4. D	8. D	12. D	16. B	20. D	24. B	28. C	32. B	36. B

Coding Exercise #3

1. A	5. C	9. C	13. D	17. A	21. D	25. D	29. C	33. C
2. B	6. A	10. B	14. C	18. C	22. A	26. B	30. C	34. D
3. A	7. A	11. D	15. A	19. C	23. A	27. D	31. D	35. A
4. C	8. D	12. A	16. C	20. C	24. C	28. A	32. A	36. A

Coding Exercise #4

1. A	5. B	9. A	13. D	17. C	21. C	25. D	29. C	33. D
2. A	6. C	10. C	14. B	18. C	22. B	26. A	30. A	34. A
3. C	7. C	11. C	15. C	19. A	23. C	27. D	31. C	35. C
4. B	8. D	12. A	16. A	20. D	24. B	28. B	32. B	36. B

Coding Exercise #5

1. B	5. A	9. D	13. B	17. D	21. D	25. A	29. C	33. B
2. A	6. C	10. C	14. C	18. B	22. B	26. C	30. A	34. C
3. D	7. C	11. A	15. A	19. A	23. C	27. C	31. B	35. B
4. C	8. B	12. D	16. C	20. A	24. D	28. B	32. C	36. C

Part	Time Allowed	Number of Ques.	Description of Question
4. Memory (of coding examples, above)	7 minutes	36	Memorize address codes (which are same as codes in the "Coding" section part of the test.)

In the **MEMORY** part of the test you will be asked to determine the delivery routes of 36 addresses. The coding guide will be the same as in the preceding coding questions section of the test.

HOWEVER, in MEMORY CODING you must determine the delivery routes by using your MEMORY of the coding guide.

In other words, you will **not** have the coding guide in front of you and you are not permitted to refer to it.

The coding guide will be the <u>same</u> coding guide that you will have used in the preceding coding section of the test.

One or two short sample coding sessions (which are not graded) may be provided for you to practice before you begin the actual coding by memory test.

During these practice examples (which may last for several minutes) you may want to memorize further the coding table.

Example of Coding Guide

Range of Addresses	Delivery Route
1 - 99 Rochester Avenue 100 - 1000 Bleeker Street 20 - 90 S. 18th Road	A
100 - 300 Rochester Avenue 91 - 200 S. 18th Road	B
5000 - 15000 Jefferson Lane 1 - 100 Rural Route 12 1001 - 5000 Bleeker Street	C
All mail that does not fall in one of address ranges listed above	D

Directions for the following 5 Coding By Memory Exercises

Each of the following 5 MEMORY exercises has 36 addresses which you must code by using your memory of the "Coding Guide" that is provided.

For each address, you will have to determine whether the address belongs to Delivery Route A, B, C or D, and mark your answer sheet accordingly.

You will be allowed 7 minutes to complete each of the following 5 coding exercises.

———————

Note: On the actual test the MEMORY section will probably come right after the CODING section and you will already have had experience with the specific coding guide.

(The same coding guide is used for both the CODING and MEMORY sections.)

On the 7 practice tests in this book we will follow that pattern (CODING questions first and then MEMORY questions right after that.)

———————

However, for now and for study purposes, for the following 5 MEMORY exercises follow these instructions:

1. Allow yourself 5 minutes (like in the actual test) to memorize the coding guide.

2. After that, cover the guide and code the 36 addresses (A, B, C, D). (Allow yourself 7 minutes to code the 36 addresses.)

Good Luck!

Memory Exercise #1:   Coding Guide

Range of Addresses	Delivery Route
1 – 99 Ferndale Avenue 100 - 1000 Hazel Street 20 - 90 S. 12th Road	A
100 - 300 Ferndale Avenue 91 - 200 S. 12th Road	B
5000 - 15000 Lincoln Lane 1 - 100 Rural Route 2 1001 - 5000 Hazel Street	C
All mail that does not fall in one of address ranges listed above	D

	Delivery Address	Delivery Route				Answer Grid
1	12000 Lincoln Lane	A	B	C	D	Ⓐ Ⓑ Ⓒ Ⓓ
2	345 Hazel Street	A	B	C	D	Ⓐ Ⓑ Ⓒ Ⓓ
3	79 S. 12th Road	A	B	C	D	Ⓐ Ⓑ Ⓒ Ⓓ
4	20 Rural Route 2	A	B	C	D	Ⓐ Ⓑ Ⓒ Ⓓ
5	25 Ferndale Avenue	A	B	C	D	Ⓐ Ⓑ Ⓒ Ⓓ
6	6000 Hazel Street	A	B	C	D	Ⓐ Ⓑ Ⓒ Ⓓ
7	95 S. 12th Road	A	B	C	D	Ⓐ Ⓑ Ⓒ Ⓓ
8	290 Ferndale Avenue	A	B	C	D	Ⓐ Ⓑ Ⓒ Ⓓ
9	11000 Lincoln Lane	A	B	C	D	Ⓐ Ⓑ Ⓒ Ⓓ
10	2400 Rural Route 2	A	B	C	D	Ⓐ Ⓑ Ⓒ Ⓓ
11	634 Hazel Street	A	B	C	D	Ⓐ Ⓑ Ⓒ Ⓓ
12	50 Rural Route 2	A	B	C	D	Ⓐ Ⓑ Ⓒ Ⓓ
13	400 Ferndale Avenue	A	B	C	D	Ⓐ Ⓑ Ⓒ Ⓓ
14	260 S. 12th Road	A	B	C	D	Ⓐ Ⓑ Ⓒ Ⓓ

	Delivery Address	Delivery Route				Answer Grid
15	300 Ferndale Avenue	A	B	C	D	Ⓐ Ⓑ Ⓒ Ⓓ
16	76 Ferndale Avenue	A	B	C	D	Ⓐ Ⓑ Ⓒ Ⓓ
17	13000 Lincoln Lane	A	B	C	D	Ⓐ Ⓑ Ⓒ Ⓓ
18	24 Watkins Avenue	A	B	C	D	Ⓐ Ⓑ Ⓒ Ⓓ
19	240 Hazel Street	A	B	C	D	Ⓐ Ⓑ Ⓒ Ⓓ
20	2000 Hazel Street	A	B	C	D	Ⓐ Ⓑ Ⓒ Ⓓ
21	120 Ferndale Avenue	A	B	C	D	Ⓐ Ⓑ Ⓒ Ⓓ
22	76 S. 12th Road	A	B	C	D	Ⓐ Ⓑ Ⓒ Ⓓ
23	777 Ferndale Avenue	A	B	C	D	Ⓐ Ⓑ Ⓒ Ⓓ
24	75 Rural Route 2	A	B	C	D	Ⓐ Ⓑ Ⓒ Ⓓ
25	88 Ferndale Avenue	A	B	C	D	Ⓐ Ⓑ Ⓒ Ⓓ
26	150 S. 12th Road	A	B	C	D	Ⓐ Ⓑ Ⓒ Ⓓ
27	5500 Lincoln Lane	A	B	C	D	Ⓐ Ⓑ Ⓒ Ⓓ
28	600 Albert Lane	A	B	C	D	Ⓐ Ⓑ Ⓒ Ⓓ
29	800 Hazel Street	A	B	C	D	Ⓐ Ⓑ Ⓒ Ⓓ
30	6500 Hazel Street	A	B	C	D	Ⓐ Ⓑ Ⓒ Ⓓ
31	168 Ferndale Avenue	A	B	C	D	Ⓐ Ⓑ Ⓒ Ⓓ
32	4000 Hazel Street	A	B	C	D	Ⓐ Ⓑ Ⓒ Ⓓ
33	60 S. 12th Road	A	B	C	D	Ⓐ Ⓑ Ⓒ Ⓓ
34	95 Rural Route 2	A	B	C	D	Ⓐ Ⓑ Ⓒ Ⓓ
35	52 Ferndale Avenue	A	B	C	D	Ⓐ Ⓑ Ⓒ Ⓓ
36	6100 Lincoln Lane	A	B	C	D	Ⓐ Ⓑ Ⓒ Ⓓ

Memory Exercise #2:   Coding Guide

Range of Addresses	Delivery Route
1 - 49 Western Lane 200 - 900 Jennings Street 25 - 75 North Circle	A
50 - 200 Western Lane 76 - 200 North Circle	B
100 - 1200 King Ave. 1 - 100 Furman Route 10 901 - 1000 Jennings Street	C
All mail that doesn't fall in one of the address ranges listed above	D

	Delivery Address	Delivery Route				Answer Grid
1	25 Western Lane	A	B	C	D	Ⓐ Ⓑ Ⓒ Ⓓ
2	77 North Circle	A	B	C	D	Ⓐ Ⓑ Ⓒ Ⓓ
3	50 Western Lane	A	B	C	D	Ⓐ Ⓑ Ⓒ Ⓓ
4	45 Furman Route 10	A	B	C	D	Ⓐ Ⓑ Ⓒ Ⓓ
5	748 Jennings Street	A	B	C	D	Ⓐ Ⓑ Ⓒ Ⓓ
6	125 King Ave.	A	B	C	D	Ⓐ Ⓑ Ⓒ Ⓓ
7	990 Jennings Street	A	B	C	D	Ⓐ Ⓑ Ⓒ Ⓓ
8	55 North Circle	A	B	C	D	Ⓐ Ⓑ Ⓒ Ⓓ
9	88 Furman Route 10	A	B	C	D	Ⓐ Ⓑ Ⓒ Ⓓ
10	22 Western Lane	A	B	C	D	Ⓐ Ⓑ Ⓒ Ⓓ
11	220 Western Lane	A	B	C	D	Ⓐ Ⓑ Ⓒ Ⓓ
12	105 North Circle	A	B	C	D	Ⓐ Ⓑ Ⓒ Ⓓ
13	980 Jennings Street	A	B	C	D	Ⓐ Ⓑ Ⓒ Ⓓ
14	75 North Circle	A	B	C	D	Ⓐ Ⓑ Ⓒ Ⓓ

	Delivery Address	Delivery Route				Answer Grid
15	500 Jennings Street	A	B	C	D	Ⓐ Ⓑ Ⓒ Ⓓ
16	1200 Jennings Street	A	B	C	D	Ⓐ Ⓑ Ⓒ Ⓓ
17	150 Western Lane	A	B	C	D	Ⓐ Ⓑ Ⓒ Ⓓ
18	85 Furman Route 10	A	B	C	D	Ⓐ Ⓑ Ⓒ Ⓓ
19	30 North Circle	A	B	C	D	Ⓐ Ⓑ Ⓒ Ⓓ
20	940 Jennings Street	A	B	C	D	Ⓐ Ⓑ Ⓒ Ⓓ
21	45 Western Lane	A	B	C	D	Ⓐ Ⓑ Ⓒ Ⓓ
22	50 King Avenue	A	B	C	D	Ⓐ Ⓑ Ⓒ Ⓓ
23	600 King Ave.	A	B	C	D	Ⓐ Ⓑ Ⓒ Ⓓ
24	325 Jennings Street	A	B	C	D	Ⓐ Ⓑ Ⓒ Ⓓ
25	215 North Circle	A	B	C	D	Ⓐ Ⓑ Ⓒ Ⓓ
26	169 North Circle	A	B	C	D	Ⓐ Ⓑ Ⓒ Ⓓ
27	800 Bedford Avenue	A	B	C	D	Ⓐ Ⓑ Ⓒ Ⓓ
28	632 Jennings Street	A	B	C	D	Ⓐ Ⓑ Ⓒ Ⓓ
29	16 Wilkes Road	A	B	C	D	Ⓐ Ⓑ Ⓒ Ⓓ
30	190 Western Lane	A	B	C	D	Ⓐ Ⓑ Ⓒ Ⓓ
31	46 Furman Route 10	A	B	C	D	Ⓐ Ⓑ Ⓒ Ⓓ
32	105 Western Lane	A	B	C	D	Ⓐ Ⓑ Ⓒ Ⓓ
33	778 King Ave.	A	B	C	D	Ⓐ Ⓑ Ⓒ Ⓓ
34	1800 Jennings Street	A	B	C	D	Ⓐ Ⓑ Ⓒ Ⓓ
35	40 Western Lane	A	B	C	D	Ⓐ Ⓑ Ⓒ Ⓓ
36	97 North Circle	A	B	C	D	Ⓐ Ⓑ Ⓒ Ⓓ

Memory Exercise #3: Coding Guide

Range of Addresses	Delivery Route
1000 – 9900 Solomon Lane 1 - 500 Walker Road 50 -100 Western Street	A
9901 – 10000 Solomon Lane 101 - 500 Western Street	B
25 – 400 Crawley Ave. 1 – 200 Vernell Route 1 501 – 1000 Walker Road	C
All mail that doesn't fall in one of the address ranges listed above	D

	Delivery Address	Delivery Route				Answer Grid
1	400 Walker Road	A	B	C	D	Ⓐ Ⓑ Ⓒ Ⓓ
2	2000 Walker Road	A	B	C	D	Ⓐ Ⓑ Ⓒ Ⓓ
3	50 Western Street	A	B	C	D	Ⓐ Ⓑ Ⓒ Ⓓ
4	30 Crawley Ave.	A	B	C	D	Ⓐ Ⓑ Ⓒ Ⓓ
5	500 Crawley Ave.	A	B	C	D	Ⓐ Ⓑ Ⓒ Ⓓ
6	2055 Solomon Lane	A	B	C	D	Ⓐ Ⓑ Ⓒ Ⓓ
7	9910 Solomon Lane	A	B	C	D	Ⓐ Ⓑ Ⓒ Ⓓ
8	650 Walker Road	A	B	C	D	Ⓐ Ⓑ Ⓒ Ⓓ
9	75 Western Street	A	B	C	D	Ⓐ Ⓑ Ⓒ Ⓓ
10	105 Vernell Route 1	A	B	C	D	Ⓐ Ⓑ Ⓒ Ⓓ
11	9950 Solomon Lane	A	B	C	D	Ⓐ Ⓑ Ⓒ Ⓓ
12	800 Crawley Ave.	A	B	C	D	Ⓐ Ⓑ Ⓒ Ⓓ
13	488 Walker Road	A	B	C	D	Ⓐ Ⓑ Ⓒ Ⓓ
14	360 Western Street	A	B	C	D	Ⓐ Ⓑ Ⓒ Ⓓ

	Delivery Address	Delivery Route				Answer Grid
15	5400 Solomon Lane	A	B	C	D	Ⓐ Ⓑ Ⓒ Ⓓ
16	32 Crawley Ave.	A	B	C	D	Ⓐ Ⓑ Ⓒ Ⓓ
17	850 Abington Road	A	B	C	D	Ⓐ Ⓑ Ⓒ Ⓓ
18	470 Walker Road	A	B	C	D	Ⓐ Ⓑ Ⓒ Ⓓ
19	9989 Solomon Lane	A	B	C	D	Ⓐ Ⓑ Ⓒ Ⓓ
20	69 Western Street	A	B	C	D	Ⓐ Ⓑ Ⓒ Ⓓ
21	932 Walker Road	A	B	C	D	Ⓐ Ⓑ Ⓒ Ⓓ
22	10 Vernell Route 1	A	B	C	D	Ⓐ Ⓑ Ⓒ Ⓓ
23	2000 Solomon Lane	A	B	C	D	Ⓐ Ⓑ Ⓒ Ⓓ
24	700 Walker Road	A	B	C	D	Ⓐ Ⓑ Ⓒ Ⓓ
25	125 Western Street	A	B	C	D	Ⓐ Ⓑ Ⓒ Ⓓ
26	9990 Solomon Lane	A	B	C	D	Ⓐ Ⓑ Ⓒ Ⓓ
27	476 Western Street	A	B	C	D	Ⓐ Ⓑ Ⓒ Ⓓ
28	900 Hampton Road	A	B	C	D	Ⓐ Ⓑ Ⓒ Ⓓ
29	325 Walker Road	A	B	C	D	Ⓐ Ⓑ Ⓒ Ⓓ
30	370 Crawley Ave.	A	B	C	D	Ⓐ Ⓑ Ⓒ Ⓓ
31	88 Pimrose Street	A	B	C	D	Ⓐ Ⓑ Ⓒ Ⓓ
32	56 Vernell Route 1	A	B	C	D	Ⓐ Ⓑ Ⓒ Ⓓ
33	3000 Walker Road	A	B	C	D	Ⓐ Ⓑ Ⓒ Ⓓ
34	99 Western Street	A	B	C	D	Ⓐ Ⓑ Ⓒ Ⓓ
35	800 Walker Road	A	B	C	D	Ⓐ Ⓑ Ⓒ Ⓓ
36	8600 Solomon Lane	A	B	C	D	Ⓐ Ⓑ Ⓒ Ⓓ

Memory Exercise #4:   Coding Guide

Range of Addresses	Delivery Route
10 - 200 Hudson Drive 50 - 300 Postal Ave. 5 - 25 N. 38th Street	A
201 - 300 Hudson Drive 26 - 90 N. 38th Street	B
300 - 700 Cohen Ave. 1 - 99 Vander Route 1 301 - 900 Postal Ave.	C
All mail that doesn't fall in one of the address ranges listed above	D

	Delivery Address	Delivery Route				Answer Grid
1	10 N. 38th Street	A	B	C	D	Ⓐ Ⓑ Ⓒ Ⓓ
2	237 Hudson Drive	A	B	C	D	Ⓐ Ⓑ Ⓒ Ⓓ
3	82 N. 38th Street	A	B	C	D	Ⓐ Ⓑ Ⓒ Ⓓ
4	58 Hudson Drive	A	B	C	D	Ⓐ Ⓑ Ⓒ Ⓓ
5	54 Vander Route 1	A	B	C	D	Ⓐ Ⓑ Ⓒ Ⓓ
6	94 Postal Ave.	A	B	C	D	Ⓐ Ⓑ Ⓒ Ⓓ
7	91 Wilkins Road	A	B	C	D	Ⓐ Ⓑ Ⓒ Ⓓ
8	290 Hudson Drive	A	B	C	D	Ⓐ Ⓑ Ⓒ Ⓓ
9	340 Cohen Ave.	A	B	C	D	Ⓐ Ⓑ Ⓒ Ⓓ
10	790 Postal Ave.	A	B	C	D	Ⓐ Ⓑ Ⓒ Ⓓ
11	20 N. 38th Street	A	B	C	D	Ⓐ Ⓑ Ⓒ Ⓓ
12	405 Hudson Drive	A	B	C	D	Ⓐ Ⓑ Ⓒ Ⓓ
13	300 Cohen Ave.	A	B	C	D	Ⓐ Ⓑ Ⓒ Ⓓ
14	84 N. 38th Street	A	B	C	D	Ⓐ Ⓑ Ⓒ Ⓓ

	Delivery Address	Delivery Route				Answer Grid
15	86 Postal Ave.	A	B	C	D	Ⓐ Ⓑ Ⓒ Ⓓ
16	77 N. 38th Street	A	B	C	D	Ⓐ Ⓑ Ⓒ Ⓓ
17	788 Hudson Drive	A	B	C	D	Ⓐ Ⓑ Ⓒ Ⓓ
18	195 Hudson Drive	A	B	C	D	Ⓐ Ⓑ Ⓒ Ⓓ
19	15 N. 38th Street	A	B	C	D	Ⓐ Ⓑ Ⓒ Ⓓ
20	561 Postal Ave.	A	B	C	D	Ⓐ Ⓑ Ⓒ Ⓓ
21	250 Hudson Drive	A	B	C	D	Ⓐ Ⓑ Ⓒ Ⓓ
22	70 Vander Route 1	A	B	C	D	Ⓐ Ⓑ Ⓒ Ⓓ
23	100 Hudson Drive	A	B	C	D	Ⓐ Ⓑ Ⓒ Ⓓ
24	348 Hudson Drive	A	B	C	D	Ⓐ Ⓑ Ⓒ Ⓓ
25	22 N. 38th Street	A	B	C	D	Ⓐ Ⓑ Ⓒ Ⓓ
26	1001 Postal Ave.	A	B	C	D	Ⓐ Ⓑ Ⓒ Ⓓ
27	278 Hudson Drive	A	B	C	D	Ⓐ Ⓑ Ⓒ Ⓓ
28	678 Postal Ave.	A	B	C	D	Ⓐ Ⓑ Ⓒ Ⓓ
29	320 Postal Ave.	A	B	C	D	Ⓐ Ⓑ Ⓒ Ⓓ
30	550 Cohen Ave.	A	B	C	D	Ⓐ Ⓑ Ⓒ Ⓓ
31	210 Hudson Drive	A	B	C	D	Ⓐ Ⓑ Ⓒ Ⓓ
32	195 N. 38th Street	A	B	C	D	Ⓐ Ⓑ Ⓒ Ⓓ
33	135 Hudson Drive	A	B	C	D	Ⓐ Ⓑ Ⓒ Ⓓ
34	84 Vander Route 1	A	B	C	D	Ⓐ Ⓑ Ⓒ Ⓓ
35	270 Postal Ave.	A	B	C	D	Ⓐ Ⓑ Ⓒ Ⓓ
36	488 Cohen Ave.	A	B	C	D	Ⓐ Ⓑ Ⓒ Ⓓ

Memory Exercise #5:   Coding Guide

Range of Addresses	Delivery Route
1 - 49 Manor Lane 10 - 300 Zebra Ave. 50 - 150 E. 8th Street	A
50 - 200 Manor Lane 151 - 300 E. 8th Street	B
1 - 2000 Belmont Road 200 - 800 Vegas Circle 301 - 1500 Zebra Ave.	C
All mail that doesn't fall in one of the address ranges listed above	D

	Delivery Address	Delivery Route				Answer Grid
1	25 Manor Lane	A	B	C	D	Ⓐ Ⓑ Ⓒ Ⓓ
2	224 Belmont Road	A	B	C	D	Ⓐ Ⓑ Ⓒ Ⓓ
3	26 Zebra Ave.	A	B	C	D	Ⓐ Ⓑ Ⓒ Ⓓ
4	124 Manor Lane	A	B	C	D	Ⓐ Ⓑ Ⓒ Ⓓ
5	900 Vegas Circle	A	B	C	D	Ⓐ Ⓑ Ⓒ Ⓓ
6	143 E. 8th Street	A	B	C	D	Ⓐ Ⓑ Ⓒ Ⓓ
7	401 Zebra Ave.	A	B	C	D	Ⓐ Ⓑ Ⓒ Ⓓ
8	469 Vegas Circle	A	B	C	D	Ⓐ Ⓑ Ⓒ Ⓓ
9	277 Zebra Ave.	A	B	C	D	Ⓐ Ⓑ Ⓒ Ⓓ
10	73 Manor Lane	A	B	C	D	Ⓐ Ⓑ Ⓒ Ⓓ
11	124 Adams Ave.	A	B	C	D	Ⓐ Ⓑ Ⓒ Ⓓ
12	131 E. 8th Street	A	B	C	D	Ⓐ Ⓑ Ⓒ Ⓓ
13	1021 Belmont Road	A	B	C	D	Ⓐ Ⓑ Ⓒ Ⓓ
14	113 E. 8th Street	A	B	C	D	Ⓐ Ⓑ Ⓒ Ⓓ

	Delivery Address	Delivery Route				Answer Grid
15	101 Manor Lane	A	B	C	D	Ⓐ Ⓑ Ⓒ Ⓓ
16	24 Belmont Road	A	B	C	D	Ⓐ Ⓑ Ⓒ Ⓓ
17	28 Smith Ave.	A	B	C	D	Ⓐ Ⓑ Ⓒ Ⓓ
18	300 Zebra Ave.	A	B	C	D	Ⓐ Ⓑ Ⓒ Ⓓ
19	27 E. 8th Street	A	B	C	D	Ⓐ Ⓑ Ⓒ Ⓓ
20	390 Mandarin Ave.	A	B	C	D	Ⓐ Ⓑ Ⓒ Ⓓ
21	244 Vegas Circle	A	B	C	D	Ⓐ Ⓑ Ⓒ Ⓓ
22	33 Manor Lane	A	B	C	D	Ⓐ Ⓑ Ⓒ Ⓓ
23	59 Zebra Ave.	A	B	C	D	Ⓐ Ⓑ Ⓒ Ⓓ
24	55 Garcy Street	A	B	C	D	Ⓐ Ⓑ Ⓒ Ⓓ
25	122 E. 8th Street	A	B	C	D	Ⓐ Ⓑ Ⓒ Ⓓ
26	987 Zebra Ave.	A	B	C	D	Ⓐ Ⓑ Ⓒ Ⓓ
27	16 E. 8th Street	A	B	C	D	Ⓐ Ⓑ Ⓒ Ⓓ
28	458 Vegas Circle	A	B	C	D	Ⓐ Ⓑ Ⓒ Ⓓ
29	67 E. 8th Street	A	B	C	D	Ⓐ Ⓑ Ⓒ Ⓓ
30	379 Zebra Ave.	A	B	C	D	Ⓐ Ⓑ Ⓒ Ⓓ
31	15 Manor Lane	A	B	C	D	Ⓐ Ⓑ Ⓒ Ⓓ
32	256 Zebra Ave.	A	B	C	D	Ⓐ Ⓑ Ⓒ Ⓓ
33	955 Vegas Circle	A	B	C	D	Ⓐ Ⓑ Ⓒ Ⓓ
34	125 E. 8th Street	A	B	C	D	Ⓐ Ⓑ Ⓒ Ⓓ
35	148 Belmont Road	A	B	C	D	Ⓐ Ⓑ Ⓒ Ⓓ
36	46 Manor Lane	A	B	C	D	Ⓐ Ⓑ Ⓒ Ⓓ

Answers to Memory Coding Exercises

Exercise #1

1. C	5. A	9. C	13. D	17. C	21. B	25. A	29. A	33. A
2. A	6. D	10. D	14. D	18. D	22. A	26. B	30. D	34. C
3. A	7. B	11. A	15. B	19. A	23. D	27. C	31. B	35. A
4. C	8. B	12. C	16. A	20. C	24. C	28. D	32. C	36. C

Exercise #2

1. A	5. A	9. C	13. C	17. B	21. A	25. D	29. D	33. C
2. B	6. C	10. A	14. A	18. C	22. D	26. B	30. B	34. D
3. B	7. C	11. D	15. A	19. A	23. C	27. D	31. C	35. A
4. C	8. A	12. B	16. D	20. C	24. A	28. A	32. B	36. B

Exercise #3

1. A	5. D	9. A	13. A	17. D	21. C	25. B	29. A	33. D
2. D	6. A	10. C	14. B	18. A	22. C	26. B	30. C	34. A
3. A	7. B	11. B	15. A	19. B	23. A	27. B	31. D	35. C
4. C	8. C	12. D	16. C	20. A	24. C	28. D	32. C	36. A

Exercise #4

1. A	5. C	9. C	13. C	17. D	21. B	25. A	29. C	33. A
2. B	6. A	10. C	14. B	18. A	22. C	26. D	30. C	34. C
3. B	7. D	11. A	15. A	19. A	23. A	27. B	31. B	35. A
4. A	8. B	12. D	16. B	20. C	24. D	28. C	32. D	36. C

Exercise #5

1. A	5. D	9. A	13. C	17. D	21. C	25. A	29. A	33. D
2. C	6. A	10. B	14. A	18. A	22. A	26. C	30. C	34. A
3. A	7. C	11. D	15. B	19. D	23. A	27. D	31. A	35. C
4. B	8. C	12. A	16. C	20. D	24. D	28. C	32. A	36. A

PERSONAL CHARACTERISTICS AND EXPERIENCE INVENTORY

5

Part	Time Allowed	Number of Ques.	Description of Question
5. Personal Characteristics and Experience Inventory	90 minutes	236	Tests for experience and job-related tendencies.

Would you ask someone to play basketball with you if you knew that he did not like the game?

Would you ask someone to see a movie with you if you knew that he did not like that particular movie?

Of course not.

If you were an employer, would you want to hire someone who did not like to work?

Would you hire someone who admitted that he could never get out of bed and was therefore frequently late?

Of course not.

> **The United States Postal Service has to be very careful that the employees it hires have the right attitude, motivation, and psychological state to help them succeed in their work.**

According to the USPS, the personal characteristics and experience inventory questions can be classified into 3 types:

1. Questions that call for an Agree/Disagree answer.
2. Questions that ask the frequency of something.
3. Questions that relate to your experience.

Examples

1. Questions that call for an Agree/Disagree answer.

I always like to work alone.

A. Strongly agree

B. Agree

C. Disagree

D. Strongly disagree

---

2. Questions that ask the frequency of something.

I become angry if I have to work overtime.

A. Very often

B. Often

C. Sometimes

D. Rarely

3. Questions that <u>relate to your experience</u>.

What type of a supervisor would you like the least?

A. a supervisor who is younger than me

B. a supervisor who is older than me

C. a supervisor who is more knowledgeable than me

D. a female supervisor

E. a male supervisor

F. would not mind any of the above supervisors

G. I am not sure.

Your responses to these questions are evaluated to help determine whether or not you are a suitable candidate for employment with the postal service. Because there are no strict "right" or "wrong" answers, practicing these types of questions is not advisable.

PRACTICE TESTS

The Postal test 473E consists of 5 parts:

   1. Address Checking

   2. Forms Completion

   3. Coding

   4. Memory

   5. Personal Characteristics and Experience Inventory

In the following 7 practice tests you will practice test sections 1 – 4.

Each section is timed. (You are only allowed to work on the questions in that part during the allotted time. You **cannot** go to questions from a different part.)

Part	Time Allowed	Number of Ques.	Description of Question
1. Address Checking	11 minutes	60	Compare two addresses.
2. Forms Completion	15 minutes	30	Correctly complete forms.
3. Coding	6 minutes	36	Find correct code for an address.
4. Memory (of coding examples, above)	7 minutes	36	Memorize address codes (which are same as codes in the "Coding" section part of the test.)
5. Personal Characteristics and Experience Inventory	90 minutes	236	Tests for experience and job-related tendencies.

When you practice with these tests, try to simulate test conditions:

1. Find a quiet place where you will not be interrupted.

2. Follow the time allowed directions carefully (STOP at the end of the allotted time.)

3. Try to complete sections 1 – 4 for each test at one sitting.

Part	Time Allowed	Number of Ques.	Description of Question
1. Address Checking	**11 minutes**	**60**	**Compare two addresses.**
2. Forms Completion	15 minutes	30	Correctly complete forms.
3. Coding	6 minutes	36	Find correct code for an address.
4. Memory (of coding examples, above)	7 minutes	36	Memorize address codes (which are same as codes in the "Coding" section part of the test.)

The first Part of this practice test is ADDRESS CHECKING.

(You have 11 minutes to complete this part of the test.)

When you are ready, turn the page and start the test.

———

FREE INTERACTIVE Access Code for PostalTest.com website is: 437347

Address Checking Practice Test 1: Below are 60 pairs of addresses. You have 11 minutes to compare each pair for errors and mark the answer sheet to indicate errors found as follows:

A. No Errors   **B.** Address Only   **C.** Zip Code Only   **D.** Both Address and ZIP Code

	Correct List of Addresses		Address List to be Checked		
	Address	**ZIP**	**Address**	**ZIP**	**Answer Grid**
1	373 Commerc Ave. Norman, VA	32195	373 Comers Ave. Norman, VA	32195	Ⓐ Ⓑ Ⓒ Ⓓ
2	525 Island Cir. Misnsky, NY	78921-2114	525 Island Cir. Misnsky, NY	78921-2114	Ⓐ Ⓑ Ⓒ Ⓓ
3	8985 Liberty Ln. Lola, FL	40558	8935 Liberty Ln. Lola, FL	40523	Ⓐ Ⓑ Ⓒ Ⓓ
4	2571 Carson St. Paradise, AK	33843-0208	2571 Carson St. Paradise, AK	33843-0208	Ⓐ Ⓑ Ⓒ Ⓓ
5	1837 Jones Road Beidly, FL	80562-0208	1887 Jones Road Beidly, FL	80562-0208	Ⓐ Ⓑ Ⓒ Ⓓ
6	690 Keller Lane Poplar, IL	41504-7421	690 Keller Lane Poplar, IL	41504-7421	Ⓐ Ⓑ Ⓒ Ⓓ
7	7831 Forest Ct. Kings, MI	74857	7831 Forest Ct. Kings, MI	74857	Ⓐ Ⓑ Ⓒ Ⓓ
8	4932 Holms Way Questor, MN	34685	4932 Holms Way Questor, MN	34985	Ⓐ Ⓑ Ⓒ Ⓓ
9	987 Justice St. Elk, CT	10501-7463	9887 Justice St Elk, CT	10501-1463	Ⓐ Ⓑ Ⓒ Ⓓ
10	564 Caraco Ave. Davin, CT	74630	564 Caraco Ave. Davin, CT	74630	Ⓐ Ⓑ Ⓒ Ⓓ
11	318 Mecal Pkwy. Kalb, TX	39205	378 Mecal Pkwy. Kalb, TX	39205	Ⓐ Ⓑ Ⓒ Ⓓ
12	1516 Roller Lane Corier, MA	04172-3143	1516 Roller Lane Corier, MA	04175-3143	Ⓐ Ⓑ Ⓒ Ⓓ
13	60 Butler Rd. Tandy, WA	90211	60 Butler Rd. Tandy, WA	98211	Ⓐ Ⓑ Ⓒ Ⓓ
14	P.O. Box 2044 Manor, WA	40382-2354	P.O. Box 2044 Manor, WA	40382-2354	Ⓐ Ⓑ Ⓒ Ⓓ
15	7824 Danfill Ter. Livingston, CA	09365-1014	7824 Danfil Ter. Livingston, CA	09365-1014	Ⓐ Ⓑ Ⓒ Ⓓ

Address Checking Practice Test 1 (cont'd): Continue to compare each pair of addresses for errors and mark the answer sheet as follows:

A. No Errors   **B.** Address Only   **C.** Zip Code Only   **D.** Both Address and ZIP Code

	Correct List of Addresses		Address List to be Checked		
	Address	**ZIP**	**Address**	**ZIP**	**Answer Grid**
16	667 Point Ln. Akron, MN	56802-3182	667 Point Ln. Akron, MA	56802-3782	A B C D
17	P.O. Box 3109 Pelham, AR	54410-4172	P.O. Box 3106 Pelham, AR	54410-4172	A B C D
18	3317 Church St. Midland, MA	85745	3317 Church St. Midland, MA	85745	A B C D
19	1762 West 18th St. Helena, CT	68845	1762 East 18th St. Helena, CT	68345	A B C D
20	4259 Kotter Ave. Kinsey, ME	7012-4613	4259 Kotter Ave. Kinsey, ME	7012-4613	A B C D
21	2183 Delroy Cir. Brenton, FL	43760	2183 Delroy Cir. Brenton, FL	43160	A B C D
22	7287 Benson Way Elba, MS	25390	7287 Benson Way Elby, MS	25390	A B C D
23	3639 Kawanis Rd. Heflin, MN	73010-4644	3639 Kawanis Rd. Heflin, MN	73010-4644	A B C D
24	54 Campfield Rd. Cardiff, IL	29110	54 Campfield Rd. Cardiff, IL	59110	A B C D
25	1620 Charles St. Newton, OR	38402-4224	1920 Charles St. Newton, OR	38402-4234	A B C D
26	4182 Stock Ave. Grant, NY	36096-0204	4182 Stock Ave. Grant, NY	36096-0204	A B C D
27	716 Riverdale Ct. Dozier, AR	43011-9127	116 Riverdale Ct. Dozier, AR	43011-9127	A B C D
28	868 Country Lane Elberta, MI	38978	863 Country Lane Elberta, MI	38918	A B C D
29	384 Best Terrace Samson, SC	24117-3491	384 Best Terrace Samson, SC	24117-3491	A B C D
30	514 Asalon Pkwy. Calera, CA	10204	514 Azalon Pkwy. Calera, CA	10204	A B C D

Address Checking Practice Test 1 (cont'd): Continue to compare each pair of addresses for errors and mark the answer sheet as follows:

A. No Errors   **B.** Address Only   **C.** Zip Code Only   **D.** Both Address and ZIP Code

	Correct List of Addresses		Address List to be Checked		
	Address	**ZIP**	**Address**	**ZIP**	**Answer Grid**
31	1689 Durnet St. Oxford, OH	26028-1948	1607 Durnet St. Oxford, OH	26023-1948	A B C D
32	81 Seneg Pkwy. Madrid, OH	97522	81 Seneg Pkwy. Madrid, AK	97522	A B C D
33	6133 Century St. Dayton, AK	92697	6133 Century St. Dayton, AK	92697	A B C D
34	3658 Placid Rd. Idler, MD	19048-9347	365 Placid Rd. Idler, MD	19048-9341	A B C D
35	8782 Conner Ave. Dora, WA	94897-9746	8782 Coner Ave. Dora, WA	94897-9746	A B C D
36	226 Junior Cir. Brent, RI	26137-6254	226 Junior Cir. Brent, RI	26137-6254	A B C D
37	4748 Point St. Hoover, PA	18247	4748 Point St. Hoover, PA	18547	A B C D
38	1000 Collins Ave. Grimes, VA	19232-9783	100 Collins Ave. Grimes, VA	19232-9183	A B C D
39	286 Rainbow Ct. Argo, ME	24563	286 Rainbow Ct. Argo, ME	24568	A B C D
40	4519 Ridge Way Auburn, KS	13102-1265	4519 Ridge Way Auburn, KS	13102-1265	A B C D
41	721 Veteran Ln. Centre, NY	54258	721 Veterans Ln. Centre, NY	54758	A B C D
42	P.O. Box 9183 Geiger, WA	19325	P.O. Box 9183 Geiger, WA	19322	A B C D
43	946 Tourist Rd. Leeds, NJ	92782-1372	9463 Tourist Rd. Leeds, NJ	92782-1312	A B C D
44	3121 Master Ave Lincoln, MI	52403	312 Master Ave. Lincoln, MI	55403	A B C D
45	1629 Eastern Ln. Florence, TX	83134-0103	1629 Eastern Ln. Florence, TX	83134-0103	A B C D

Address Checking Practice Test 1 (cont'd): Continue to compare each pair of addresses for errors and mark the answer sheet as follows:

A. No Errors   **B.** Address Only   **C.** Zip Code Only   **D.** Both Address and ZIP Code

	Correct List of Addresses		Address List to be Checked		
	Address	**ZIP**	**Address**	**ZIP**	**Answer Grid**
46	3317 China Street Seward, MO	05354	3317 China Street Seward, MO	05324	Ⓐ Ⓑ Ⓒ Ⓓ
47	8159 Brinks Lane Tanker, VA	38433-0201	859 Brinks Lane Tanker, VA	38433-2001	Ⓐ Ⓑ Ⓒ Ⓓ
48	114 Rockaway Ct. Youngs, NY	05268-8372	114 Rockaway Ct. Youngs, NY	05268-8375	Ⓐ Ⓑ Ⓒ Ⓓ
49	2090 Hatter Ave. Vance, WA	15044-7412	2090 Hater Ave. Vance, WA	15044-7412	Ⓐ Ⓑ Ⓒ Ⓓ
50	3162 Overton Rd. Williams, MD	48557	362 Overton Rd. Williams, MD	48527	Ⓐ Ⓑ Ⓒ Ⓓ
51	6274 North Way Ruby, NJ	46583	6274 North Way Ruby, NY	46583	Ⓐ Ⓑ Ⓒ Ⓓ
52	567 Memorial Ln. Larsen, KS	64073	567 Memorial Ln. Larsen, KS	64013	Ⓐ Ⓑ Ⓒ Ⓓ
53	711 Reves Pkwy. Adak, SC	07210-1436	771 Reves Pkwy. Adak, SC	07210-1436	Ⓐ Ⓑ Ⓒ Ⓓ
54	4683 Clinton St. Kodiak, PA	92053	4683 Clinton St. Kodiak, PA	92058	Ⓐ Ⓑ Ⓒ Ⓓ
55	2716 Meteor Cir. St. Paul, MN	17030-6432	2716 Meteor Cir. St. Paul, MN	17080-6432	Ⓐ Ⓑ Ⓒ Ⓓ
56	3241 Colonial Ave. Monroe, RI	15090	324 Colonial Ave. Monroe, RI	12090	Ⓐ Ⓑ Ⓒ Ⓓ
57	P.O. Box 7882 Barrow, TX	03284-3524	P.O. Box 7382 Barrow, TX	03284-3524	Ⓐ Ⓑ Ⓒ Ⓓ
58	4553 Broad Rd. Craig, ME	93660-1089	4553 Broad Rd. Craig, ME	93660-1039	Ⓐ Ⓑ Ⓒ Ⓓ
59	479 Power Street Willow, AK	44001-2917	479 Power Street Willow, AK	44001-2917	Ⓐ Ⓑ Ⓒ Ⓓ
60	924 North Terrace Waldez, OH	13889	924 North Terrace Waldez, OR	13889	Ⓐ Ⓑ Ⓒ Ⓓ

Forms Completion Practice Test 1

This part of the test consists of 5 different forms and 30 questions relating to the 5 forms. Study each form and then answer the questions following each of the forms. (Time allowed: 15 minutes for 30 questions).

Answer questions 1 – 6 based on the following form:

1. RECEIPT FOR INSURED MAIL		
15.	2. Postage	6. ☐ Fragile 7. ☐ Perishable
		8. ☐ Liquid 9. ☐ Hazardous
	3. Insurance Fee	10.
		11. Stamp Postmark Here
	4. Handling Fee	
	5. Total (Postage plus Fees) $\$_____$	
12. Addressee (Sent to):		
13. Street, Apt. Number; or PO Box Number		
14. City, State and ZIP		

	Question	Answer Grid
1	The postmark should be stamped in box: A. 2 B. 15 C. 10 D. 11	Ⓐ Ⓑ Ⓒ Ⓓ
2	The name of the person to whom the mail is being sent should be written in box: A. 15 B. 11 C. 12 D. 10	Ⓐ Ⓑ Ⓒ Ⓓ
3	Where on this form should the ZIP number of the addressee be entered? A. 11 B. 14 C. 3 D. 13	Ⓐ Ⓑ Ⓒ Ⓓ
4	The mail includes fresh pears that are perishable. This should be indicated by a checkmark in box: A. B. 4 C. 7 D. 6	Ⓐ Ⓑ Ⓒ Ⓓ
5	The address of addressee includes "21 West Street." This should be recorded in box: A. 11 B. 8 C. 13 D. 14	Ⓐ Ⓑ Ⓒ Ⓓ
6	David Kim, a Postal Clerk, processes this receipt. He should sign his name in box: A. 15 B. 12 C. 11 D. He should not sign his name.	Ⓐ Ⓑ Ⓒ Ⓓ

Answer questions 7 – 12 based on the following form:

1. RETURN RECEIPT FOR DOMESTIC MAIL	
THIS WHITE SECTION IS TO BE COMPLETED BY THE SENDER	**THIS DARK SECTION IS TO BE COMPLETED UPON DELIVERY OF THE ITEM**

2. ▶Sender must complete items 5, 6, 12, 13, 14, 15, 16, 17 (and 18 if Restricted Delivery is desired.) 3. ▶Sender must print sender's name and address on the reverse side of this card so that card can be returned to sender. 4. ▶Peel off glue protector strips on opposite side and attach to the back of the mail, or on the front if there is enough space.	7. Signature □ Addressee ▶ □ Agent

8. Received by (PRINT)	9. Delivery Date

10. Is delivery address same or different from item 5?   □ Same   □ Different (If different, write delivery address below:

5. Article addressed to:	Type of mail service:	
	12. □ Registered	15. □ C.O.D.
	13. □ Insured	16. □ Express
	14. □ Certified	17. □ Merchandise Return receipt
	18. Restricted delivery (Additional fee) $_____ □ Yes	

6. Article number (from service label)	

	Question	Answer Grid
7	The sender should complete all of the following boxes, except box: A. 5 B. 12 C. 6 D. 7	Ⓐ Ⓑ Ⓒ Ⓓ
8	Upon receipt of the mail, the recipient should sign in box: A. 6 B. 8 C. 7 D. 5	Ⓐ Ⓑ Ⓒ Ⓓ
9	Where on this form should the ZIP number of the person to whom mail is addressed be entered? A. 5 B. 6 C. 8 D. 7	Ⓐ Ⓑ Ⓒ Ⓓ
10	If restricted delivery is requested, that information should be recorded in box: A. 5 B. 7 C. 12 D. 18	Ⓐ Ⓑ Ⓒ Ⓓ
11	The service label has the article number "3864952978." This information should be recorded in box: A. 5 B. 6 C. 14 D. 12	Ⓐ Ⓑ Ⓒ Ⓓ
12	If the delivery address is the same as from item 5, in which box should this be indicated? A. 10 B. 11 C. 18 D. 6	Ⓐ Ⓑ Ⓒ Ⓓ

Answer questions 13 – 18 based on the following form:

STATEMENT FOR PICKUP SERVICE			
1. Information (Product)		**2. Information (Customer)**	
Type of pickup service	**Quantity**	13. First and Last Name	
3. Priority Mail	8.	14. Company Name	
4. Express Mail	9.	15. Address 1.	
5. Parcel Post	10.	16. Address 2	
6.Global Express Guaranteed	11.	17. City	
		18. State.	
7. Estimated weight (total) of all packages (in pounds)	12.	19. Zip + 4	
29.			
20. Affix stamps or Meter Strip in this space		**Method of Payment**	
		21. □ Metered Postage or Stamps	
		22. ☑ Postage Due Account	
		23. □ Express Mail Corporate Account Number	
		24. □ Check (Payable to Postmaster)	
		25. □ Label For Merchandise Return	
26. Signature of Customer		27. Signature of USPS employee	28. Pickup Date and Time

	Question	Answer Grid
13	The postal employee should sign in which box? A. 20　　　　B. 13　　　　C. 27　　　　D. 29	(A) (B) (C) (D)
14	The number of Express Mail items picked up is indicated in box: A. 29　　　　B. 12　　　　C. 3　　　　D. 9	(A) (B) (C) (D)
15	Payment is made with postage stamps. The stamps should be affixed in box: A. 21　　　　B. 20　　　　C. 22　　　　D. 29	(A) (B) (C) (D)
16	If payment is made by check, a checkmark should be placed in box: A. 19　　　　B. 6　　　　C. 24　　　　D. 16	(A) (B) (C) (D)
17	If payment is made by check, it must be made payable to: A. USPS Clerk　B. Postmaster　C. Carrier　　D. Cash	(A) (B) (C) (D)
18	Which of the following is a correct entry for box 12? A. 14 kg.　　　B. 11 lbs.　　　C. 8 pints　　　D. 19 gm.	(A) (B) (C) (D)

Answer questions 19 – 24 based on the following form:

CUSTOMS DECLARATION	
FROM (SENDER): 1. Last and First Name (and Business Name, if any) 2. Street 3. City 4. State 5. Zip	11. Insured Amount
	12. Insured Fees (U.S. $)
	13. Importer's Name and Telephone Number

TO (ADDRESSEE):
6. Last and First Name (and Business Name, if any)
 	
7. Street
 	
8. City
 	
9. State 10. Zip
	14. Sender's instructions in case cannot be delivered:
	15. □ Treat as abandoned
	  □ Return to sender
	  □ Redirect to following address (#16):
	16.

17. Specific description of contents	18. Qty	19. Lbs.	20. Oz.
21. Comments			
22. Check one 23. □ Airmail/Priority 24. □ Surface/Non priority			
25. Check one 26. □ Documents 27. □ Merchandise 28. □ Gift 29. □ Other _____			
30. Date Signed 31. Sender's Signature			

	Question	Answer Grid
19	The contents of the article is "Children's books." This information should be recorded in box: A. 15 B. 16 C. 17 D. 18	(A) (B) (C) (D)
20	The customer wishes this article to be shipped by Airmail. This should be indicated with a checkmark in box: A. 15 B. 26 C. 27 D. 23	(A) (B) (C) (D)
21	Where on this form should the ZIP number of the addressee be entered? A. 5 B. 7 C. 4 D. 10	(A) (B) (C) (D)
22	The insured amount is $325.00. This should be recorded in box: A. 12 B. 11 C. 29 D. 16	(A) (B) (C) (D)
23	The customer signed this form on 11/22/2010. This date should be written in box: A. 18 B. 19 C. 30 D. 7	(A) (B) (C) (D)
24	The contents weigh 6 pounds. The number "6" should be written in box: A. 18 B. 19 C. 30 D. 20	(A) (B) (C) (D)

Answer questions 25 – 30 based on the following form:

Application for Nonprofit Standard Mail Prices	
1. Legal Name of Organization	2. Street Address (including Street/Suite Number)
	3. City, State, Zip
4. Telephone	5. E-mail address
6. Alternate mailing address (if any)	
Type of Organization (Check only one box) 7. □ Educational 8. □ Religious 9. □ Scientific 10. □ Labor 11. □ Veterans	
12. Has this organization previously mailed at nonprofit standard prices? 13. □ YES 14. □ NO	15. If the answer to 12 is "YES", have standard mail privileges ever been revoked? 16. □ YES 17. □ NO
18. Signature of applicant	19. Title of applicant
20. Date this request is submitted.	

	Question	Answer Grid
25	The name of the person requesting Nonprofit Standard Mail Prices is "William Bentley." He should sign in box: A. 1 B. 2 C. 10 D. 18	Ⓐ Ⓑ Ⓒ Ⓓ
26	The applicant "William Bentley" is the president of ABC Charities, Inc. He should write "President" in box: A. 10 B. 19 C. 1 D. 5	Ⓐ Ⓑ Ⓒ Ⓓ

27	The fact that this organization previously mailed at nonprofit standard prices must be indicated by checking box: A. 14 B. 19 C. 13 D. 6	(A) (B) (C) (D)
28	The date that this request is submitted should be indicated in box: A. 19 B. 6 C. 1 D. 20	(A) (B) (C) (D)
29	The postal service received the form on 9/25/10. This date should be recorded in box: A. 19 B. 8 C. 20 D. 7	(A) (B) (C) (D)
30	The applicant's charitable company, "ABC Charities, Inc." is a religious organization. Which box should be checked to indicate the type of organization? A. 14 B. 11 C. 8 D. 19	(A) (B) (C) (D)

Directions for the following 36 Coding Questions

For each of the following 36 "Delivery Addresses" determine based on the coding guide whether the address belongs to Delivery Route A, B, C or D, and mark your answer grid accordingly. You have 6 minutes to code the 36 addresses.

Coding Practice Test #1:   Coding Guide

Range of Addresses	Delivery Route
100 – 999 Elton Parkway 1 - 200 Walters Ave. 50 - 150 N. 32nd Street	A
1000 – 2000 Elton Parkway 151 – 300 N. 32nd Street	B
500 – 6000 Veronica Ave. 1 – 1000 Victory Blvd. 201 – 1500 Walters Ave.	C
All mail that doesn't fall in one of the address ranges listed above	D

	Delivery Address	Delivery Route				Answer Grid
1	161 N. 32nd Street	A	B	C	D	Ⓐ Ⓑ Ⓒ Ⓓ
2	150 Elton Parkway	A	B	C	D	Ⓐ Ⓑ Ⓒ Ⓓ
3	510 Veronica Ave.	A	B	C	D	Ⓐ Ⓑ Ⓒ Ⓓ
4	125 Walters Ave.	A	B	C	D	Ⓐ Ⓑ Ⓒ Ⓓ
5	1000 Elton Parkway	A	B	C	D	Ⓐ Ⓑ Ⓒ Ⓓ
6	201 Walters Ave.	A	B	C	D	Ⓐ Ⓑ Ⓒ Ⓓ
7	195 Walters Ave.	A	B	C	D	Ⓐ Ⓑ Ⓒ Ⓓ
8	100 Victory Blvd.	A	B	C	D	Ⓐ Ⓑ Ⓒ Ⓓ
9	900 Elton Parkway	A	B	C	D	Ⓐ Ⓑ Ⓒ Ⓓ
10	245 Bradford Ave.	A	B	C	D	Ⓐ Ⓑ Ⓒ Ⓓ
11	50 N. 32nd Street	A	B	C	D	Ⓐ Ⓑ Ⓒ Ⓓ
12	1820 Wycoff Street	A	B	C	D	Ⓐ Ⓑ Ⓒ Ⓓ
13	1400 Walters Ave.	A	B	C	D	Ⓐ Ⓑ Ⓒ Ⓓ
14	200 N. 32nd Street	A	B	C	D	Ⓐ Ⓑ Ⓒ Ⓓ

PASS THE NEW POSTAL TEST 473E - 2010 EDITION

	Delivery Address	Delivery Route				Answer Grid
15	110 Walters Ave.	A	B	C	D	Ⓐ Ⓑ Ⓒ Ⓓ
16	1100 Elton Parkway	A	B	C	D	Ⓐ Ⓑ Ⓒ Ⓓ
17	1500 Veronica Ave.	A	B	C	D	Ⓐ Ⓑ Ⓒ Ⓓ
18	850 Elton Parkway	A	B	C	D	Ⓐ Ⓑ Ⓒ Ⓓ
19	500 Victory Blvd.	A	B	C	D	Ⓐ Ⓑ Ⓒ Ⓓ
20	55 N. 32nd Street	A	B	C	D	Ⓐ Ⓑ Ⓒ Ⓓ
21	897 Wilmington Drive	A	B	C	D	Ⓐ Ⓑ Ⓒ Ⓓ
22	400 Decatur Ave.	A	B	C	D	Ⓐ Ⓑ Ⓒ Ⓓ
23	300 N. 32nd Street	A	B	C	D	Ⓐ Ⓑ Ⓒ Ⓓ
24	1201 Walters Ave.	A	B	C	D	Ⓐ Ⓑ Ⓒ Ⓓ
25	200 Walters Ave.	A	B	C	D	Ⓐ Ⓑ Ⓒ Ⓓ
26	908 Fillmore Ave.	A	B	C	D	Ⓐ Ⓑ Ⓒ Ⓓ
27	1500 Elton Parkway	A	B	C	D	Ⓐ Ⓑ Ⓒ Ⓓ
28	1300 Walters Ave.	A	B	C	D	Ⓐ Ⓑ Ⓒ Ⓓ
29	2500 Veronica Ave.	A	B	C	D	Ⓐ Ⓑ Ⓒ Ⓓ
30	900 Victory Blvd.	A	B	C	D	Ⓐ Ⓑ Ⓒ Ⓓ
31	150 N. 32nd Street	A	B	C	D	Ⓐ Ⓑ Ⓒ Ⓓ
32	2500 Walters Ave.	A	B	C	D	Ⓐ Ⓑ Ⓒ Ⓓ
33	250 N. 32nd Street	A	B	C	D	Ⓐ Ⓑ Ⓒ Ⓓ
34	4000 Veronica Ave.	A	B	C	D	Ⓐ Ⓑ Ⓒ Ⓓ
35	1800 Elton Parkway	A	B	C	D	Ⓐ Ⓑ Ⓒ Ⓓ
36	745 Elton Parkway	A	B	C	D	Ⓐ Ⓑ Ⓒ Ⓓ

Memory Practice Test #1:   Coding Guide

Range of Addresses	Delivery Route

You have 5 minutes to memorize the Coding Guide on page 98, then code the following 36 addresses based on your **memory** of the coding guide. (On the actual test you will probably have several minutes to practice answering coding questions. Those minutes can also be used, if you wish, to further memorize the codes.)

You have 7 minutes to answer the following 36 coding questions.

	Delivery Address	Delivery Route				Answer Grid
1	200 Elton Parkway	A	B	C	D	Ⓐ Ⓑ Ⓒ Ⓓ
2	190 N. 32nd Street	A	B	C	D	Ⓐ Ⓑ Ⓒ Ⓓ
3	150 Walters Ave.	A	B	C	D	Ⓐ Ⓑ Ⓒ Ⓓ
4	600 Veronica Ave.	A	B	C	D	Ⓐ Ⓑ Ⓒ Ⓓ
5	1100 Elton Parkway	A	B	C	D	Ⓐ Ⓑ Ⓒ Ⓓ
6	50 N. 32nd Street	A	B	C	D	Ⓐ Ⓑ Ⓒ Ⓓ
7	210 Walters Ave.	A	B	C	D	Ⓐ Ⓑ Ⓒ Ⓓ
8	900 Walker Ave.	A	B	C	D	Ⓐ Ⓑ Ⓒ Ⓓ
9	175 Walters Ave.	A	B	C	D	Ⓐ Ⓑ Ⓒ Ⓓ
10	7000 Veronica Ave.	A	B	C	D	Ⓐ Ⓑ Ⓒ Ⓓ
11	2000 Elton Parkway	A	B	C	D	Ⓐ Ⓑ Ⓒ Ⓓ
12	150 N. 32nd Street	A	B	C	D	Ⓐ Ⓑ Ⓒ Ⓓ
13	900 Elton Parkway	A	B	C	D	Ⓐ Ⓑ Ⓒ Ⓓ
14	1900 Victory Blvd.	A	B	C	D	Ⓐ Ⓑ Ⓒ Ⓓ

	Delivery Address	Delivery Route				Answer Grid
15	100 Victory Blvd.	A	B	C	D	Ⓐ Ⓑ Ⓒ Ⓓ
16	75 Delmar Street	A	B	C	D	Ⓐ Ⓑ Ⓒ Ⓓ
17	400 Elton Parkway	A	B	C	D	Ⓐ Ⓑ Ⓒ Ⓓ
18	2175 Marville Ave.	A	B	C	D	Ⓐ Ⓑ Ⓒ Ⓓ
19	450 N. 32nd Street	A	B	C	D	Ⓐ Ⓑ Ⓒ Ⓓ
20	1201 Walters Ave.	A	B	C	D	Ⓐ Ⓑ Ⓒ Ⓓ
21	200 Walters Ave.	A	B	C	D	Ⓐ Ⓑ Ⓒ Ⓓ
22	900 Victory Blvd.	A	B	C	D	Ⓐ Ⓑ Ⓒ Ⓓ
23	120 N. 32nd Street	A	B	C	D	Ⓐ Ⓑ Ⓒ Ⓓ
24	375 Bakers Ave.	A	B	C	D	Ⓐ Ⓑ Ⓒ Ⓓ
25	900 Veronica Ave.	A	B	C	D	Ⓐ Ⓑ Ⓒ Ⓓ
26	200 Farmers Ave.	A	B	C	D	Ⓐ Ⓑ Ⓒ Ⓓ
27	1500 Elton Parkway	A	B	C	D	Ⓐ Ⓑ Ⓒ Ⓓ
28	125 Victory Blvd.	A	B	C	D	Ⓐ Ⓑ Ⓒ Ⓓ
29	2500 Walters Ave.	A	B	C	D	Ⓐ Ⓑ Ⓒ Ⓓ
30	5000 Veronica Ave.	A	B	C	D	Ⓐ Ⓑ Ⓒ Ⓓ
31	190 Walters Ave.	A	B	C	D	Ⓐ Ⓑ Ⓒ Ⓓ
32	290 N. 32nd Street	A	B	C	D	Ⓐ Ⓑ Ⓒ Ⓓ
33	1500 Walters Ave.	A	B	C	D	Ⓐ Ⓑ Ⓒ Ⓓ
34	840 Furman Street	A	B	C	D	Ⓐ Ⓑ Ⓒ Ⓓ
35	550 Elton Parkway	A	B	C	D	Ⓐ Ⓑ Ⓒ Ⓓ
36	225 N. 32nd Street	A	B	C	D	Ⓐ Ⓑ Ⓒ Ⓓ

Answers: Practice Test #1

Address Checking

1. B	7. A	13. C	19. D	25. D	31. D	37. C	43. D	49. B	55. C
2. A	8. C	14. A	20. A	26. A	32. B	38. D	44. D	50. D	56. D
3. D	9. D	15. B	21. C	27. B	33. A	39. C	45. A	51. B	57. B
4. A	10. A	16. D	22. B	28. D	34. D	40. A	46. C	52. C	58. C
5. B	11. B	17. B	23. A	29. A	35. B	41. D	47. D	53. B	59. A
6. A	12. C	18. A	24. C	30. B	36. A	42. C	48. C	54. C	60. B

Forms Completion

1. D	6. D	11. B	16. C	21. D	26. B
2. C	7. D	12. A	17. B	22. B	27. C
3. B	8. C	13. C	18. B	23. C	28. D
4. C	9. A	14. D	19. C	24. B	29. C
5. C	10. D	15. B	20. D	25. D	30. C

Coding

1. B	5. B	9. A	13. C	17. C	21. D	25. A	29. C	33. B
2. A	6. C	10. D	14. B	18. A	22. D	26. D	30. C	34. C
3. C	7. A	11. A	15. A	19. C	23. B	27. B	31. A	35. B
4. A	8. C	12. D	16. B	20. A	24. C	28. C	32. D	36. A

Memory

1. A	5. B	9. A	13. A	17. A	21. A	25. C	29. D	33. C
2. B	6. A	10. D	14. D	18. D	22. C	26. D	30. C	34. D
3. A	7. C	11. B	15. C	19. D	23. A	27. B	31. A	35. A
4. C	8. D	12. A	16. D	20. C	24. D	28. C	32. B	36. B

Part	Time Allowed	Number of Ques.	Description of Question
1. Address Checking	**11 minutes**	**60**	**Compare two addresses.**
2. Forms Completion	15 minutes	30	Correctly complete forms.
3. Coding	6 minutes	36	Find correct code for an address.
4. Memory (of coding examples, above)	7 minutes	36	Memorize address codes (which are same as codes in the "Coding" section part of the test.)

The first Part of this practice test is ADDRESS CHECKING.

(You have 11 minutes to complete this part of the test.)

When you are ready, turn the page and start the test.

Address Checking Practice Test 2: Below are 60 pairs of addresses. You have 11 minutes to compare each pair for errors and mark the answer sheet to indicate errors found as follows:

A. No Errors   **B.** Address Only   **C.** Zip Code Only   **D.** Both Address and ZIP Code

Correct List of Addresses   Address List to be Checked

	Address	ZIP	Address	ZIP	Answer Grid
1	650 Bouldor Ave. Yuma, MN	30467	620 Boulder Ave. Yuma, MN	30467	A B C D
2	1040 Narrow Rd. Williams, MS	09391	1040 Narrow Rd. Williams, MS	00391	A B C D
3	P.O. Box 6062 Payson, SC	02018-3798	P.O. Box 6065 Payson, SC	02018-3793	A B C D
4	4238 Felder Way Glendale, AK	10912	4238 Felder Way Glendale, AK	10912	A B C D
5	563 Trader Ave. Miami, TX	42803-3425	563 Trader Ave. Miami, TX	42803-3455	A B C D
6	2671 JFK Pkwy. Willis, NY	06693-1012	2671 JFK Pkwy. Willis, NY	06693-1012	A B C D
7	3542 Carren St. Sedonia, MI	11004-2779	3542 Careen St. Sedonia, MI	11004-2719	A B C D
8	196 Venen Ct. Mesa, MA	98813	196 Venen Ave. Mesa, MA	98813	A B C D
9	663 Delva Street Florence, AR	12412-4343	663 Delva Street Florence, AR	12412-4343	A B C D
10	900 Reyes St. Chandler, CA	54001	90 Reyes St. Chandler, CA	24001	A B C D
11	4224 York Road Sierra, OR	03662-4891	4225 York Road Sierra, OR	03662-4891	A B C D
12	562 Trader Ave. Somerton, CT	52729	562 Trader Ave. Somerton, CT	55729	A B C D
13	6084 Overton Ln. Peoria, OH	47901-4189	608 Overton Ln. Peoria, OH	47901-4139	A B C D
14	9372 Island Cir. Eloy, IL	07400-4070	9372 Island Cir. Eloy, IL	07400 4070	A B C D
15	2876 Elderts Ln. Jamaica, NY	11302	2376 Elderts Ln. Jamaica, NY	11302	A B C D

Address Checking Practice Test 2 (cont'd): Continue to compare each pair of addresses for errors and mark the answer sheet as follows:

A. No Errors   **B.** Address Only   **C.** Zip Code Only   **D.** Both Address and ZIP Code

	Correct List of Addresses		Address List to be Checked		
	Address	**ZIP**	**Address**	**ZIP**	**Answer Grid**
16	4325 Ludder Rd. Walton, MS	70467	4325 Ludder Rd. Walton, MA	70467	A B C D
17	3254 Barnes St. Willerd, MS	03391	3254 Barn St. Willerd, MS	03891	A B C D
18	P.O. Box 4039 Quiet, NY	02028-3743	P.O. Box 4039 Quiet, NY	02028-3743	A B C D
19	7738 Field Way Ferndale, CA	90412	738 Field Way Ferndale, CA	90412	A B C D
20	8634 Tungs Ave. Atlas, TX	52603-7422	8684 Tungs Ave. Atlas, TX	52603-7425	A B C D
21	6671 Acer Pkwy. James, FL	04653-5392	6671 Acer Pkwy. James, FL	04653-5392	A B C D
22	4542 Karns St. Seldon, MI	31044-3713	4542 Karns St. Seldon, MI	31044-3718	A B C D
23	7963 Mirage Ct. Lima, MA	57893	796 Mirage Ct. Lima, MA	57863	A B C D
24	2632 Herker St. Rome, MN	32413-2347	2632 Herken St. Rome, MN	32413-2347	A B C D
25	5990 Marina St. Charmer, CA	84401	5990 Marina St. Charmer, CA	84401	A B C D
26	2254 Jersey Road Niece, OR	33429-4921	2254 Jersey Road Neice, OR	33429-4921	A B C D
27	8375 Turk Ave. Sonya, NJ	22325	8375 Turk Ave. Sonya, NJ	22322	A B C D
28	1039 Linker Ln. Newton, IL	47267	1039 Linker Ln. Newton, IL	47267	A B C D
29	1599 Somer Lane Perry, WA	87207-3189	1599 Sumer Lane Perry, WA	87201-3189	A B C D
30	7292 Island Cir. Danker, SC	87684	7292 Island Cir. Danker, SC	87634	A B C D

Address Checking Practice Test 2 (cont'd): Continue to compare each pair of addresses for errors and mark the answer sheet as follows:

A. No Errors   **B.** Address Only   **C.** Zip Code Only   **D.** Both Address and ZIP Code

Correct List of Addresses   **Address List to be Checked**

	Address	ZIP	Address	ZIP	Answer Grid
31	3325 Lumer Rd. Felton, FL	27662-5256	325 Lumer Rd. Felton, FL	27662-5256	(A) (B) (C) (D)
32	527 Comfort Ln. Tempe, WA	27840	527 Cumfort Ln. Tempe, WA	27340	(A) (B) (C) (D)
33	4413 Rama Ave. Taylor, MO	22920-8319	4413 Ramu Ave. Taylor, MO	22920-8319	(A) (B) (C) (D)
34	109 Binion Street Prescott, RI	54462	109 Binion Street Prescott, RI	24462	(A) (B) (C) (D)
35	1537 Venian Ct. Fredonia, FL	11301-6166	1537 Venian Ct. Fredonia, FL	11301-6166	(A) (B) (C) (D)
36	P.O. Box 4012 Gilbert, MS	78454	P.O. Box 4012 Gilbert, MD	78424	(A) (B) (C) (D)
37	291 Ventura Ter. Stafford, AK	35912	291 Ventura Ter. Stafford, AR	35912	(A) (B) (C) (D)
38	5784 Manor Way San Luis, MD	72298-2120	5784 Manor Way San Leo, MD	72298-2120	(A) (B) (C) (D)
39	3739 Spring St. Hayden, NJ	43550	3739 Spring St. Hayden, NJ	43500	(A) (B) (C) (D)
40	854 Center Ave. Clark, VA	33483-0108	854 Center Ave. Clark, VA	33483-1008	(A) (B) (C) (D)
41	672 Bahama Cir. Avon, ME	82601-8273	672 Bahama Cir. Avon, ME	82601-8273	(A) (B) (C) (D)
42	4153 Clay Ave. Parker, KS	40451-7214	453 Clay Ave. Parker, KS	40451-7514	(A) (B) (C) (D)
43	737 Grand Lane Marana, PA	75684	737 Grand Lane Marana, PA	75684	(A) (B) (C) (D)
44	1591 Custard St. Hudson, IL	38564	1591 Custerd St. Hudson, IL	38564	(A) (B) (C) (D)
45	1618 Huron Rd. Duncan, NJ	20127-4341	1618 Horon Rd. Duncan, NJ	20157-4341	(A) (B) (C) (D)

Address Checking Practice Test 2 (cont'd): Continue to compare each pair of addresses for errors and mark the answer sheet as follows:

A. No Errors   **B.** Address Only   **C.** Zip Code Only   **D.** Both Address and ZIP Code

	Correct List of Addresses		Address List to be Checked		
	Address	**ZIP**	**Address**	**ZIP**	**Answer Grid**
46	4617 Indy Ln. Warren, AR	07016-4361	4617 Indy Ln. Warren, AR	07016-4367	Ⓐ Ⓑ Ⓒ Ⓓ
47	2729 Over Ave. Tucker, NY	47603	2729 Over Ave. Tucker, NY	47603	Ⓐ Ⓑ Ⓒ Ⓓ
48	3415 Bonner Rd. Rector, OH	35029	3415 Boner Rd. Rector, OH	35029	Ⓐ Ⓑ Ⓒ Ⓓ
49	9624 Gator Way Wynne, OR	01702-4177	9624 Gator Way Wynne, OR	01702-4117	Ⓐ Ⓑ Ⓒ Ⓓ
50	6617 Coral Lane Prescott, AK	07214	667 Coral Lane Prescott, AK	07224	Ⓐ Ⓑ Ⓒ Ⓓ
51	5779 China Pkwy. Branch, NJ	84203-3254	579 China Pkwy. Branch, NJ	84208-3254	Ⓐ Ⓑ Ⓒ Ⓓ
52	1167 Wells Ct. Viola, MD	60396-1009	167 Wells Ct. Viola, MD	60396-1009	Ⓐ Ⓑ Ⓒ Ⓓ
53	1244 Slattery St. Marshall, FL	12010-1297	1244 Slattery St. Marshall, FL	12010-1297	Ⓐ Ⓑ Ⓒ Ⓓ
54	2439 Harbor St. Conway, VA	89313	2439 Harbor St. Conway, VA	89318	Ⓐ Ⓑ Ⓒ Ⓓ
55	3429 Shop Ave. Jersey, PA	11242-4433	349 Shop Ave. Jersey, PA	11242-4433	Ⓐ Ⓑ Ⓒ Ⓓ
56	5705 Ash St. Buffalo, KS	24001	5705 Ash St. Buffalo, KS	54001	Ⓐ Ⓑ Ⓒ Ⓓ
57	2112 Dawn Cir. Marion, MS	23602-7151	2112 Dawn Cir. Marion, MS	23602-7151	Ⓐ Ⓑ Ⓒ Ⓓ
58	6794 Center St. Eudora, RI	57922	674 Center St. Eudora, RI	57923	Ⓐ Ⓑ Ⓒ Ⓓ
59	P.O. Box 0712 Gentry, WA	62976	P.O. Box 0712 Gentry, WA	62979	Ⓐ Ⓑ Ⓒ Ⓓ
60	1719 East Rd. Wright, MO	90147-3194	1719 East Rd. Wright, MO	90147-3194	Ⓐ Ⓑ Ⓒ Ⓓ

Forms Completion Practice Test 2

This part of the test consists of 5 different forms and 30 questions relating to the 5 forms. Study each form and then answer the questions following each of the forms. (Time allowed: 15 minutes for 30 questions).

Answer questions 1 – 6 based on the following form:

STATEMENT FOR PICKUP SERVICE		
1. Information (Product)		**2. Information (Customer)**
Type of pickup service	**Quantity**	13. First and Last Name
3. Priority Mail	8.	14. Company Name
4. Express Mail	9.	15. Address 1.
5. Parcel Post	10.	16. Address 2
6.Global Express Guaranteed	11.	17. City
		18. State.
7. Estimated weight (total) of all packages (in pounds)	12.	19. Zip + 4

20. Affix stamps or Meter Strip in this space	Method of Payment
	21. □ Metered Postage or Stamps
	22. □ Postage Due Account
	23. □ Express Mail Corporate Account Number
	24. □ Check (Payable to Postmaster)
	25. □ Label For Merchandise Return

26. Signature of Customer	27. Signature of USPS employee	28. Pickup Date and Time

Question	Answer Grid
1 In which box would you indicate that the mail articles were picked up on September 12, 2010? A. 20　　　　　B. 26　　　　　C. 28　　　　　D. 2	Ⓐ Ⓑ Ⓒ Ⓓ
2 The stamps should be affixed in box: A. 8　　　　　B. 20　　　　　C. 5　　　　　D. 8	Ⓐ Ⓑ Ⓒ Ⓓ
3 Where on this form should the postal employee sign? A. 26　　　　　B. 27　　　　　C. 13　　　　　D. 28	Ⓐ Ⓑ Ⓒ Ⓓ
4 Which of the following is a correct entry for box 10? A. Express　　　B. 9/10/10　　　C. $4.50　　　D. 8	Ⓐ Ⓑ Ⓒ Ⓓ
5 The customer paid $13.00 in the form of stamps. Which box should be checked? A. 21　　　　　B. 7　　　　　C. 24　　　　　D. 22	Ⓐ Ⓑ Ⓒ Ⓓ
6 The customer's Zip+4 number is 11201-3765. This should be indicated in box: A. 19　　　　　B. 9　　　　　C. 10　　　　　D. 20	Ⓐ Ⓑ Ⓒ Ⓓ

Answer questions 7 – 12 based on the following form:

RECEIVE FOR REGISTERED MAIL		
RECEIPT FOR REGISTERED MAIL		

1. This section is to be completed by the post office.	2. Registered Number:	4. Date Stamp	
		5. Charge for Handling	8. Fee for Return Receipt
	3. Registration Fee $ _____	6. Postage Amount	9. Fee for Restricted Delivery
		7. Received by	
10. This section is to be completed by the postal customer. **Please PRINT with ballpoint pen, or TYPE.**	11. TO:		
	12. FROM:		
FORM # 7477 (Copy 1 – Customer) (Copy 2 – Post Office)			
(See information on reverse side of this form.)			

Question	Answer Grid
7 The Registration Fee is $9.75 and the Postage Amount is $2.85. What amount should be entered in box 6? A. 12.60 B. 2.85 C. 9.75 D. 12	Ⓐ Ⓑ Ⓒ Ⓓ
8 The address where the mail is being sent to should be entered in box: A. 11 B. 12 C. 7 D. 4	Ⓐ Ⓑ Ⓒ Ⓓ
9 The customer wishes Restricted Delivery. In which box should the fee for restricted delivery be entered? A. 5 B. 6 C. 8 D. 9	Ⓐ Ⓑ Ⓒ Ⓓ
10 Which of the following boxes should be completed by the postal customer? A. 7 B. 9 C. 3 D. 11	Ⓐ Ⓑ Ⓒ Ⓓ
11 The name of the postal employee who processes the Receipt For Registered Mail should be entered in which box? A. 11 B. 12 C. 1 D. 7	Ⓐ Ⓑ Ⓒ Ⓓ
12 The date stamp should be stamped in box: A. 1 B. 2 C. 3 D. 4	Ⓐ Ⓑ Ⓒ Ⓓ

Answer questions 13 – 18 based on the following form:

1. RECEIPT FOR INSURED MAIL		
15.	2. Postage	6. ☐ Fragile 7. ☐ Perishable
		8. ☐ Liquid 9. ☐ Hazardous
	3. Insurance Fee	10.
		11. Stamp Postmark Here
	4. Handling Fee	
	5. Total (Postage plus Fees) $\$$_____	
12. Addressee (Sent to):		
13. Street, Apt. Number; or PO Box Number		
14. City, State and ZIP		

Question	Answer Grid
13 The first and last name of the person to whom the mail is being sent should be entered in box: A. 14 B. 13 C. 9 D. 12	Ⓐ Ⓑ Ⓒ Ⓓ
14 The postmark should be stamped in box: A. 8 B. 9 C. 5 D. 11	Ⓐ Ⓑ Ⓒ Ⓓ
15 The ZIP code of the addressee must be entered in box: A. 12 B. 13 C. 14 D. 15	Ⓐ Ⓑ Ⓒ Ⓓ
16 In which of the following boxes is a "check mark" appropriate? A. 6 B. 15 C. 2 D. 10	Ⓐ Ⓑ Ⓒ Ⓓ
17 Postage is $2.00. Handling Fee is $4.50. Insurance Fee is $3.25. What is the correct amount to be entered in box 5? A. 8.75: B. 9.75 C. 7.75 D. 9.00	Ⓐ Ⓑ Ⓒ Ⓓ
18 The PO Box Number of the addressee must be entered in which box? A. 14 B. 13 C. 10 D. 11	Ⓐ Ⓑ Ⓒ Ⓓ

Answer questions 19 – 24 based on the following form:

Application for Nonprofit Standard Mail Prices	
1. Legal Name of Organization	2. Street Address (including Street/Suite Number)
	3. City, State, Zip
4. Telephone	5. E-mail address
6. Alternate mailing address (if any)	
Type of Organization (Check only one box) 7. □ Educational 8. □ Religious 9. □ Scientific 10. □ Labor 11. □ Veterans	
12. Has this organization previously mailed at nonprofit standard prices? 13. □ YES 14. □ NO	15. If the answer to 12 is "YES", have standard mail privileges ever been revoked? 16. □ YES 17. □ NO
18. Signature of applicant	19. Title of applicant
20. Date this request is submitted.	21.

	Question	Answer Grid
19	In which box should the name of the organization be entered? A. 1　　　B. 2　　　C. 3　　　D. 21	Ⓐ Ⓑ Ⓒ Ⓓ
20	The organization is a non-profit Labor organization. Based on this, box ___ should be checked. A. 8　　　B. 9　　　C. 5　　　D. 10	Ⓐ Ⓑ Ⓒ Ⓓ
21	Where on this form should the applicant sign? A. 18　　　B. 20　　　C. 1　　　D. 3	Ⓐ Ⓑ Ⓒ Ⓓ
22	Which of the following is a correct entry for box 4? A. 11214B　　B. 718-674-2456　C. 1/10　　D. 16	Ⓐ Ⓑ Ⓒ Ⓓ
23	The customer previously mailed at nonprofit standard prices. Based on this, which box should be checked? A. 12　　　B. 13　　　C. 14　　　D. 21	Ⓐ Ⓑ Ⓒ Ⓓ
24	The Application for Nonprofit Standard Mail Prices was submitted on July 7, 2010. This date should be entered in which box? A. 1　　　B. 18　　　C. 21　　　D. 20	Ⓐ Ⓑ Ⓒ Ⓓ

Answer questions 25 – 30 based on the following form:

CLAIM FOR DOMESTIC OR INTERNATIONAL MAIL					
2. Addressee Information			**3. Mailer Information**		
4. Last Name	5.MI	6. First Name	7. Last Name	8.MI	9. First Name
10. Business Name (if addressee is a company)			11. Business Name (if mailer is a company)		
12. Address (Number and Street)			13. Address (Number and Street)		
14. Address (Suite or Apartment Number)			15. Address (Suite or Apartment Number)		
16. City State Zip			17. City State Zip		
18. E-mail Address (Optional)			19. E-mail Address (Optional)		

20. Description of Missing Lost or Damaged Contents
21. Item codes: 01 Jewelry, 02 Electronics, 03 Computers, 04 Animals, 05 Firearms, 06 Event Tickets,   07 Sports Equipment, 08 Collectibles, 09 Clothing, 10 Cash, 11 Other.
22. Describe the contents and check off (L) for Lost or (D) for damaged

23.Item	24. Description of contents	25.(L)or(D)	26.Item code	27.Value or Repair Cost in $
1		L ☐ D ☐		
2		L ☐ D ☐		
3		L ☐ D ☐		
		28. Total Value or Repair Cost in $		

29. The customer submitting the claim is the ☐ Mailer ☐ Addressee	
30. Payment is to be made to the ☐ Mailer ☐ Addressee	
31. Signature of Postal Customer submitting Claim	32. Date signed (MM/DD/YYYY)

	Question	Answer Grid
25	The first name of the customer who mailed the article should be entered in which box? A. 6　　　B. 4　　　C. 7　　　D. 9	(A) (B) (C) (D)
26	The e-mail address of the Addressee should be entered in which box? A. 18　　　B. 19　　　C. 12　　　D. 13	(A) (B) (C) (D)
27	In which box on this form should the customer submitting the claim sign? A. 32　　　B. 31　　　C. 4　　　D. 7	(A) (B) (C) (D)
28	The missing item is a computer. The item code is therefore: A. 21　　　B. 01　　　C. 02　　　D. 03	(A) (B) (C) (D)
29	Which of the following is a correct entry for box 32? A. May 21, 2010　B. 7/21/10　　C. 10/20/2010　　D. 1/9	(A) (B) (C) (D)
30	The middle initial of the Mailer should be entered in which box? A. 5　　　B. 8　　　C. 4　　　D. 7	(A) (B) (C) (D)

Directions for the following 36 Coding Questions

For each of the following 36 "Delivery Addresses" determine based on the coding guide whether the address belongs to Delivery Route A, B, C or D, and mark your answer grid accordingly. You have 6 minutes to code the 36 addresses.

Coding Practice Test # 2:   Coding Guide

Range of Addresses	Delivery Route
50 – 400 S. 9th Street 10 – 99 Jackson Lane 10 – 200 Willis Ave.	A
100 – 500 Jackson Lane 401 – 1000 S. 9th Street	B
2000 – 8000 Dover Place 1 – 100 Emperor Drive 201 – 2500 Willis Ave.	C
All mail that doesn't fall in one of the address ranges listed above	D

	Delivery Address	Delivery Route				Answer Grid
1	10 Willis Ave.	A	B	C	D	Ⓐ Ⓑ Ⓒ Ⓓ
2	105 Jackson Lane	A	B	C	D	Ⓐ Ⓑ Ⓒ Ⓓ
3	2000 Dover Place	A	B	C	D	Ⓐ Ⓑ Ⓒ Ⓓ
4	420 S. 9th Street	A	B	C	D	Ⓐ Ⓑ Ⓒ Ⓓ
5	300 Willis Ave.	A	B	C	D	Ⓐ Ⓑ Ⓒ Ⓓ
6	80 S. 9th Street	A	B	C	D	Ⓐ Ⓑ Ⓒ Ⓓ
7	350 Jackson Lane	A	B	C	D	Ⓐ Ⓑ Ⓒ Ⓓ
8	10 Jackson Lane	A	B	C	D	Ⓐ Ⓑ Ⓒ Ⓓ
9	9000 Dover Place	A	B	C	D	Ⓐ Ⓑ Ⓒ Ⓓ
10	200 Willis Ave.	A	B	C	D	Ⓐ Ⓑ Ⓒ Ⓓ
11	6000 Dover Place	A	B	C	D	Ⓐ Ⓑ Ⓒ Ⓓ
12	250 S. 9th Street	A	B	C	D	Ⓐ Ⓑ Ⓒ Ⓓ
13	10 Emperor Drive	A	B	C	D	Ⓐ Ⓑ Ⓒ Ⓓ
14	89 Jackson Lane	A	B	C	D	Ⓐ Ⓑ Ⓒ Ⓓ

	Delivery Address	Delivery Route				Answer Grid
15	501 S. 9th Street	A	B	C	D	Ⓐ Ⓑ Ⓒ Ⓓ
16	379 Jackson Lane	A	B	C	D	Ⓐ Ⓑ Ⓒ Ⓓ
17	649 Prospect Park	A	B	C	D	Ⓐ Ⓑ Ⓒ Ⓓ
18	350 S. 9th Street	A	B	C	D	Ⓐ Ⓑ Ⓒ Ⓓ
19	7650 Dover Place	A	B	C	D	Ⓐ Ⓑ Ⓒ Ⓓ
20	620 Willis Ave.	A	B	C	D	Ⓐ Ⓑ Ⓒ Ⓓ
21	867 S. 9th Street	A	B	C	D	Ⓐ Ⓑ Ⓒ Ⓓ
22	2800 Dinkens Ave.	A	B	C	D	Ⓐ Ⓑ Ⓒ Ⓓ
23	375 S. 9th Street	A	B	C	D	Ⓐ Ⓑ Ⓒ Ⓓ
24	8100 Dover Place	A	B	C	D	Ⓐ Ⓑ Ⓒ Ⓓ
25	75 Emperor Drive	A	B	C	D	Ⓐ Ⓑ Ⓒ Ⓓ
26	100 Willis Ave.	A	B	C	D	Ⓐ Ⓑ Ⓒ Ⓓ
27	770 S. 9th Street	A	B	C	D	Ⓐ Ⓑ Ⓒ Ⓓ
28	100 Emperor Drive	A	B	C	D	Ⓐ Ⓑ Ⓒ Ⓓ
29	2400 Willis Ave.	A	B	C	D	Ⓐ Ⓑ Ⓒ Ⓓ
30	99 Jackson Lane	A	B	C	D	Ⓐ Ⓑ Ⓒ Ⓓ
31	145 Willis Ave.	A	B	C	D	Ⓐ Ⓑ Ⓒ Ⓓ
32	90 Emperor Drive	A	B	C	D	Ⓐ Ⓑ Ⓒ Ⓓ
33	55 Jackson Lane	A	B	C	D	Ⓐ Ⓑ Ⓒ Ⓓ
34	470 Jackson Lane	A	B	C	D	Ⓐ Ⓑ Ⓒ Ⓓ
35	490 Fennimore Lane	A	B	C	D	Ⓐ Ⓑ Ⓒ Ⓓ
36	6500 Dover Place	A	B	C	D	Ⓐ Ⓑ Ⓒ Ⓓ

Memory Practice Test #2:   Coding Guide

Range of Addresses	Delivery Route

You have 5 minutes to memorize the Coding Guide on page 118, then code the following 36 addresses based on your <u>memory</u> of the coding guide. (On the actual test you will probably have several minutes to practice answering coding questions. Those minutes can also be used, if you wish, to further memorize the codes.)

You have 7 minutes to answer the following 36 coding questions.

	Delivery Address	Delivery Route				Answer Grid
1	50 Jackson Lane	A	B	C	D	Ⓐ Ⓑ Ⓒ Ⓓ
2	2000 Dover Place	A	B	C	D	Ⓐ Ⓑ Ⓒ Ⓓ
3	200 Willis Ave.	A	B	C	D	Ⓐ Ⓑ Ⓒ Ⓓ
4	890 Blanding Road	A	B	C	D	Ⓐ Ⓑ Ⓒ Ⓓ
5	400 Jackson Lane	A	B	C	D	Ⓐ Ⓑ Ⓒ Ⓓ
6	90 Jackson Lane	A	B	C	D	Ⓐ Ⓑ Ⓒ Ⓓ
7	3500 Willis Ave.	A	B	C	D	Ⓐ Ⓑ Ⓒ Ⓓ
8	444 S. 9th Street	A	B	C	D	Ⓐ Ⓑ Ⓒ Ⓓ
9	2800 Charles Drive	A	B	C	D	Ⓐ Ⓑ Ⓒ Ⓓ
10	210 Willis Ave.	A	B	C	D	Ⓐ Ⓑ Ⓒ Ⓓ
11	50 S. 9th Street	A	B	C	D	Ⓐ Ⓑ Ⓒ Ⓓ
12	10 Emperor Drive	A	B	C	D	Ⓐ Ⓑ Ⓒ Ⓓ
13	100 Jackson Lane	A	B	C	D	Ⓐ Ⓑ Ⓒ Ⓓ
14	100 Willis Ave.	A	B	C	D	Ⓐ Ⓑ Ⓒ Ⓓ

	Delivery Address	Delivery Route				Answer Grid
15	6000 Dover Place	A	B	C	D	Ⓐ Ⓑ Ⓒ Ⓓ
16	410 Jackson Lane	A	B	C	D	Ⓐ Ⓑ Ⓒ Ⓓ
17	350 S. 9th Street	A	B	C	D	Ⓐ Ⓑ Ⓒ Ⓓ
18	777 S. 9th Street	A	B	C	D	Ⓐ Ⓑ Ⓒ Ⓓ
19	200 Emperor Drive	A	B	C	D	Ⓐ Ⓑ Ⓒ Ⓓ
20	150 Willis Ave.	A	B	C	D	Ⓐ Ⓑ Ⓒ Ⓓ
21	2500 Willis Ave.	A	B	C	D	Ⓐ Ⓑ Ⓒ Ⓓ
22	865 S. 9th Street	A	B	C	D	Ⓐ Ⓑ Ⓒ Ⓓ
23	100 Elmers Lane	A	B	C	D	Ⓐ Ⓑ Ⓒ Ⓓ
24	200 S. 9th Street	A	B	C	D	Ⓐ Ⓑ Ⓒ Ⓓ
25	120 Willis Ave.	A	B	C	D	Ⓐ Ⓑ Ⓒ Ⓓ
26	90 Emperor Drive	A	B	C	D	Ⓐ Ⓑ Ⓒ Ⓓ
27	60 Jackson Lane	A	B	C	D	Ⓐ Ⓑ Ⓒ Ⓓ
28	7000 Dover Place	A	B	C	D	Ⓐ Ⓑ Ⓒ Ⓓ
29	436 Jackson Lane	A	B	C	D	Ⓐ Ⓑ Ⓒ Ⓓ
30	50 Emperor Drive	A	B	C	D	Ⓐ Ⓑ Ⓒ Ⓓ
31	280 S. 9th Street	A	B	C	D	Ⓐ Ⓑ Ⓒ Ⓓ
32	1000 Emperor Drive	A	B	C	D	Ⓐ Ⓑ Ⓒ Ⓓ
33	900 S. 9th Street	A	B	C	D	Ⓐ Ⓑ Ⓒ Ⓓ
34	820 Willis Ave.	A	B	C	D	Ⓐ Ⓑ Ⓒ Ⓓ
35	75 Jackson Lane	A	B	C	D	Ⓐ Ⓑ Ⓒ Ⓓ
36	5500 Dover Place	A	B	C	D	Ⓐ Ⓑ Ⓒ Ⓓ

Answers: Practice Test #2

Address Checking

1. B	7. D	13. D	19. B	25. A	31. B	37. B	43. A	49. C	55. B
2. C	8. B	14. C	20. D	26. B	32. D	38. B	44. B	50. D	56. C
3. D	9. A	15. B	21. A	27. C	33. B	39. C	45. D	51. D	57. A
4. A	10. D	16. B	22. C	28. A	34. C	40. C	46. C	52. B	58. D
5. C	11. B	17. D	23. D	29. D	35. A	41. A	47. A	53. A	59. C
6. A	12. C	18. A	24. B	30. C	36. D	42. D	48. B	54. C	60. A

Forms Completion

1. C	6. A	11. D	16. A	21. A	26. A
2. B	7. B	12. D	17. B	22. B	27. B
3. B	8. A	13. D	18. B	23. B	28. D
4. D	9. D	14. D	19. A	24. D	29. C
5. A	10. D	15. C	20. D	25. D	30. B

Coding

1. A	5. C	9. D	13. C	17. D	21. B	25. C	29. C	33. A
2. B	6. A	10. A	14. A	18. A	22. D	26. A	30. A	34. B
3. C	7. B	11. C	15. B	19. C	23. A	27. B	31. A	35. D
4. B	8. A	12. A	16. B	20. C	24. D	28. C	32. C	36. C

Memory

1. A	5. B	9. D	13. B	17. A	21. C	25. A	29. B	33. B
2. C	6. A	10. C	14. A	18. B	22. B	26. C	30. C	34. C
3. A	7. D	11. A	15. C	19. D	23. D	27. A	31. A	35. A
4. D	8. B	12. C	16. B	20. A	24. A	28. C	32. D	36. C

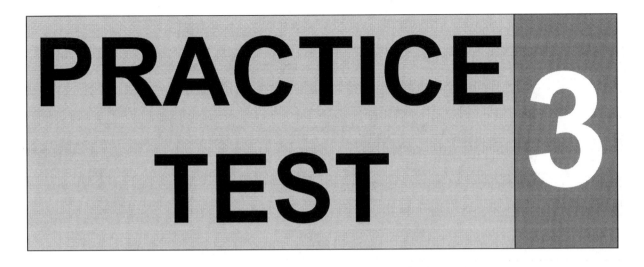

PRACTICE TEST 3

Part	Time Allowed	Number of Ques.	Description of Question
1. Address Checking	**11 minutes**	**60**	**Compare two addresses.**
2. Forms Completion	15 minutes	30	Correctly complete forms.
3. Coding	6 minutes	36	Find correct code for an address.
4. Memory (of coding examples, above)	7 minutes	36	Memorize address codes (which are same as codes in the "Coding" section part of the test.)

The first Part of this practice test is ADDRESS CHECKING.

(You have 11 minutes to complete this part of the test.)

When you are ready, turn the page and start the test.

Address Checking Practice Test 3: Below are 60 pairs of addresses. You have 11 minutes to compare each pair for errors and mark the answer sheet to indicate errors found as follows:

A. No Errors   **B.** Address Only   **C.** Zip Code Only   **D.** Both Address and ZIP Code

	Correct List of Addresses		Address List to be Checked		
	Address	**ZIP**	**Address**	**ZIP**	**Answer Grid**
1	4617 India Ln. Warren, AR	07016-4362	4617 India Ln Watren, AR	07016-4362	A B C D
2	2729 Overly Ave. Tucker, NY	47603	2729 Overly Ave. Tucker, NJ	47603	A B C D
3	3415 Bonner Rd. Rector, OH	35029	3415 Bonner Rd. Rector, OH	35209	A B C D
4	9624 Kator Way Wynne, OR	01703-4717	9624 Gator Way Wynne, OR	01703-4117	A B C D
5	6617 Coral Lane Prescott, AK	07214	6617 Coral Lane Prescott, AK	07214	A B C D
6	779 China Pkwy. Brach, NJ	84203-8254	779 China Pkwy. Brach, NJ	84203-3254	A B C D
7	167 Welay Ct. Viola, MD	60396-1009	167 Velay Ct. Viola, MD	60396-1009	A B C D
8	1244 Slattery St. Marshall, FL	10201-1297	124 Slattery St. Marshall, FL	10201-7297	A B C D
9	439 Harbor Ave. Conway, VA	89318	439 Harbor Ave. Conway, VA	89318	A B C D
10	3377 Shop St. Jersey, PA	11245-4433	3377 Shop St. Jersey, PA	11242-4433	A B C D
11	5705 Ash Street Buffalo, KS	24001	5705 Ark Street Buffalo, KS	24001	A B C D
12	2112 Dawn Cir. Marion, MS	23605-7151	212 Dawn Cir. Marion, MS	23602-7151	A B C D
13	6794 Center St. Eudora, RI	57922	679 Center St. Eudora, RI	57922	A B C D
14	P.O. Box 0912 Bentry, WA	62070	P.O. Box 0912 Gentry, WA	62976	A B C D
15	171 Eastern Rd. Wright, MO	90147-3194	171 Eastern Rd. Wright, MO	90174-3194	A B C D

Address Checking Practice Test 3 (cont'd): Continue to compare each pair of addresses for errors and mark the answer sheet as follows:

A. No Errors   **B.** Address Only   **C.** Zip Code Only   **D.** Both Address and ZIP Code

	Correct List of Addresses		Address List to be Checked		
	Address	ZIP	Address	ZIP	Answer Grid
16	47 Kings Road Truman, PA	48779-4769	47 Kings Road Truman, PA	48779-4769	Ⓐ Ⓑ Ⓒ Ⓓ
17	2237 Tiger Street West Fork, SC	62627-5257	2237 Tiger Street East Fork, SC	62627-5257	Ⓐ Ⓑ Ⓒ Ⓓ
18	4326 Mirage Cir. Salem, KS	82047	4326 Mirage Cir. Salem, KS	82047	Ⓐ Ⓑ Ⓒ Ⓓ
19	5934 Paeder Ct. Rogers, CA	92328-8193	5934 Paeder Ct. Rogers, CA	92328-8193	Ⓐ Ⓑ Ⓒ Ⓓ
20	P.O. Box 3196 Stuggord, ME	55467	P.O. Box 3196 Stuggard, ME	55461	Ⓐ Ⓑ Ⓒ Ⓓ
21	7787 Capital St. Sidney, CT	31108-2772	7737 Capital St. Sidney, CT	31108-2772	Ⓐ Ⓑ Ⓒ Ⓓ
22	1482 Keller Way Atkins, TX	47482	1482 Keller Way Atkins, TX	47485	Ⓐ Ⓑ Ⓒ Ⓓ
23	630 Park Terrace Cabot, MI	92185	630 Park Terrace Cabot, MI	92135	Ⓐ Ⓑ Ⓒ Ⓓ
24	5534 Trump St. Newport, AR	27985-2419	5534 Trump St. Newport, AK	27982-2419	Ⓐ Ⓑ Ⓒ Ⓓ
25	3200 Faith Pkwy. Boles, NY	54035	3200 Faith Pkwy. Boles, NY	54035	Ⓐ Ⓑ Ⓒ Ⓓ
26	4394 Brock Ave. Gurdon, OR	43814-0702	4394 Brick Ave. Gurdon, OR	43814-0702	Ⓐ Ⓑ Ⓒ Ⓓ
27	632 Freedom Ln. Lowell, MA	68051-7281	6321 Freedom Ln. Lowell, MA	68051-7231	Ⓐ Ⓑ Ⓒ Ⓓ
28	527 Cactus Road Diaz, MN	14116-3293	527 Cactus Road Diaz, MN	14116-3293	Ⓐ Ⓑ Ⓒ Ⓓ
29	1698 Myers Cir. St. Joe, IL	28617	1693 Myers Cir. St. Joe, IL	28677	Ⓐ Ⓑ Ⓒ Ⓓ
30	2937 Justice Lane Stark City, MS	17490-9345	2937 Justice Lane Star City, MS	17490-9345	Ⓐ Ⓑ Ⓒ Ⓓ

Address Checking Practice Test 3 (cont'd): Continue to compare each pair of addresses for errors and mark the answer sheet as follows:

A. No Errors   **B.** Address Only   **C.** Zip Code Only   **D.** Both Address and ZIP Code

	Correct List — Address	ZIP	Checked — Address	ZIP	Answer Grid
31	9723 Jazon Lane, Phoenix, KS	18221	9723 Jason Lane, Phoenix, KS	18221	A B C D
32	72 Boulder Ct. Freemont, WA	39214-5245	72 Boulder Ct. Freemont, WA	39514-5245	A B C D
33	4653 Caserto St. Boise, ME	77104-1127	4653 Caserta St. Boise, ME	77104-1121	A B C D
34	583 Diamond St. Akron, MA	21175-8230	583 Damond St. Akron, MA	21115-8230	A B C D
35	3627 Hills Ave. Gilbert, CT	99024	3627 Hills Ave. Gilbert, CT	99024	A B C D
36	P.O. Box 7137 Garfand, NY	35223-4554	P.O. Box 7137 Garland, NY	35223-4554	A B C D
37	4388 Lewis Way Newark, SC	51812	4388 Lewis Way Newark, SC	51312	A B C D
38	747 Main Street Winston, MO	47303-9052	747 Main Street Winston, MO	47303-9052	A B C D
39	584 Fox Lane Stockton, IL	33630	5184 Fox Lane Stockton, IL	38630	A B C D
40	3116 Laker Road Jerome, TX	83701	3116 Laker Road Jerome, TX	83707	A B C D
41	612 Reasure Cir. Madison, MI	80152-2450	612 Reasure Cir. Madison, MI	80152-2450	A B C D
42	7417 Potters Ave. Scotti, OR	85900-7850	7417 Potter Ave. Scotti, OR	85900-7850	A B C D
43	427 Overons Ave. Tulsa, OH	08373-3697	427 Overon Ave. Tulsa, OH	08373-3667	A B C D
44	165 Square St. Durham, MN	89358	1165 Square St. Durham, MN	89350	A B C D
45	853 Queens Rd. Laredo, MD	30331-4590	853 Queens Rd. Lareto, MD	30331-4290	A B C D

Address Checking Practice Test 3 (cont'd): Continue to compare each pair of addresses for errors and mark the answer sheet as follows:

A. No Errors   **B.** Address Only   **C.** Zip Code Only   **D.** Both Address and ZIP Code

	Correct List of Addresses		Address List to be Checked		
	Address	**ZIP**	**Address**	**ZIP**	**Answer Grid**
46	4837 Holder Rd. Chandler, PA	55673	4837 Holder Rd. Chandler, PA	55673	Ⓐ Ⓑ Ⓒ Ⓓ
47	1743 Broad Street Glendale, KS	96869	1743 Broad Street Glendale, KS	96866	Ⓐ Ⓑ Ⓒ Ⓓ
48	3561 Thunder Ave. Plano, MD	24212-7372	356 Thunder Ave. Plano, MD	24212-7372	Ⓐ Ⓑ Ⓒ Ⓓ
49	172 Waller Ave. Lincoln, WA	60435	172 Wall Ave. Lincoln, WA	60432	Ⓐ Ⓑ Ⓒ Ⓓ
50	8282 Young St. Buffalo, MS	33890-3322	8282 Young St. Buffalo, MS	33890-3322	Ⓐ Ⓑ Ⓒ Ⓓ
51	4171 Sheps Way Austin, FL	46516	4171 Shepps Way Austin, FL	46516	Ⓐ Ⓑ Ⓒ Ⓓ
52	2922 Bancor St. Henderson, MJ	54438-1113	2922 Bancor St. Henderson, MJ	54438-1113	Ⓐ Ⓑ Ⓒ Ⓓ
53	667 Springer Way Raleigh, AK	37916-3896	667 Springer Way Raleigh, AK	37916-3894	Ⓐ Ⓑ Ⓒ Ⓓ
54	5182 Trader Ave. Memphis, MO	15226-3285	5182 Traker Ave. Memphis, MO	15526-3285	Ⓐ Ⓑ Ⓒ Ⓓ
55	2583 Election Ln. Tempo, VA	69859	2583 Election Ln. Tempo, VA	66859	Ⓐ Ⓑ Ⓒ Ⓓ
56	176 Numeral Ct. Aurora, RI	69457	1716 Numeral Ct. Aurora, RI	69457	Ⓐ Ⓑ Ⓒ Ⓓ
57	4896 Rastern St. Riverside, IL	21107-4724	489 Rastern St. Riverside, IL	27107-4724	Ⓐ Ⓑ Ⓒ Ⓓ
58	921 Soldiers Rd. Columbus, AR	14814	92 Soldiers Rd. Columbus, AR	14874	Ⓐ Ⓑ Ⓒ Ⓓ
59	3374 Happer Ln. El Paso, CA	16403	3374 Happer Ln. El Paso, CA	16403	Ⓐ Ⓑ Ⓒ Ⓓ
60	P.O. Box 1208 Toledo, IL	27071-6755	P.O. Box 1203 Toledo, IL	27071-6755	Ⓐ Ⓑ Ⓒ Ⓓ

Forms Completion Practice Test 3

This part of the test consists of 5 different forms and 30 questions relating to the 5 forms. Study each form and then answer the questions following each of the forms. (Time allowed: 15 minutes for 30 questions).

Answer questions 1 – 6 based on the following form:

RECEIPT FOR REGISTERED MAIL			
1. This section is to be completed by the post office.	2.Registered Number:	4. Date Stamp	
	3. Registration Fee $ _____	5. Charge for Handling	8. Fee for Return Receipt
		6. Postage Amount	9. Fee for Restricted Delivery
		7. Received by	
10. This section is to be completed by the postal customer. Please PRINT with ballpoint pen, or TYPE.	11. TO:		
	12. FROM:		
FORM # 7477 (Copy 1 – Customer) (Copy 2 – Post Office) (See information on reverse side of this form.)			

	Question	Answer Grid
1	The fee for Return Receipt should be entered in which box? A. 3　　　　B. 7　　　　C. 8　　　　D. 2	Ⓐ Ⓑ Ⓒ Ⓓ
2	Which of the following boxes should not be completed by the post office? A. 5　　　　B. 7　　　　C. 6　　　　D. 12	Ⓐ Ⓑ Ⓒ Ⓓ
3	Where on this form should the customer enter his name and address? A. 7　　　　B. 11　　　　C. 12　　　　D. 4	Ⓐ Ⓑ Ⓒ Ⓓ
4	Which of the following is a correct entry for box 3? A. done　　B. 9/12/10　　C. 6.50　　D. 9:13	Ⓐ Ⓑ Ⓒ Ⓓ
5	The customer paid $16.00 charge for handling. This amount should be recorded in which box? A. 2　　　　B. 5　　　　C. 7　　　　D. 12	Ⓐ Ⓑ Ⓒ Ⓓ
6	In which box should the Registered Number be entered? A. 5　　　　B. 9　　　　C. 8　　　　D. 2	Ⓐ Ⓑ Ⓒ Ⓓ

Answer questions 7 – 12 based on the following form:

1. RECEIPT FOR INSURED MAIL		
15.	2. Postage	6. ☐ Fragile 7. ☐ Perishable
		8. ☐ Liquid 9. ☐ Hazardous
	3. Insurance Fee	10.
		11. Stamp Postmark Here
	4. Handling Fee	
	5. Total (Postage plus Fees) $_____	
12. Addressee (Sent to):		
13. Street, Apt. Number; or PO Box Number		
14. City, State and ZIP		

	Question	Answer Grid
7	The first and last name of the addressee should be entered in box: A. 14 B. 13 C. 9 D. 12	Ⓐ Ⓑ Ⓒ Ⓓ
8	The postmark should be stamped in which box? A. 8 B. 10 C. 11 D. 15	Ⓐ Ⓑ Ⓒ Ⓓ
9	The State of the Addressee should be entered in which box? A. 14 B. 13 C. 12 D. 15	Ⓐ Ⓑ Ⓒ Ⓓ
10	Which of the following is a correct entry for box 4? A. 8/11 B. 9/1/10 C. $3.25 D. CM	Ⓐ Ⓑ Ⓒ Ⓓ
11	The contents of the article is a glass bottle. Which box should be checked? A. 6 B. 7 C. 8 D. 9	Ⓐ Ⓑ Ⓒ Ⓓ
12	The postage is $4.25. This should be entered in which box? A. 4 B. 3 C. 2 D. 11	Ⓐ Ⓑ Ⓒ Ⓓ

Answer questions 13 – 18 based on the following form:

CUSTOMS DECLARATION	
FROM (SENDER): 1. Last and First Name (and Business Name, if any) _____ 2. Street _____ 3. City _____ 4. State _____ 5. Zip	11. Insured Amount 12. Insured Fees (U.S. $) 13. Importer's Name and Telephone Number

TO (ADDRESSEE):
 	
6. Last and First Name (and Business Name, if any)
 	
_____
7. Street
 	
_____
8. City
 	
_____
9. State   10. Zip
	14. Sender's instructions in case cannot be delivered:
	15. □ Treat as abandoned
	    □ Return to sender
	    □ Redirect to following address (#16):
	16.
	_____
	_____
	_____

17. Specific description of contents	18. Qty	19. Lbs.	20. Oz.

21. Comments

22. Check one   23. □ Airmail/Priority   24. □ Surface/Non priority

25. Check one   26 □ Documents   27. □ Merchandise 28. □ Gift 29. □ Other _____

30. Date Signed   31. Sender's Signature

	Question	Answer Grid
13	The Insured Amount is $300.00 and the Insured Fees are $9.75. Which amount should be entered in box 12? A. 309.75 B. 9.75 C. 300.00 D. 39	Ⓐ Ⓑ Ⓒ Ⓓ
14	The contents should be specifically described in which box? A. 16 B. 21 C. 17 D. 25	Ⓐ Ⓑ Ⓒ Ⓓ
15	Where on this form should the customer sign? A. 1 B. 29 C. 6 D. 31	Ⓐ Ⓑ Ⓒ Ⓓ
16	Which of the following is a correct entry for box 30? A. done B. 9/12/10 C. March D. N/A	Ⓐ Ⓑ Ⓒ Ⓓ
17	If the article cannot be delivered, the customer wishes that it be returned to him. To convey this, the customer must check off the appropriate box in section: A. 27 B. 15 C. 24 D. 26	Ⓐ Ⓑ Ⓒ Ⓓ
18	The sender signs the customs declaration on 7/25/10. In which box should this date be indicated? A. 1 B. 30 C. 10 D. 11	Ⓐ Ⓑ Ⓒ Ⓓ

Answer questions 19 – 24 based on the following form:

HOLD MAIL (AUTHORIZATION)
1. This form authorizes the USPS to hold mail for a minimum of 3 days but not more than 30 days for the following individual(s).
2. Name(s)
3. Address (including number and street, Apartment or suite number, city, state, ZIP)
4. A. □ I shall pick up my mail upon my return. I understand that if I do not pick up my mail, then mail delivery will not be made until I pick up the mail.   4.B. □ I am authorizing the USPS to deliver all held mail and resume mail delivery on the end ing date indicated below.

5. Beginning Date To Hold Mail	6. Ending Date To Hold Mail (This date can only be changed by the customer – in writing)	7. Signature of Customer

Shaded section is for Post Office (USPS) use only.		
8. Date this form received:		
9. Carrier name and ID Number receiving this form:	10. Carrier Name	11. Carrier ID Number
12. Clerk name and ID Number receiving this form	13. Clerk Name	14. Clerk ID Number

15. If option B was selected, complete this section:

16. □ All mail has been picked up on (Date)_____

17. □ Regular mail delivery to be resumed on (Date) _____

Signature of:

18. USPS Employee: _____19. Date Signed: _____

	Question	Answer Grid
19	Which of the following boxes is not to be completed by the customer? A. 10　　　B. 5　　　C. 3　　　D. 2	Ⓐ Ⓑ Ⓒ Ⓓ
20	The customer signs in which box? A. 18　　　B. 7　　　C. 2　　　D. 10	Ⓐ Ⓑ Ⓒ Ⓓ
21	Where on this form should the clerk or carrier sign? A. 2　　　B. 7　　　C. 18　　　D. 19	Ⓐ Ⓑ Ⓒ Ⓓ
22	Which of the following is a correct entry for box 6? A. done　　　B. 6/1/10　　　C. $6.50　　　D. 1	Ⓐ Ⓑ Ⓒ Ⓓ
23	This form authorizes the USPS to hold mail for a maximum of how many days? A. 13　　　B. 13　　　C. 33　　　D. 30	Ⓐ Ⓑ Ⓒ Ⓓ
24	If a clerk receives this form, the clerk's I.D. number must be entered in which box? A. 11　　　B. 7　　　C. 14　　　D. 19	Ⓐ Ⓑ Ⓒ Ⓓ

Answer questions 25 – 30 based on the following form:

Application for Nonprofit Standard Mail Prices	
1. Legal Name of Organization	2. Street Address (including Street/Suite Number)
	3. City, State, Zip
4. Telephone	5. E-mail address
6. Alternate mailing address (if any)	
Type of Organization (Check only one box) 7. □ Educational　　　8. □ Religious　　　9. □ Scientific　　　10. □ Labor　　　11. □ Veterans	
12. Has this organization previously mailed at nonprofit standard prices? 13. □ YES　　　14. □ NO	15. If the answer to 12 is "YES", have standard mail privileges ever been revoked? 16. □ YES　　　17. □ NO
18. Signature of applicant	19. Title of applicant
20. Date this request is submitted.	21.

	Question	Answer Grid
25	The telephone number of the organization is entered in which box? A. 1　　　　B. 2　　　　C. 3　　　　D. 4	Ⓐ Ⓑ Ⓒ Ⓓ
26	The applicant signs in which box? A. 1　　　B. 19　　　C. 18　　　D. 20	Ⓐ Ⓑ Ⓒ Ⓓ

27	Where on this form should the date the request is submitted be entered? A. 7　　　　B. 19　　　　C. 20　　　　D. 18	Ⓐ Ⓑ Ⓒ Ⓓ
28	Which of the following is a correct entry for box 19? A. done　　B. Pres.　　C. $6.50　　D. $5	Ⓐ Ⓑ Ⓒ Ⓓ
29	The organization is a nonprofit Veterans organization. This is indicated by checking box: A. 8　　　　B. 7　　　　C. 9　　　　D. 11	Ⓐ Ⓑ Ⓒ Ⓓ
30	The E-mail address of the organization should be entered in box: A. 1　　　　B. 2　　　　C. 3　　　　D. 5	Ⓐ Ⓑ Ⓒ Ⓓ

Directions for the following 36 Coding Questions

For each of the following 36 "Delivery Addresses" determine based on the coding guide whether the address belongs to Delivery Route A, B, C or D, and mark your answer grid accordingly. You have 6 minutes to code the 36 addresses.

Coding Practice Test #3:   Coding Guide

Range of Addresses	Delivery Route
50 – 600 London Lane 1 – 500 Condor Ave. 100 – 1200 N. 69th Street	A
601– 1200 London Lane 1201 - 2000 N. 69th Street	B
1000 – 1900 Gordon Ave, 200 – 1500 Patterson Circle 501 – 2000 Condor Ave.	C
All mail that doesn't fall in one of the address ranges listed above	D

	Delivery Address	Delivery Route				Answer Grid
1	500 London Lane	A	B	C	D	Ⓐ Ⓑ Ⓒ Ⓓ
2	1000 Gordon Ave.	A	B	C	D	Ⓐ Ⓑ Ⓒ Ⓓ
3	1 Condor Ave.	A	B	C	D	Ⓐ Ⓑ Ⓒ Ⓓ
4	610 London Lane	A	B	C	D	Ⓐ Ⓑ Ⓒ Ⓓ
5	3000 Condor Ave.	A	B	C	D	Ⓐ Ⓑ Ⓒ Ⓓ
6	700 N. 69th Street	A	B	C	D	Ⓐ Ⓑ Ⓒ Ⓓ
7	1901 N. 69th Street	A	B	C	D	Ⓐ Ⓑ Ⓒ Ⓓ
8	2000 Gordon Ave.	A	B	C	D	Ⓐ Ⓑ Ⓒ Ⓓ
9	425 London Lane	A	B	C	D	Ⓐ Ⓑ Ⓒ Ⓓ
10	690 Condor Ave.	A	B	C	D	Ⓐ Ⓑ Ⓒ Ⓓ
11	200 Patterson Circle	A	B	C	D	Ⓐ Ⓑ Ⓒ Ⓓ
12	1100 N. 69th Street	A	B	C	D	Ⓐ Ⓑ Ⓒ Ⓓ
13	1249 Gordon Ave.	A	B	C	D	Ⓐ Ⓑ Ⓒ Ⓓ
14	469 Condor Ave.	A	B	C	D	Ⓐ Ⓑ Ⓒ Ⓓ

	Delivery Address	Delivery Route				Answer Grid
15	1500 Patterson Circle	A	B	C	D	Ⓐ Ⓑ Ⓒ Ⓓ
16	600 London Lane	A	B	C	D	Ⓐ Ⓑ Ⓒ Ⓓ
17	1585 N. 69th Street	A	B	C	D	Ⓐ Ⓑ Ⓒ Ⓓ
18	860 London Lane	A	B	C	D	Ⓐ Ⓑ Ⓒ Ⓓ
19	1000 Billings Way	A	B	C	D	Ⓐ Ⓑ Ⓒ Ⓓ
20	125 Condor Ave.	A	B	C	D	Ⓐ Ⓑ Ⓒ Ⓓ
21	1340 Gordon Ave.	A	B	C	D	Ⓐ Ⓑ Ⓒ Ⓓ
22	3247 Gordon Ave.	A	B	C	D	Ⓐ Ⓑ Ⓒ Ⓓ
23	625 N. 69th Street	A	B	C	D	Ⓐ Ⓑ Ⓒ Ⓓ
24	907 Condor Ave.	A	B	C	D	Ⓐ Ⓑ Ⓒ Ⓓ
25	1678 Ridge Pkwy.	A	B	C	D	Ⓐ Ⓑ Ⓒ Ⓓ
26	987 London Lane	A	B	C	D	Ⓐ Ⓑ Ⓒ Ⓓ
27	459 Patterson Circle	A	B	C	D	Ⓐ Ⓑ Ⓒ Ⓓ
28	1290 Gordon Ave.	A	B	C	D	Ⓐ Ⓑ Ⓒ Ⓓ
29	4956 Hartman Road	A	B	C	D	Ⓐ Ⓑ Ⓒ Ⓓ
30	411 Condor Ave.	A	B	C	D	Ⓐ Ⓑ Ⓒ Ⓓ
31	1357 Condor Ave.	A	B	C	D	Ⓐ Ⓑ Ⓒ Ⓓ
32	1050 London Lane	A	B	C	D	Ⓐ Ⓑ Ⓒ Ⓓ
33	1777 N. 69th Street	A	B	C	D	Ⓐ Ⓑ Ⓒ Ⓓ
34	335 London Lane	A	B	C	D	Ⓐ Ⓑ Ⓒ Ⓓ
35	1200 Patterson Circle	A	B	C	D	Ⓐ Ⓑ Ⓒ Ⓓ
36	879 N. 69th Street	A	B	C	D	Ⓐ Ⓑ Ⓒ Ⓓ

Memory Practice Test #3:   Coding Guide

Range of Addresses	Delivery Route

You have 5 minutes to memorize the Coding Guide on page 138, then code the following 36 addresses based on your <u>memory</u> of the coding guide. (On the actual test you will probably have several minutes to practice answering coding questions. Those minutes can also be used, if you wish, to further memorize the codes.)

You have 7 minutes to answer the following 36 coding questions.

	Delivery Address	Delivery Route				Answer Grid
1	125 Condor Ave.	A	B	C	D	(A) (B) (C) (D)
2	609 London Lane	A	B	C	D	(A) (B) (C) (D)
3	1000 N. 69th Street	A	B	C	D	(A) (B) (C) (D)
4	9000 Condor Ave.	A	B	C	D	(A) (B) (C) (D)
5	1100 Gordon Ave.	A	B	C	D	(A) (B) (C) (D)
6	334 Condor Ave.	A	B	C	D	(A) (B) (C) (D)
7	1500 Patterson Circle	A	B	C	D	(A) (B) (C) (D)
8	860 London Lane	A	B	C	D	(A) (B) (C) (D)
9	1290 N. 69th Street	A	B	C	D	(A) (B) (C) (D)
10	907 Condor Ave.	A	B	C	D	(A) (B) (C) (D)
11	997 N. 69th Street	A	B	C	D	(A) (B) (C) (D)
12	876 Neiman Place	A	B	C	D	(A) (B) (C) (D)
13	50 London Lane	A	B	C	D	(A) (B) (C) (D)
14	1556 Gordon Ave.	A	B	C	D	(A) (B) (C) (D)

	Delivery Address	Delivery Route				Answer Grid
15	100 N. 69th Street	A	B	C	D	Ⓐ Ⓑ Ⓒ Ⓓ
16	1720 N. 69th Street	A	B	C	D	Ⓐ Ⓑ Ⓒ Ⓓ
17	2500 Patterson Circle	A	B	C	D	Ⓐ Ⓑ Ⓒ Ⓓ
18	500 London Lane	A	B	C	D	Ⓐ Ⓑ Ⓒ Ⓓ
19	1444 Condor Ave.	A	B	C	D	Ⓐ Ⓑ Ⓒ Ⓓ
20	245 Patterson Circle	A	B	C	D	Ⓐ Ⓑ Ⓒ Ⓓ
21	245 Condor Ave.	A	B	C	D	Ⓐ Ⓑ Ⓒ Ⓓ
22	1648 Gordon Ave.	A	B	C	D	Ⓐ Ⓑ Ⓒ Ⓓ
23	933 Fuller Street	A	B	C	D	Ⓐ Ⓑ Ⓒ Ⓓ
24	1500 N. 69th Street	A	B	C	D	Ⓐ Ⓑ Ⓒ Ⓓ
25	450 London Lane	A	B	C	D	Ⓐ Ⓑ Ⓒ Ⓓ
26	200 Peterson Circle	A	B	C	D	Ⓐ Ⓑ Ⓒ Ⓓ
27	955 London Lane	A	B	C	D	Ⓐ Ⓑ Ⓒ Ⓓ
28	1900 Gordon Ave.	A	B	C	D	Ⓐ Ⓑ Ⓒ Ⓓ
29	1550 Patterson Circle	A	B	C	D	Ⓐ Ⓑ Ⓒ Ⓓ
30	1100 N. 69th Street	A	B	C	D	Ⓐ Ⓑ Ⓒ Ⓓ
31	769 London Lane	A	B	C	D	Ⓐ Ⓑ Ⓒ Ⓓ
32	1200 Patterson Circle	A	B	C	D	Ⓐ Ⓑ Ⓒ Ⓓ
33	477 London Lane	A	B	C	D	Ⓐ Ⓑ Ⓒ Ⓓ
34	2000 Condor Ave.	A	B	C	D	Ⓐ Ⓑ Ⓒ Ⓓ
35	1775 N. 69th Street	A	B	C	D	Ⓐ Ⓑ Ⓒ Ⓓ
36	465 Condor Ave.	A	B	C	D	Ⓐ Ⓑ Ⓒ Ⓓ

Answers: Practice Test #3

Address Checking

1. B	7. B	13. B	19. A	25. A	31. B	37. C	43. D	49. D	55. C
2. B	8. D	14. D	20. D	26. B	32. C	38. A	44. D	50. A	56. B
3. C	9. A	15. C	21. B	27. D	33. D	39. D	45. D	51. B	57. D
4. D	10. C	16. A	22. C	28. A	34. D	40. C	46. A	52. A	58. D
5. A	11. B	17. B	23. C	29. D	35. A	41. A	47. C	53. C	59. A
6. C	12. D	18. A	24. D	30. B	36. B	42. B	48. B	54. D	60. B

Forms Completion

1. C	6. D	11. A	16. B	21. C	26. C
2. D	7. D	12. C	17. B	22. B	27. C
3. C	8. C	13. B	18. B	23. D	28. B
4. C	9. A	14. C	19. A	24. C	29. D
5. B	10. C	15. D	20. B	25. D	30. D

Coding

1. A	5. D	9. A	13. C	17. B	21. C	25. D	29. D	33. B
2. C	6. A	10. C	14. A	18. B	22. D	26. B	30. A	34. A
3. A	7. B	11. C	15. C	19. D	23. A	27. C	31. C	35. C
4. B	8. D	12. A	16. A	20. A	24. C	28. C	32. B	36. A

Memory

1. A	5. C	9. B	13. A	17. D	21. A	25. A	29. D	33. A
2. B	6. A	10. C	14. C	18. A	22. C	26. D	30. A	34. C
3. A	7. C	11. A	15. A	19. C	23. D	27. B	31. B	35. B
4. D	8. B	12. D	16. B	20. C	24. B	28. C	32. C	36. A

Part	Time Allowed	Number of Ques.	Description of Question
1. Address Checking	**11 minutes**	**60**	**Compare two addresses.**
2. Forms Completion	15 minutes	30	Correctly complete forms.
3. Coding	6 minutes	36	Find correct code for an address.
4. Memory (of coding examples, above)	7 minutes	36	Memorize address codes (which are same as codes in the "Coding" section part of the test.)

The first Part of this practice test is ADDRESS CHECKING.

(You have 11 minutes to complete this part of the test.)

When you are ready, turn the page and start the test.

———

Address Checking Practice Test 4: Below are 60 pairs of addresses. You have 11 minutes to compare each pair for errors and mark the answer sheet to indicate errors found as follows:

A. No Errors   **B.** Address Only   **C.** Zip Code Only   **D.** Both Address and ZIP Code

	Correct List of Addresses		Address List to be Checked		
	Address	ZIP	Address	ZIP	Answer Grid
1	493 Holders Road Chandler, PA	55673	493 Holder Road Chandler, PA	55673	A B C D
2	174 Thunder Cir. Plano, MD	24512-7372	174 Thunder Cir. Plano, MD	24212-7372	A B C D
3	356 Broad Street Glendale, KS	95866	356 Broad Street Glendale, KS	95866	A B C D
4	1172 Wall Ave. Lincoln, WA	60482	172 Wall Ave. Lincoln, WA	60432	A B C D
5	8282 Young St. Buffalo, MS	33890-3322	8282 Young St. Buffalo, MS	33890-3322	A B C D
6	4171 Shepps Ter. Austin, FL	46519	4171 Shepps Ter. Austin, FL	46516	A B C D
7	2822 Bancor St. Henderson, NJ	54438-1113	2822 Bankor St. Henderson, NJ	54438-1113	A B C D
8	6676 Spring Way Raleigh, AK	37916-3894	6676 Spring Way Raleigh, AK	37916-3894	A B C D
9	5182 Trader Ave. Memphis, MO	15256-3285	5182 Trader Ave. Memphis, MO	15526-3285	A B C D
10	258 Elena Lane Temko, VA	69859	258 Elena Lane Tempo, VA	66859	A B C D
11	1716 Numeral Ct. Aurora, RI	69451	176 Numeral Ct. Aurora, RI	69457	A B C D
12	4896 East Pkwy. Riverside, IL	21107-4724	4896 East St. Riverside, IL	21107-4724	A B C D
13	92 Soldiers Road Columbus, AR	14374	92 Soldiers Road Columbus, AR	14874	A B C D
14	3374 Happer Ln. El Paso, CA	10400	3374 Happer Ln. El Paso, PA	16403	A B C D
15	P.O. Box 1208 Toledo, IL	27071-6755	P.O. Box 1203 Toledo, IL	27071-6755	A B C D

Address Checking Practice Test 4 (cont'd): Continue to compare each pair of addresses for errors and mark the answer sheet as follows:

A. No Errors   **B.** Address Only   **C.** Zip Code Only   **D.** Both Address and ZIP Code

	Correct List of Addresses		Address List to be Checked		
	Address	**ZIP**	**Address**	**ZIP**	**Answer Grid**
16	4391 Coffey St. Torrance, WA	87908	4391 Coffey St. Torrance, WA	87908	Ⓐ Ⓑ Ⓒ Ⓓ
17	2721 Korean Rd. Hayward, MD	18051	2721 Korean Rd. Hayward, MD	18021	Ⓐ Ⓑ Ⓒ Ⓓ
18	8784 Reserve Ln. Salinas, TX	27174-6112	8784 Reserve St. Salinas, TX	27174-6112	Ⓐ Ⓑ Ⓒ Ⓓ
19	6602 Corner Ave. Lanchester, FL	18253-1927	6602 Corner Ave. Lancester, FL	18223-1927	Ⓐ Ⓑ Ⓒ Ⓓ
20	3472 Trokker St. Hampton, NJ	48821	3472 Trotter St. Hampton, NJ	48827	Ⓐ Ⓑ Ⓒ Ⓓ
21	5128 Tillard Ave. Paterson, KS	62453	5128 Tilard Ave. Paterson, KS	62453	Ⓐ Ⓑ Ⓒ Ⓓ
22	8216 Harlow Rd. Joliet, MO	45426	8216 Harlow Rd. Joliet, MO	45429	Ⓐ Ⓑ Ⓒ Ⓓ
23	6728 Stewart Way Paladen, RI	91012	6728 Stewart Way Paladen, RI	91012	Ⓐ Ⓑ Ⓒ Ⓓ
24	7944 Craw Pkwy. Corona, SC	84230-2533	7944 Craw Pkwy. Corona, SC	84230-2538	Ⓐ Ⓑ Ⓒ Ⓓ
25	2451 Donner St. Eugene, MS	65141-2002	2451 Doner St. Eugene, MS	65141-2002	Ⓐ Ⓑ Ⓒ Ⓓ
26	325 Bueffer Cir. Pomona, WA	04160-2716	325 Buffer Cir. Pomona, WA	04130-2716	Ⓐ Ⓑ Ⓒ Ⓓ
27	1896 Column Ct. Salem, MN	89183	1896 Column Ct. Salem, MN	89183	Ⓐ Ⓑ Ⓒ Ⓓ
28	P.O. Box 2917 Dayton, AR	11422-3543	P.O. Box 2917 Dayton, AR	11422-3343	Ⓐ Ⓑ Ⓒ Ⓓ
29	4253 Hills St. Cape Coral, PA	12236	425 Hills St. Cape Coral, PA	12236	Ⓐ Ⓑ Ⓒ Ⓓ
30	9216 Devry Lane Rockford, CT	96101-2314	9216 Devry Lane Rockford, CT	96101-2314	Ⓐ Ⓑ Ⓒ Ⓓ

Address Checking Practice Test 4 (cont'd): Continue to compare each pair of addresses for errors and mark the answer sheet as follows:

A. No Errors   **B.** Address Only   **C.** Zip Code Only   **D.** Both Address and ZIP Code

	Correct List of Addresses		**Address List to be Checked**		
	Address	**ZIP**	**Address**	**ZIP**	**Answer Grid**
31	8183 Mater Pkwy. Oceanside, MA	82327	883 Mater Pkwy. Oceanside, MA	82327	Ⓐ Ⓑ Ⓒ Ⓓ
32	2673 Clinton Ln. Providence, NY	61704-5115	2673 Clinton Ln. Providence, NY	61704-5115	Ⓐ Ⓑ Ⓒ Ⓓ
33	6624 Scenic Rd. Ontario, AK	24346	6624 Scenic Rd. Ontario, AK	24346	Ⓐ Ⓑ Ⓒ Ⓓ
34	1794 Spruil Rd. Kaskin, CA	87754	1794 Spruil Rd. Kaskin, CA	37754	Ⓐ Ⓑ Ⓒ Ⓓ
35	7800 Sony St. Jackson, OR	65268-3411	7800 Sony St. Jacksen, OR	65263-3411	Ⓐ Ⓑ Ⓒ Ⓓ
36	353 Tavern Ave. Tempo, MI	57217	353 Tavern Ave. Tempor, MI	57217	Ⓐ Ⓑ Ⓒ Ⓓ
37	4392 Folger St. Huntsville, VA	25518-1973	492 Folger St. Huntsville, VA	25518-1913	Ⓐ Ⓑ Ⓒ Ⓓ
38	P.O. Box 1283 Oxnard, ME	17715-1674	P.O. Box 1283 Oxnard, ME	17714-1674	Ⓐ Ⓑ Ⓒ Ⓓ
39	173 Boxley Ct. Columbus, AK	23526-3291	173 Boxley Ct. Columbus, AK	23326-3291	Ⓐ Ⓑ Ⓒ Ⓓ
40	6211 Court Way Mobile, IL	92517	621 Court Way Mobile, IL	92517	Ⓐ Ⓑ Ⓒ Ⓓ
41	1899 Becker St. Glendale, OR	83165	1899 Becker St. Glendale, OR	83165	Ⓐ Ⓑ Ⓒ Ⓓ
42	4285 Manor Ave. Tacoma, WA	11853-1749	4285 Manor Ave. Tacoma, WA	11823-1749	Ⓐ Ⓑ Ⓒ Ⓓ
43	5924 Pillow Cir. Irving, FL	30823	5924 Pillow Cir. Irvina, FL	30853	Ⓐ Ⓑ Ⓒ Ⓓ
44	7253 Farmers St. Yonkers, MN	24914	7253 Farmer St. Yonkers, MN	24914	Ⓐ Ⓑ Ⓒ Ⓓ
45	916 Diamond Ln. Richmond, OH	21071-3533	916 Diamond Ln. Richmond, OH	21071-3533	Ⓐ Ⓑ Ⓒ Ⓓ

Address Checking Practice Test 4 (cont'd): Continue to compare each pair of addresses for errors and mark the answer sheet as follows:

A. No Errors   **B.** Address Only   **C.** Zip Code Only   **D.** Both Address and ZIP Code

	Correct List of Addresses		Address List to be Checked		
	Address	**ZIP**	**Address**	**ZIP**	**Answer Grid**
46	8004 April Ln. Syracuse, KS	76662-3325	8004 April Ln. Syracuse, KS	76662-3235	A B C D
47	3911 Canary Ave. Orange, MS	59238-5250	3911 Canary Ave. Orange, MS	59538-5250	A B C D
48	P.O. Box 3415 Warren, IL	37748-5441	P.O. Box 3415 Warren, IL	37748-5441	A B C D
49	772 Bedding Ct. Fuller, CA	28415	772 Beding Ct. Fuller, CA	28415	A B C D
50	9714 Spring St. Cary, MI	85019	9714 Spring St. Cary, MI	85019	A B C D
51	4319 Lake Road Columbia, TX	43034-0374	4316 Lake Road Columbia, TX	43034-0347	A B C D
52	1679 Mirror Cir. Coral, ME	36487	1679 Mirror Cir. Coral, ME	36437	A B C D
53	4411 Bedford Ave. New Haven, AR	32695	441 Bedford Ave. New Haven, AR	32665	A B C D
54	5840 Booker St. Waco, VA	36344-1911	5840 Bocker St. Waco, VA	36344-1911	A B C D
55	3114 Century St. Topeka, OR	36445	314 Century St. Topeka, OR	36445	A B C D
56	6789 Lanser Way El Monte, MA	55136-7563	6789 Lanse Way El Monte, MA	55136-7568	A B C D
57	216 Clover Lane Concord, WA	33860-3043	216 Clover Lane Concord, WA	33360-3043	A B C D
58	8432 Zone Street Visalia, NY	40101-4146	8432 Zone Street Visalia, NY	40101-4146	A B C D
59	1199 Tourist Road Denton, SC	58649	199 Tourist Road Denton, SC	58646	A B C D
60	5367 Milan St. Provo, NJ	57342-6743	5367 Milan St. Provo, NJ	57342-6743	A B C D

Forms Completion Practice Test 4

This part of the test consists of 5 different forms and 30 questions relating to the 5 forms. Study each form and then answer the questions following each of the forms. (Time allowed: 15 minutes for 30 questions).

Answer questions 1 – 6 based on the following form:

HOLD MAIL (AUTHORIZATION)		
1. This form authorizes the USPS to hold mail for a minimum of 3 days but not more than 30 days for the following individual(s).		
2. Name(s)		
3. Address (including number and street, Apartment or suite number, city, state, ZIP)		
4. A. ☐ I shall pick up my mail upon my return. I understand that if I do not pick up my mail, then mail delivery will not be made until I pick up the mail.		
4.B. ☐ I am authorizing the USPS to deliver all held mail and resume mail delivery on the end ing date indicated below.		
5. Beginning Date To Hold Mail	6. Ending Date To Hold Mail (This date can only be changed by the customer – in writing)	7. Signature of Customer
Shaded section is for Post Office (USPS) use only.		
8. Date this form received:		
9. Carrier name and ID Number receiving this form:	10. Carrier Name	11. Carrier ID Number
12. Clerk name and ID Number receiving this form	13. Clerk Name	14. Clerk ID Number
15. If option B was selected, complete this section:		
16. ☐ All mail has been picked up on (Date)_____		
17. ☐ Regular mail delivery to be resumed on (Date) _____		
Signature of:		
18. USPS Employee: _____	19. Date Signed: _____	

Question	Answer Grid
1 The first and last name(s) of the customer(s) whose mail is to held should be entered in box: A. 1　　　B. 2　　　C. 3　　　D. 4	Ⓐ Ⓑ Ⓒ Ⓓ
2 The first date that mail is to be held should be entered in box: A. 3　　　B. 4　　　C. 29　　　D. 5	Ⓐ Ⓑ Ⓒ Ⓓ
3 Where on this form should the customer sign? A. 18　　　B. 7　　　C. 2　　　D. 10	Ⓐ Ⓑ Ⓒ Ⓓ
4 The ID Number of the clerk who received this form should be entered in which box? A. 11　　　B. 3　　　C. 14　　　D. 9	Ⓐ Ⓑ Ⓒ Ⓓ
5 The ending date to hold the mail should be entered in which box? A. 5　　　B. 6　　　C. 8　　　D. 19	Ⓐ Ⓑ Ⓒ Ⓓ
6 Which of the following boxes must be completed by the postal customer? A. 8　　　B. 9　　　C. 10　　　D. 5	Ⓐ Ⓑ Ⓒ Ⓓ

Answer questions 7 – 12 based on the following form:

1. RECEIPT FOR INSURED MAIL			
	2. Postage	6. ☐ Fragile 7. ☐ Perishable	
		8. ☐ Liquid 9. ☐ Hazardous	
	3. Insurance Fee	10.	
	4. Handling Fee	11. Stamp Postmark Here	
	5. Total (Postage plus Fees) $\$\underline{\hspace{3cm}}$		
12. Addressee (Sent to):			
13. Street, Apt. Number; or PO Box Number			
14. City, State and ZIP			

	Question	Answer Grid
7	The first and last name of the addressee should be entered in box: A. 14 B. 13 C. 9 D. 12	Ⓐ Ⓑ Ⓒ Ⓓ
8	The postmark should be stamped in box: A. 2 B. 4 C. 11 D. 14	Ⓐ Ⓑ Ⓒ Ⓓ
9	Where on this form should the customer indicate that the item being mailed is a delicate vase? A. 8 B. 6 C. 9 D. 12	Ⓐ Ⓑ Ⓒ Ⓓ
10	Which is a correct entry for box 8? A. 2 B. a "check mark" C. $2.50 D. Zip	Ⓐ Ⓑ Ⓒ Ⓓ
11	In which box should the City of the addressee be entered? A. 12 B. 13 C. 14 D. 11	Ⓐ Ⓑ Ⓒ Ⓓ
12	The handling fee should be entered in which box? A. 2 B. 3 C. 4 D. 5	Ⓐ Ⓑ Ⓒ Ⓓ

Answer questions 13 – 18 based on the following form:

RECEIPT FOR REGISTERED MAIL			
1.This section is to be completed by the post office.	2.Registered Number:	4. Date Stamp	
	3. Registration Fee $ _____	5. Charge for Handling	8. Fee for Return Receipt
		6. Postage Amount	9. Fee for Restricted Delivery
		7. Received by	
10. This section is to be completed by the postal customer. Please PRINT with ballpoint pen, or TYPE.	11. TO:		
	12. FROM:		
FORM # 7477 (Copy 1 – Customer) (Copy 2 – Post Office) (See information on reverse side of this form.)			

	Question	Answer Grid
13	The first and last name of the customer who is mailing the item should be entered in which box? A. 11 B. 7 C. 9 D. 12	Ⓐ Ⓑ Ⓒ Ⓓ
14	The date should be stamped in which box? A. 1 B. 2 C. 3 D. 4	Ⓐ Ⓑ Ⓒ Ⓓ
15	According to the directions on this form, the Customer keeps which numbered copy of the form? A. 1 B. 2 C. 3 D. 4	Ⓐ Ⓑ Ⓒ Ⓓ
16	Which of the following is a correct entry for box 8? A. X-5 B. 9:15 a.m. C. $4.75 D. 12	Ⓐ Ⓑ Ⓒ Ⓓ
17	Which of the following boxes should not be completed by the postal employee? A. 5 B. 7 C. 2 D. 12	Ⓐ Ⓑ Ⓒ Ⓓ
18	The Street Number of the postal customer should be entered in which box? A. 8 B. 12 C. 7 D. 11	Ⓐ Ⓑ Ⓒ Ⓓ

Answer questions 19 – 24 based on the following form:

REPORT TO POSTAL INSPECTOR OF NON-RECEIPT OF CREDIT CARD			
Dear Postal Inspector:			
The addressee named below has informed the credit card company that he/she did not receive the credit card mailed by the credit card company.			
Addressee Information			
1. Last Name	2. First Name		
3. Street Address	4. City	5. State	6. Zip
7. Telephone Number	8. E-mail Address (if any)		
9. Card type (Visa, American Express, etc.)			
10. Were purchases made using this card? 11. ☐ YES 12. ☐ NO	13. If answer to 11 is "YES" where were purchases made? City State		
Mailer Information			
14. Mailer Name			
15. Street Address	16. City	17. State	18. Zip
19. Telephone Number	20. E-mail Address (if any)		
21. Mailed at Location	city	state	Zip
22. Credit card number	23. Credit card expiration date		
24. Date that purchases began (MM/DD/YYYY)	25. Total amount of purchases made with this credit card: $ ____		

	Question	Answer Grid
19	The name of the mailer should be entered in box: A. 14 B. 13 C. 1 D. 2	ⒶⒷⒸⒹ
20	The state where purchases were made should be entered in which box? A. 3 B. 15 C. 13 D. 21	ⒶⒷⒸⒹ
21	The credit card expiration date should be entered in which box? A. 25 B. 23 C. 24 D. 25	ⒶⒷⒸⒹ
22	Which of the following is a correct entry for box 11? A. a "check mark" B. some C. $306.50 D. None	ⒶⒷⒸⒹ
23	The type of card, "VISA", should be entered in which box? A. 1 B. 10 C. 20 D. 9	ⒶⒷⒸⒹ
24	The "Mailer name" is the person or company that mailed: the: A. this form B. credit card C. fruit D. gem	ⒶⒷⒸⒹ

Answer questions 25 – 30 based on the following form:

1. CLAIM FOR DOMESTIC OR INTERNATIONAL MAIL					
2. Addressee Information			**3. Mailer Information**		
4. Last Name	5.MI	6. First Name	7. Last Name	8.MI	9. First Name
10. Business Name (if addressee is a company)			11. Business Name (if mailer is a company)		
12. Address (Number and Street)			13. Address (Number and Street)		
14. Address (Suite or Apartment Number)			15. Address (Suite or Apartment Number)		
16. City State Zip			17. City State Zip		
18. E-mail Address (Optional)			19. E-mail Address (Optional)		
20. Description of Missing Lost or Damaged Contents					

21. Item codes: 01 Jewelry, 02 Electronics, 03 Computers, 04 Animals, 05 Firearms, 06 Event Tickets, 07 Sports Equipment, 08 Collectibles, 09 Clothing, 10 Cash, 11 Other.

22. Describe the contents and check off (L) for Lost or (D) for damaged

23.Item	24. Description of contents	25.(L)or(D)	26.Item code	27.Value or Repair Cost in $
1		L ☐ D ☐		
2		L ☐ D ☐		
3		L ☐ D ☐		
		28. Total Value or Repair Cost in $		

29. The customer submitting the claim is the ☐ Mailer   ☐ Addressee

30. Payment is to be made to the ☐ Mailer   ☐ Addressee

31. Signature of Postal Customer submitting Claim	32. Date signed (MM/DD/YYYY)

Question	Answer Grid
25 The last name of the customer who mailed the article should be entered in box: A. 4　　B. 7　　C. 10　　D. 9	Ⓐ Ⓑ Ⓒ Ⓓ
26 The code for the missing item "Clothing" is: A. 08　　B. 09　　C. 01　　D. 02	Ⓐ Ⓑ Ⓒ Ⓓ
27 Where on this form should the customer sign? A. 27　　B. 28　　C. 29　　D. 31	Ⓐ Ⓑ Ⓒ Ⓓ
28 Which of the following is a correct entry for box 5? A. MIE　　B. 6　　C. A　　D. 4	Ⓐ Ⓑ Ⓒ Ⓓ
29 The ZIP number of the addressee should be entered in which box? A. 16　　B. 17　　C. 24　　D. 29	Ⓐ Ⓑ Ⓒ Ⓓ
30 Which of the following is a correct entry for box 32? A. 8　　B. 12/11/2010　　C. $17.00　　D. 11	Ⓐ Ⓑ Ⓒ Ⓓ

Directions for the following 36 Coding Questions

For each of the following 36 "Delivery Addresses" determine based on the coding guide whether the address belongs to Delivery Route A, B, C or D, and mark your answer grid accordingly. You have 6 minutes to code the 36 addresses.

Coding Practice Test #4:   Coding Guide

Range of Addresses	Delivery Route
1 - 900 Rome Avenue 200 – 1000 Caton Lane 300 – 1400 South Street	A
901– 1000 Rome Avenue 1401 - 3000 South Street	B
1001 – 2000 Caton Lane 300 – 1200 Rockefeller Plaza 900 – 3000 Clinton Ave.	C
All mail that doesn't fall in one of the address ranges listed above	D

	Delivery Address	Delivery Route				Answer Grid
1	200 Caton Lane	A	B	C	D	Ⓐ Ⓑ Ⓒ Ⓓ
2	4000 Clinton Ave.	A	B	C	D	Ⓐ Ⓑ Ⓒ Ⓓ
3	901 Rome Avenue	A	B	C	D	Ⓐ Ⓑ Ⓒ Ⓓ
4	1501 South Street	A	B	C	D	Ⓐ Ⓑ Ⓒ Ⓓ
5	100 Rome Avenue	A	B	C	D	Ⓐ Ⓑ Ⓒ Ⓓ
6	2450 Clinton Ave.	A	B	C	D	Ⓐ Ⓑ Ⓒ Ⓓ
7	800 South Street	A	B	C	D	Ⓐ Ⓑ Ⓒ Ⓓ
8	1400 Rockefeller Plaza	A	B	C	D	Ⓐ Ⓑ Ⓒ Ⓓ
9	800 Caton Lane	A	B	C	D	Ⓐ Ⓑ Ⓒ Ⓓ
10	310 Rockefeller Plaza	A	B	C	D	Ⓐ Ⓑ Ⓒ Ⓓ
11	1500 Caton Lane	A	B	C	D	Ⓐ Ⓑ Ⓒ Ⓓ
12	3000 South Street	A	B	C	D	Ⓐ Ⓑ Ⓒ Ⓓ
13	978 Rome Avenue	A	B	C	D	Ⓐ Ⓑ Ⓒ Ⓓ
14	670 Rome Avenue	A	B	C	D	Ⓐ Ⓑ Ⓒ Ⓓ

	Delivery Address	Delivery Route				Answer Grid
15	1100 Rockefeller Plaza	A	B	C	D	Ⓐ Ⓑ Ⓒ Ⓓ
16	777 Caton Lane	A	B	C	D	Ⓐ Ⓑ Ⓒ Ⓓ
17	4985 Hagerty Road	A	B	C	D	Ⓐ Ⓑ Ⓒ Ⓓ
18	1943 Caton Lane	A	B	C	D	Ⓐ Ⓑ Ⓒ Ⓓ
19	1300 South Street	A	B	C	D	Ⓐ Ⓑ Ⓒ Ⓓ
20	800 Rome Avenue	A	B	C	D	Ⓐ Ⓑ Ⓒ Ⓓ
21	45 Yonkers Avenue	A	B	C	D	Ⓐ Ⓑ Ⓒ Ⓓ
22	900 Rockefeller Plaza	A	B	C	D	Ⓐ Ⓑ Ⓒ Ⓓ
23	969 Rome Avenue	A	B	C	D	Ⓐ Ⓑ Ⓒ Ⓓ
24	900 Clinton Ave.	A	B	C	D	Ⓐ Ⓑ Ⓒ Ⓓ
25	300 Fuller Plaza	A	B	C	D	Ⓐ Ⓑ Ⓒ Ⓓ
26	690 Rome Avenue	A	B	C	D	Ⓐ Ⓑ Ⓒ Ⓓ
27	2000 Clinton Ave.	A	B	C	D	Ⓐ Ⓑ Ⓒ Ⓓ
28	2000 South Street	A	B	C	D	Ⓐ Ⓑ Ⓒ Ⓓ
29	1477 Caton Lane	A	B	C	D	Ⓐ Ⓑ Ⓒ Ⓓ
30	1300 Postell Way	A	B	C	D	Ⓐ Ⓑ Ⓒ Ⓓ
31	668 South Street	A	B	C	D	Ⓐ Ⓑ Ⓒ Ⓓ
32	1954 Caton Lane	A	B	C	D	Ⓐ Ⓑ Ⓒ Ⓓ
33	999 Rome Avenue	A	B	C	D	Ⓐ Ⓑ Ⓒ Ⓓ
34	2500 South Street	A	B	C	D	Ⓐ Ⓑ Ⓒ Ⓓ
35	780 Caton Lane	A	B	C	D	Ⓐ Ⓑ Ⓒ Ⓓ
36	1000 Rockefeller Plaza	A	B	C	D	Ⓐ Ⓑ Ⓒ Ⓓ

Memory Practice Test #4: Coding Guide

Range of Addresses	Delivery Route
You have 5 minutes to memorize the Coding Guide on page 158, then code the following 36 addresses based on your <u>memory</u> of the coding guide. (On the actual test you will probably have several minutes to practice answering coding questions. Those minutes can also be used, if you wish, to further memorize the codes.) You have 7 minutes to answer the following 36 coding questions.	

#	Delivery Address	Delivery Route	Answer Grid
1	205 Caton Lane	A B C D	Ⓐ Ⓑ Ⓒ Ⓓ
2	300 South Street	A B C D	Ⓐ Ⓑ Ⓒ Ⓓ
3	360 Rockefeller Plaza	A B C D	Ⓐ Ⓑ Ⓒ Ⓓ
4	944 Rome Avenue	A B C D	Ⓐ Ⓑ Ⓒ Ⓓ
5	1410 South Street	A B C D	Ⓐ Ⓑ Ⓒ Ⓓ
6	140 Rome Avenue	A B C D	Ⓐ Ⓑ Ⓒ Ⓓ
7	1600 Caton Lane	A B C D	Ⓐ Ⓑ Ⓒ Ⓓ
8	4000 Clinton Ave.	A B C D	Ⓐ Ⓑ Ⓒ Ⓓ
9	1200 Rockefeller Plaza	A B C D	Ⓐ Ⓑ Ⓒ Ⓓ
10	1300 South Street	A B C D	Ⓐ Ⓑ Ⓒ Ⓓ
11	979 Clinton Ave.	A B C D	Ⓐ Ⓑ Ⓒ Ⓓ
12	200 Rockefeller Plaza	A B C D	Ⓐ Ⓑ Ⓒ Ⓓ
13	933 Caton Lane	A B C D	Ⓐ Ⓑ Ⓒ Ⓓ
14	2460 Clinton Ave.	A B C D	Ⓐ Ⓑ Ⓒ Ⓓ

	Delivery Address	Delivery Route				Answer Grid
15	900 Rome Avenue	A	B	C	D	Ⓐ Ⓑ Ⓒ Ⓓ
16	1701 South Street	A	B	C	D	Ⓐ Ⓑ Ⓒ Ⓓ
17	534 Caton Lane	A	B	C	D	Ⓐ Ⓑ Ⓒ Ⓓ
18	300 Youmans Plaza	A	B	C	D	Ⓐ Ⓑ Ⓒ Ⓓ
19	901 Rome Avenue	A	B	C	D	Ⓐ Ⓑ Ⓒ Ⓓ
20	800 Rockefeller Plaza	A	B	C	D	Ⓐ Ⓑ Ⓒ Ⓓ
21	456 South Street	A	B	C	D	Ⓐ Ⓑ Ⓒ Ⓓ
22	1945 Caton Lane	A	B	C	D	Ⓐ Ⓑ Ⓒ Ⓓ
23	1200 Peterson Street	A	B	C	D	Ⓐ Ⓑ Ⓒ Ⓓ
24	765 Rome Avenue	A	B	C	D	Ⓐ Ⓑ Ⓒ Ⓓ
25	1030 Caton Lane	A	B	C	D	Ⓐ Ⓑ Ⓒ Ⓓ
26	987 Rome Avenue	A	B	C	D	Ⓐ Ⓑ Ⓒ Ⓓ
27	4200 Rockefeller Plaza	A	B	C	D	Ⓐ Ⓑ Ⓒ Ⓓ
28	750 Caton Lane	A	B	C	D	Ⓐ Ⓑ Ⓒ Ⓓ
29	2401 South Street	A	B	C	D	Ⓐ Ⓑ Ⓒ Ⓓ
30	1900 Clinton Ave.	A	B	C	D	Ⓐ Ⓑ Ⓒ Ⓓ
31	689 South Street	A	B	C	D	Ⓐ Ⓑ Ⓒ Ⓓ
32	1464 Caton Lane	A	B	C	D	Ⓐ Ⓑ Ⓒ Ⓓ
33	2225 South Street	A	B	C	D	Ⓐ Ⓑ Ⓒ Ⓓ
34	150 Rome Avenue	A	B	C	D	Ⓐ Ⓑ Ⓒ Ⓓ
35	1300 Bowford Plaza	A	B	C	D	Ⓐ Ⓑ Ⓒ Ⓓ
36	922 Rome Avenue	A	B	C	D	Ⓐ Ⓑ Ⓒ Ⓓ

Answers: Practice Test #4

Address Checking

1. B	7. B	13. C	19. D	25. B	31. B	37. D	43. D	49. B	55. B
2. C	8. A	14. B	20. D	26. D	32. A	38. C	44. B	50. A	56. D
3. A	9. C	15. B	21. B	27. A	33. A	39. C	45. A	51. D	57. C
4. D	10. D	16. A	22. C	28. C	34. C	40. B	46. C	52. C	58. A
5. A	11. D	17. C	23. A	29. B	35. D	41. A	47. C	53. D	59. D
6. C	12. B	18. B	24. C	30. A	36. B	42. C	48. A	54. B	60. B

Forms Completion

1. B	6. D	11. C	16. C	21. B	26. B
2. D	7. D	12. C	17. D	22. A	27. D
3. B	8. C	13. D	18. B	23. D	28. C
4. C	9. B	14. D	19. A	24. B	29. A
5. B	10. B	15. A	20. C	25. B	30. B

Coding

1. A	5. A	9. A	13. B	17. D	21. D	25. D	29. C	33. B
2. D	6. C	10. C	14. A	18. C	22. C	26. A	30. D	34. B
3. B	7. A	11. C	15. C	19. A	23. B	27. C	31. A	35. A
4. B	8. D	12. B	16. A	20. A	24. C	28. B	32. C	36. C

Memory

1. A	5. B	9. C	13. A	17. A	21. A	25. C	29. B	33. B
2. A	6. A	10. A	14. C	18. D	22. C	26. B	30. C	34. A
3. C	7. C	11. C	15. A	19. B	23. D	27. D	31. A	35. D
4. B	8. D	12. D	16. B	20. C	24. A	28. A	32. C	36. B

Part	Time Allowed	Number of Ques.	Description of Question
1. Address Checking	**11 minutes**	**60**	**Compare two addresses.**
2. Forms Completion	15 minutes	30	Correctly complete forms.
3. Coding	6 minutes	36	Find correct code for an address.
4. Memory (of coding examples, above)	7 minutes	36	Memorize address codes (which are same as codes in the "Coding" section part of the test.)

The first Part of this practice test is ADDRESS CHECKING.

(You have 11 minutes to complete this part of the test.)

When you are ready, turn the page and start the test.

———

Address Checking Practice Test 5: Below are 60 pairs of addresses. You have 11 minutes to compare each pair for errors and mark the answer sheet to indicate errors found as follows:

A. No Errors   **B.** Address Only   **C.** Zip Code Only   **D.** Both Address and ZIP Code

	Correct List of Addresses		Address List to be Checked		
	Address	**ZIP**	**Address**	**ZIP**	**Answer Grid**
1	3640 Naples St Albany, KS	76662-3335	3640 Naples St. Abilene, KS	76662-3335	Ⓐ Ⓑ Ⓒ Ⓓ
2	311 Camay Ave. Orange, MS	59538-5220	311 Camay Ave. Orange, MS	59538-5250	Ⓐ Ⓑ Ⓒ Ⓓ
3	P.O. Box 3415 Warren, IL	37748-5441	P.O. Box 3415 Warren, IL	37748-5441	Ⓐ Ⓑ Ⓒ Ⓓ
4	7772 Beding Ct. Fuller, CA	28412	772 Beding Ct. Fuller, CA	28415	Ⓐ Ⓑ Ⓒ Ⓓ
5	9774 Spring St. Cary, MI	85019	9714 Spring St. Cary, MI	85019	Ⓐ Ⓑ Ⓒ Ⓓ
6	4356 Lake Road Columbia, TX	43034-0341	4316 Lake Road Columbia, TX	43034-0347	Ⓐ Ⓑ Ⓒ Ⓓ
7	1679 Mirror Cir. Corall, ME	36487	1679 Mirror Cir. Coral, ME	36437	Ⓐ Ⓑ Ⓒ Ⓓ
8	415 Bedford Ave. New Haven, AR	32665	415 Beford Ave. New Haven, AR	32665	Ⓐ Ⓑ Ⓒ Ⓓ
9	5840 Bookker St. Waco, VA	33644-1911	5840 Booker St. Waco, VA	36344-1911	Ⓐ Ⓑ Ⓒ Ⓓ
10	114 Century Ter. Topeka, OR	36445	114 Century Ter. Topeka, OR	36445	Ⓐ Ⓑ Ⓒ Ⓓ
11	6789 Lanse Way El Monte, OR	38360-3043	6789 Lanse Way El Monte, OR	33360-3043	Ⓐ Ⓑ Ⓒ Ⓓ
12	2161 Clover Lane Concord, WA	55139-7568	216 Clover Lane Concord, WA	55136-7568	Ⓐ Ⓑ Ⓒ Ⓓ
13	8432 Zone St. Visalia, NY	40101-4246	8432 Zone St. Visalia, NY	40101-4146	Ⓐ Ⓑ Ⓒ Ⓓ
14	194 Tourist Road Denton, SC	58616	194 Tourist Road Denton, SC	58646	Ⓐ Ⓑ Ⓒ Ⓓ
15	537 Milano Pkwy. Provo, NJ	57342-6743	537 Milan Pkwy. Provo, NJ	57342-6743	Ⓐ Ⓑ Ⓒ Ⓓ

Address Checking Practice Test 5 (cont'd): Continue to compare each pair of addresses for errors and mark the answer sheet as follows:

A. No Errors   **B.** Address Only   **C.** Zip Code Only   **D.** Both Address and ZIP Code

	Correct List of Addresses		Address List to be Checked		
	Address	**ZIP**	**Address**	**ZIP**	**Answer Grid**
16	1779 Pader Ave. Waterbury, SC	02171-4164	1779 Pader Ave. Waterbury, SC	02117-4164	Ⓐ Ⓑ Ⓒ Ⓓ
17	8384 Cabinet Ln. Norman, CT	30529	8334 Cabinet Ln. Norman, CT	30529	Ⓐ Ⓑ Ⓒ Ⓓ
18	510 Marlo St. Midland, PA	93704	5100 Marlo St. Midland, PA	63704	Ⓐ Ⓑ Ⓒ Ⓓ
19	2731 Amy Street Elgin, MN	11214-1913	2731 Army Street Elgin, MN	11214-1918	Ⓐ Ⓑ Ⓒ Ⓓ
20	4218 Lanse Ave. Covina, AR	35364	4218 Lanse Ave. Covina, AR	35364	Ⓐ Ⓑ Ⓒ Ⓓ
21	3412 Follins St. Clearing, KS	72855	3412 Follins St. Clearing, KS	75855	Ⓐ Ⓑ Ⓒ Ⓓ
22	6546 Tunnel Way Cambridge, OH	41540-7142	654 Tunnel Way Cambridge, OH	41540-7142	Ⓐ Ⓑ Ⓒ Ⓓ
23	P.O. Box 3568 Pueblo, AK	85065-7382	P.O. Box 3268 Pueblo, AK	85062-7382	Ⓐ Ⓑ Ⓒ Ⓓ
24	1681 Clarter Ct. Indian, MD	34841-2018	1681 Clarter Ct. Indian, MD	34841-2018	Ⓐ Ⓑ Ⓒ Ⓓ
25	998 Motor Cir. Billings, RI	45035	998 Motor Cir. Bilings, RI	45035	Ⓐ Ⓑ Ⓒ Ⓓ
26	3617 Town Ter. Erie, NJ	27983-2112	3617 Town Ter. Erie, NJ	27983-2112	Ⓐ Ⓑ Ⓒ Ⓓ
27	2709 Sports Lane S. Bend, MS	93122	2709 Sports Lane S. Bend, MS	93125	Ⓐ Ⓑ Ⓒ Ⓓ
28	3181 Norwell St. San Buren, VA	73856	3181 Norwel St. San Buren, VA	73856	Ⓐ Ⓑ Ⓒ Ⓓ
29	7652 Sunny Rd. Fairfield, FL	31162-1382	7652 Sunny Rd. Fairfield, FL	31162-1382	Ⓐ Ⓑ Ⓒ Ⓓ
30	5827 Tech Pkwy. Lowell, NY	46914	5827 Tech Pkwy. Lowell, NY	46614	Ⓐ Ⓑ Ⓒ Ⓓ

Address Checking Practice Test 5 (cont'd): Continue to compare each pair of addresses for errors and mark the answer sheet as follows:

A. No Errors **B.** Address Only **C.** Zip Code Only **D.** Both Address and ZIP Code

	Correct List of Addresses		Address List to be Checked		
	Address	ZIP	Address	ZIP	Answer Grid
31	3134 Macon St. Norwalk, VA	56553-0497	314 Macon St. Norwalk, VA	56553-6497	A B C D
32	562 Reper Lane Burban, MA	81477	562 Reper Lane Burban, MA	81417	A B C D
33	1874 Park Court Richmons, NY	62171-5162	1874 Park Court Richmond, NY	62171-5165	A B C D
34	5534 Soldier Ln. High Peak, MO	78862-7393	5534 Soldier Ln. High Point, MO	78862-7394	A B C D
35	6820 Fuller Rd. Berkely, CA	46374-3576	6820 Fuller Rd. Berkely, CA	46374-3476	A B C D
36	8084 Potter Ave. Greshan, WA	35368	8084 Potter Ave. Greshan, WA	35368	A B C D
37	870 Purpose Ln. Wichita, ME	54256	870 Purpose Ln. Wichita, ME	54256	A B C D
38	417 Trenton Way Green Bay, IL	64515-6515	411 Trenton Way Green Bay, IL	64515-6515	A B C D
39	6633 Tanker St. Daven, MI	93424	6633 Tanker St. Daven, MI	63424	A B C D
40	3444 Remo Ave. Palin Bay, TX	53414-1746	344 Remo Ave. Palin Bay, TX	53414-1746	A B C D
41	7433 Corn St. Columbia, MN	97646	7433 Corn St. Columbia, MN	97646	A B C D
42	6738 Quentin Ave. Antioch, AR	96368-3040	6738 Quentin St. Antioch, AR	96360-3040	A B C D
43	P.O. Box 8759 Willis, KS	57136-7063	P.O. Box 8756 Willis, KS	57136-7063	A B C D
44	65 Stark Rd. Adenton, SC	19821	65 Stark Rd. Adenton, SC	10021	A B C D
45	3972 India Ave. Richmond, NY	38764-8715	3972 India Ave. Richmond, NY	38764-8715	A B C D

Address Checking Practice Test 5 (cont'd): Continue to compare each pair of addresses for errors and mark the answer sheet as follows:

A. No Errors   **B.** Address Only   **C.** Zip Code Only   **D.** Both Address and ZIP Code

	Correct List of Addresses		Address List to be Checked		
	Address	**ZIP**	**Address**	**ZIP**	**Answer Grid**
46	1688 Florin St. Hillside, MN	22397	1633 Florin St. Hillside, MN	22379	A B C D
47	P.O. Box 8317 Alamo, PA	80776-9009	P.O. Box 8317 Alamo, PA	80779-9009	A B C D
48	2726 Spring Ct. Albany, ME	06867	2726 Spring Ct. Albany, ME	06867	A B C D
49	461 Shoppes Cir. Allas, WA	90868-2307	461 Shopes Cir. Allas, WA	90868-2307	A B C D
50	3607 Vacaro Ave. Oakly, NY	81083	3607 Vacaro Ave. Oakly, NJ	81083	A B C D
51	133 Quaker Lane Richmond, CT	18080	133 Quaker Lane Richmond, CT	18030	A B C D
52	4746 Pink Road Stanford, VA	13607-7903	4746 Pink Road Stanford, VA	13607-7903	A B C D
53	3192 Trior Ave. Winsted, IL	10233-0103	3192 Trio Ave. Winsted, IL	10233-0103	A B C D
54	5778 Hickory St. Clover, MI	16808-8170	5778 History St. Clover, MI	16808-8110	A B C D
55	7166 Stanley Way Orchard, MS	12009	7146 Stanley Way Orchard, MS	12006	A B C D
56	9116 Credit St. Anton, MD	14812	9116 Credit St. Anton, MD	18412	A B C D
57	8821 Winters Rd. Marcer, MA	83680-9623	8821 Winter Rd. Marcer, MA	83680-9623	A B C D
58	95 People Ter. Lona, CA	04128	95 People Ter. Lona, CA	04128	A B C D
59	3518 Niles St. Norwalk, CT	76963-1807	3518 Niles St. Norwalk, CT	79663-1807	A B C D
60	6765 Transfer Ln. Putnam, OR	20114	6762 Transfer Ln. Putnam, OR	20114	A B C D

Forms Completion Practice Test 5

This part of the test consists of 5 different forms and 30 questions relating to the 5 forms. Study each form and then answer the questions following each of the forms. (Time allowed: 15 minutes for 30 questions).

Answer questions 1 – 6 based on the following form:

1. RETURN RECEIPT FOR DOMESTIC MAIL		
THIS SECTION IS TO BE COMPLETED BY THE SENDER	**THIS SECTION IS TO BE COMPLETED UPON DELIVERY OF THE ITEM**	
2. ▶Sender must complete items 1, 2, 3 (and 4 if Restricted Delivery is desired.)	7. Signature ▶	□ Addressee □ Agent
3. ▶Sender must print sender's name and address on the reverse side of this card so that card can be returned to sender.	8. Received by (PRINT)	9. Delivery Date
4. ▶Peel off glue protector strips on opposite side and attach to the back of the mail, or on the front if there is enough space.	10. Is delivery address same or different from item 5? □ Same □ Different (If different, write delivery address below:	
5. Article addressed to:	Type of mail service:	
	12. □ Registered	15. □ C.O.D.
	13. □ Insured	16. □ Express
	14. □ Certified	17. □ Merchandise Return receipt
	18. Restricted delivery (Additional fee) $_____ □ Yes	
6. Article number (from service label)		

	Question	Answer Grid
1	The item was delivered on 9/14/2010. In which box should this date be entered? A. 7 B. 8 C. 9 D. 10	Ⓐ Ⓑ Ⓒ Ⓓ
2	The address to where the article is addressed is written in which box? A. 5 B. 10 C. 6 D. 13	Ⓐ Ⓑ Ⓒ Ⓓ
3	Where on this form should the customer who receives the item sign? A. 5 B. 7 C. 13 D. 6	Ⓐ Ⓑ Ⓒ Ⓓ
4	Which of the following is a correct entry for box 6? A. done B. 5/2/10 C. 893794878 D. OK	Ⓐ Ⓑ Ⓒ Ⓓ
5	If the article is insured, which box should be checked? A. 10 B. 11 C. 12 D. 13	Ⓐ Ⓑ Ⓒ Ⓓ
6	What would be a correct entry for the space in box 18? A. 10.00 B. YES C. NO D. CK	Ⓐ Ⓑ Ⓒ Ⓓ

Answer questions 7 – 12 based on the following form:

CUSTOMS DECLARATION	
FROM (SENDER): 1. Last and First Name (and Business Name, if any) 2. Street 3. City 4. State 5. Zip	11. Insured Amount 12. Insured Fees (U.S. $) 13. Importer's Name and Telephone Number

TO (ADDRESSEE):
 	
6. Last and First Name (and Business Name, if any)
 	
7. Street
 	
8. City
 	
9. State   10. Zip
	14. Sender's instructions in case cannot be delivered:
	15. □ Treat as abandoned
	      □ Return to sender
	      □ Redirect to following address (#16):
	16.

17. Specific description of contents	18. Qty	19. Lbs.	20. Oz.

21. Comments

22. Check one	23. □ Airmail/Priority	24. □ Surface/Non priority

25. Check one   26. □ Documents   27. □ Merchandise 28. □ Gift 29. □ Other _____

30. Date Signed	31. Sender's Signature

	Question	Answer Grid
7	Comments should be entered in which box? A. 13　　　　B. 16　　　　C. 18　　　　D. 21	Ⓐ Ⓑ Ⓒ Ⓓ
8	Which of the following is a correct entry for box 12? A. YES　　　B. $34.00　　　C. 6 Euro　　　D. OK	Ⓐ Ⓑ Ⓒ Ⓓ
9	Where on this form should the sender sign? A. 1　　　　B. 6　　　　C. 31　　　　D. 21	Ⓐ Ⓑ Ⓒ Ⓓ
10	Which of the following is a correct entry for box 11? A. done　　　B. AKJ　　　C. $400.00　　　D. OK	Ⓐ Ⓑ Ⓒ Ⓓ
11	The ZIP of the addressee should be entered in which box? A. 5　　　　B. 10　　　　C. 3　　　　D. 8	Ⓐ Ⓑ Ⓒ Ⓓ
12	If the item is being shipped Airmail/Priority which box should be checked? A. 11　　　B. 21　　　C. 30　　　D. 23	Ⓐ Ⓑ Ⓒ Ⓓ

Answer questions 13 – 18 based on the following form:

RECEIPT FOR REGISTERED MAIL		
1.This section is to be completed by the post office.	2.Registered Number:	4. Date Stamp
	3. Registration Fee $ _____	5. Charge for Handling / 8. Fee for Return Receipt 6. Postage Amount / 9. Fee for Restricted Delivery 7. Received by
10. This section is to be completed by the postal customer. Please PRINT with ballpoint pen, or TYPE.	11. TO: 12. FROM:	
13. FORM # 7477 (Copy 1 – Customer) (Copy 2 – Post Office) 14. (See information on reverse side of this form.)		

	Question	Answer Grid
13	Which of the following boxes does not relate to a fee? A. 8　　　　B. 9　　　　C. 3　　　　D. 11	Ⓐ Ⓑ Ⓒ Ⓓ
14	The date should be stamped in which box? A. 8　　　　B. 9　　　　C. 5　　　　D. 4	Ⓐ Ⓑ Ⓒ Ⓓ
15	In which box on this form should the name and address of the postal customer (sender) be entered? A. 2　　　　B. 4　　　　C. 12　　　　D. 11	Ⓐ Ⓑ Ⓒ Ⓓ
16	Which of the following is a correct entry for box 3? A. AOK　　　B. 3/12/11　　　C. 4.25　　　D. #4	Ⓐ Ⓑ Ⓒ Ⓓ
17	The location of "information" regarding this form is indicated in which numbered section of this form? A. 4　　　　B. 7　　　　C. 14　　　　D. 12	Ⓐ Ⓑ Ⓒ Ⓓ
18	What would be a correct entry for box 8? A. $12.00　　B. DF　　C. 3 ft. 1 in.　　D. 6 lbs.	Ⓐ Ⓑ Ⓒ Ⓓ

Answer questions 19 – 24 based on the following form:

Application for Nonprofit Standard Mail Prices	
1. Legal Name of Organization	2. Street Address (including Street/Suite Number)
	3. City, State, Zip
4. Telephone	5. E-mail address
6. Alternate mailing address (if any)	
Type of Organization (Check only one box) 7. ☐ Educational 8. ☐ Religious 9. ☐ Scientific 10. ☐ Labor 11. ☐ Veterans	
12. Has this organization previously mailed at nonprofit standard prices? 13. ☐ YES 14. ☐ NO	15. If the answer to 12 is "YES", have standard mail privileges ever been revoked? 16. ☐ YES 17. ☐ NO
18. Signature of applicant	19. Title of applicant
20. Date this request is submitted.	

	Question	Answer Grid
19	Tim Smith is applying for World Relief Efforts, Inc., a nonprofit organization. Tim Smith's signature should be entered in which box? A. 1　　　　　B. 6　　　　　C. 18　　　　　D. 19	Ⓐ Ⓑ Ⓒ Ⓓ
20	World Relief Efforts, Inc. should be entered in which box? A. 4　　　　　B. 3　　　　　C. 2　　　　　D. 1	Ⓐ Ⓑ Ⓒ Ⓓ
21	If the organization has a primary address and a secondary address, the secondary address should be entered in which box? A. 1　　　　　B. 2　　　　　C. 3　　　　　D. 6	Ⓐ Ⓑ Ⓒ Ⓓ
22	Which of the following is a correct entry for box 7? A. check mark　　B. 10:15 a.m.　　C. $2.50　　　　D. $3.50	Ⓐ Ⓑ Ⓒ Ⓓ
23	The organization has not previously mailed at nonprofit standard prices. Which box should be checked to indicate this? A. 7　　　　　B. 15　　　　　C. 16　　　　　D. 14	Ⓐ Ⓑ Ⓒ Ⓓ
24	What would be a correct entry for box 20? A. Today　　　　B. 6/14/10　　　C. 6/17　　　　D. 3 lbs.	Ⓐ Ⓑ Ⓒ Ⓓ

Answer questions 25 – 30 based on the following form:

HOLD MAIL (AUTHORIZATION)
1. This form authorizes the USPS to hold mail for a minimum of 3 days but not more than 30 days for the following individual(s).
2. Name(s)
3. Address (including number and street, Apartment or suite number, city, state, ZIP)
4. A. ☐ I shall pick up my mail upon my return. I understand that if I do not pick up my mail, then mail delivery will not be made until I pick up the mail.   4.B. ☐ I am authorizing the USPS to deliver all held mail and resume mail delivery on the end ing date indicated below.

5. Beginning Date To Hold Mail	6. Ending Date To Hold Mail (This date can only be changed by the customer – in writing)	7. Signature of Customer

Shaded section is for Post Office (USPS) use only.		
8. Date this form received:		
9. Carrier name and ID Number receiving this form:	10. Carrier Name	11. Carrier ID Number
12. Clerk name and ID Number receiving this form	13. Clerk Name	14. Clerk ID Number
15. If option B was selected, complete this section:		
16. ☐ All mail has been picked up on (Date)_____		
17. ☐ Regular mail delivery to be resumed on (Date) _____		
Signature of:		
18. USPS Employee: _____19. Date Signed: _____		

Question	Answer Grid
25	The first and last name of the customer(s) whose mail is to be held should be entered in box: A. 7　　　　B. 18　　　　C. 10　　　　D. 2	Ⓐ Ⓑ Ⓒ Ⓓ
26	The first date that mail is to be held is entered in which box? A. 19　　　　B. 6　　　　C. 5　　　　D. 8	Ⓐ Ⓑ Ⓒ Ⓓ
27	Where on this form should the customer sign? A. 18　　　　B. 13　　　　C. 7　　　　D. 2	Ⓐ Ⓑ Ⓒ Ⓓ
28	Which of the following is a correct entry for box 19? A. check mark　B. 7/12/10　C. $2.50　　D. OK	Ⓐ Ⓑ Ⓒ Ⓓ
29	Which of the following boxes should be completed by the postal employee? A. 6　　　　B. 4　　　　C. 3　　　　D. 8	Ⓐ Ⓑ Ⓒ Ⓓ
30	The postal employee signs in which box? A. 2　　　　B. 18　　　　C. 10　　　　D. 11	Ⓐ Ⓑ Ⓒ Ⓓ

Directions for the following 36 Coding Questions

For each of the following 36 "Delivery Addresses" determine based on the coding guide whether the address belongs to Delivery Route A, B, C or D, and mark your answer grid accordingly. You have 6 minutes to code the 36 addresses.

Coding Practice Test #5:   Coding Guide

Range of Addresses	Delivery Route
500 - 1500 Darfield Avenue 100 – 1000 Lansing Lane 200 – 1200 Eckerd Street	A
1501 – 3000 Darfield Avenue 1201 - 2000 Eckerd Street	B
1001 – 3000 Lansing Lane 500 – 1200 Kennedy Circle 100 – 3000 Forman Ave.	C
All mail that doesn't fall in one of the address ranges listed above	D

	Delivery Address	Delivery Route				Answer Grid
1	105 Lansing Lane	A	B	C	D	Ⓐ Ⓑ Ⓒ Ⓓ
2	600 Darfield Avenue	A	B	C	D	Ⓐ Ⓑ Ⓒ Ⓓ
3	1400 Eckerd Street	A	B	C	D	Ⓐ Ⓑ Ⓒ Ⓓ
4	1001 Lansing Lane	A	B	C	D	Ⓐ Ⓑ Ⓒ Ⓓ
5	258 Eckerd Street	A	B	C	D	Ⓐ Ⓑ Ⓒ Ⓓ
6	2200 Kennedy Circle	A	B	C	D	Ⓐ Ⓑ Ⓒ Ⓓ
7	1556 Darfield Avenue	A	B	C	D	Ⓐ Ⓑ Ⓒ Ⓓ
8	100 Forman Ave.	A	B	C	D	Ⓐ Ⓑ Ⓒ Ⓓ
9	1976 Eckerd Street	A	B	C	D	Ⓐ Ⓑ Ⓒ Ⓓ
10	509 Kennedy Circle	A	B	C	D	Ⓐ Ⓑ Ⓒ Ⓓ
11	798 Lansing Lane	A	B	C	D	Ⓐ Ⓑ Ⓒ Ⓓ
12	500 Kensington Circle	A	B	C	D	Ⓐ Ⓑ Ⓒ Ⓓ
13	2456 Lansing Lane	A	B	C	D	Ⓐ Ⓑ Ⓒ Ⓓ
14	1200 Eckerd Street	A	B	C	D	Ⓐ Ⓑ Ⓒ Ⓓ

	Delivery Address	Delivery Route				Answer Grid
15	2501 Darfield Avenue	A	B	C	D	Ⓐ Ⓑ Ⓒ Ⓓ
16	1250 Darfield Avenue	A	B	C	D	Ⓐ Ⓑ Ⓒ Ⓓ
17	4000 Forman Ave.	A	B	C	D	Ⓐ Ⓑ Ⓒ Ⓓ
18	1765 Eckerd Street	A	B	C	D	Ⓐ Ⓑ Ⓒ Ⓓ
19	645 Lansing Lane	A	B	C	D	Ⓐ Ⓑ Ⓒ Ⓓ
20	3000 Forman Ave.	A	B	C	D	Ⓐ Ⓑ Ⓒ Ⓓ
21	888 Kennedy Circle	A	B	C	D	Ⓐ Ⓑ Ⓒ Ⓓ
22	886 Eckerd Street	A	B	C	D	Ⓐ Ⓑ Ⓒ Ⓓ
23	2000 Darfield Avenue	A	B	C	D	Ⓐ Ⓑ Ⓒ Ⓓ
24	1922 Lansing Lane	A	B	C	D	Ⓐ Ⓑ Ⓒ Ⓓ
25	1555 Eckerd Street	A	B	C	D	Ⓐ Ⓑ Ⓒ Ⓓ
26	860 Merner Street	A	B	C	D	Ⓐ Ⓑ Ⓒ Ⓓ
27	876 Darfield Avenue	A	B	C	D	Ⓐ Ⓑ Ⓒ Ⓓ
28	2000 Forman Ave.	A	B	C	D	Ⓐ Ⓑ Ⓒ Ⓓ
29	1801 Darfield Avenue	A	B	C	D	Ⓐ Ⓑ Ⓒ Ⓓ
30	673 Kennedy Circle	A	B	C	D	Ⓐ Ⓑ Ⓒ Ⓓ
31	982 Lansing Lane	A	B	C	D	Ⓐ Ⓑ Ⓒ Ⓓ
32	3100 Forman Ave.	A	B	C	D	Ⓐ Ⓑ Ⓒ Ⓓ
33	1933 Eckerd Street	A	B	C	D	Ⓐ Ⓑ Ⓒ Ⓓ
34	940 Darfield Avenue	A	B	C	D	Ⓐ Ⓑ Ⓒ Ⓓ
35	2664 Lansing Lane	A	B	C	D	Ⓐ Ⓑ Ⓒ Ⓓ
36	1049 Eckerd Street	A	B	C	D	Ⓐ Ⓑ Ⓒ Ⓓ

Memory Practice Test #5:   Coding Guide

Range of Addresses	Delivery Route

You have 5 minutes to memorize the Coding Guide on page 178, then code the following 36 addresses based on your <u>memory</u> of the coding guide. (On the actual test you will probably have several minutes to practice answering coding questions. Those minutes can also be used, if you wish, to further memorize the codes.)

You have 7 minutes to answer the following 36 coding questions.

	Delivery Address	Delivery Route	Answer Grid
1	190 Lansing Lane	A B C D	Ⓐ Ⓑ Ⓒ Ⓓ
2	4000 Forman Ave.	A B C D	Ⓐ Ⓑ Ⓒ Ⓓ
3	309 Eckerd Street	A B C D	Ⓐ Ⓑ Ⓒ Ⓓ
4	1772 Eckerd Street	A B C D	Ⓐ Ⓑ Ⓒ Ⓓ
5	200 Kennedy Circle	A B C D	Ⓐ Ⓑ Ⓒ Ⓓ
6	1050 Lansing Lane	A B C D	Ⓐ Ⓑ Ⓒ Ⓓ
7	550 Darfield Avenue	A B C D	Ⓐ Ⓑ Ⓒ Ⓓ
8	1456 Forman Ave.	A B C D	Ⓐ Ⓑ Ⓒ Ⓓ
9	1501 Darfield Avenue	A B C D	Ⓐ Ⓑ Ⓒ Ⓓ
10	110 Forman Ave.	A B C D	Ⓐ Ⓑ Ⓒ Ⓓ
11	1501 Eckerd Street	A B C D	Ⓐ Ⓑ Ⓒ Ⓓ
12	680 Eckerd Street	A B C D	Ⓐ Ⓑ Ⓒ Ⓓ
13	500 Kennedy Circle	A B C D	Ⓐ Ⓑ Ⓒ Ⓓ
14	745 Lansing Lane	A B C D	Ⓐ Ⓑ Ⓒ Ⓓ

	Delivery Address	Delivery Route				Answer Grid
15	1450 Darfield Avenue	A	B	C	D	(A) (B) (C) (D)
16	1678 Eckerd Street	A	B	C	D	(A) (B) (C) (D)
17	276 Lansing Lane	A	B	C	D	(A) (B) (C) (D)
18	1000 Kennedy Circle	A	B	C	D	(A) (B) (C) (D)
19	1892 Darfield Avenue	A	B	C	D	(A) (B) (C) (D)
20	2412 Lansing Lane	A	B	C	D	(A) (B) (C) (D)
21	679 Darfield Avenue	A	B	C	D	(A) (B) (C) (D)
22	458 Lincoln Drive	A	B	C	D	(A) (B) (C) (D)
23	1200 Kennedy Circle	A	B	C	D	(A) (B) (C) (D)
24	1640 Kaiser Blvd.	A	B	C	D	(A) (B) (C) (D)
25	993 Eckerd Street	A	B	C	D	(A) (B) (C) (D)
26	700 Kennedy Circle	A	B	C	D	(A) (B) (C) (D)
27	500 Leiman Street	A	B	C	D	(A) (B) (C) (D)
28	1505 Eckerd Street	A	B	C	D	(A) (B) (C) (D)
29	933 Lansing Lane	A	B	C	D	(A) (B) (C) (D)
30	2100 Lansing Lane	A	B	C	D	(A) (B) (C) (D)
31	2783 Darfield Avenue	A	B	C	D	(A) (B) (C) (D)
32	2980 Lansing Lane	A	B	C	D	(A) (B) (C) (D)
33	883 Darfield Avenue	A	B	C	D	(A) (B) (C) (D)
34	1200 Underhill Road	A	B	C	D	(A) (B) (C) (D)
35	667 Eckerd Street	A	B	C	D	(A) (B) (C) (D)
36	2000 Forman Ave.	A	B	C	D	(A) (B) (C) (D)

Answers: Practice Test #5

Address Checking

1.B	7. D	13. C	19. D	25. B	31. B	37. A	43. B	49. B	55. D
2. C	8. B	14. A	20. A	26. A	32. C	38. B	44. C	50. B	56. C
3. A	9. D	15. B	21. C	27. C	33. D	39. C	45. A	51. C	57. B
4. D	10. A	16. C	22. B	28. B	34. D	40. B	46. D	52. A	58. A
5. B	11. C	17. B	23. D	29. A	35. C	41. A	47. C	53. B	59. C
6. D	12. D	18. D	24. A	30. C	36. A	42. D	48. A	54. D	60. B

Forms Completion

1. C	6. A	11. B	16. C	21. D	26. C
2. A	7. D	12. D	17. C	22. A	27. C
3. B	8. B	13. D	18. A	23. D	28. B
4. C	9. C	14. D	19. C	24. B	29. D
5. D	10. C	15: C	20. D	25. D	30. B

Coding

1. A	5. A	9. B	13. C	17. D	21. C	25. B	29. B	33. B
2. A	6. D	10. C	14. A	18. B	22. A	26. D	30. C	34. A
3. B	7. B	11. A	15. B	19. A	23. B	27. A	31. A	35. C
4. C	8. C	12. D	16. A	20. C	24. C	28. C	32. D	36. A

Memory

1. A	5. D	9. B	13. C	17. A	21. A	25. A	29. A	33. A
2. D	6. C	10. C	14. A	18. C	22. D	26. C	30. C	34. D
3. A	7. A	11. B	15. A	19. B	23. C	27. D	31. B	35. A
4. B	8. C	12. A	16. B	20. C	24. D	28. B	32. C	36. C

Part	Time Allowed	Number of Ques.	Description of Question
1. Address Checking	**11 minutes**	**60**	**Compare two addresses.**
2. Forms Completion	15 minutes	30	Correctly complete forms.
3. Coding	6 minutes	36	Find correct code for an address.
4. Memory (of coding examples, above)	7 minutes	36	Memorize address codes (which are same as codes in the "Coding" section part of the test.)

The first Part of this practice test is ADDRESS CHECKING.

(You have 11 minutes to complete this part of the test.)

When you are ready, turn the page and start the test.

___

Address Checking Practice Test 6: Below are 60 pairs of addresses. You have 11 minutes to compare each pair for errors and mark the answer sheet to indicate errors found as follows:

A. No Errors   **B.** Address Only   **C.** Zip Code Only   **D.** Both Address and ZIP Code

	Correct List of Addresses		Address List to be Checked		
	Address	**ZIP**	**Address**	**ZIP**	**Answer Grid**
1	7913 Prospect Ln. Nunn, OH	20164	7913 Project Ln. Nunn, OH	20154	Ⓐ Ⓑ Ⓒ Ⓓ
2	511 Yankee Rd. Agates, FL	43987	511 Yankee Rd. Agates, FL	43987	Ⓐ Ⓑ Ⓒ Ⓓ
3	6600 Camaro St. Fremont, SC	87765-8217	6600 Camaro St. Fremont, SC	87764-8217	Ⓐ Ⓑ Ⓒ Ⓓ
4	3800 Factory Ave. Foxtones, AR	90691	380 Factory Ave. Foxtones, AR	90661	Ⓐ Ⓑ Ⓒ Ⓓ
5	881 Marina Way Long Beach, RI	59861-6372	881 Marina Way Long Beach, RI	59861-6372	Ⓐ Ⓑ Ⓒ Ⓓ
6	4855 Brand St. Calfar, ME	80261-8820	4855 Brand St. Calfax, ME	80261-8120	Ⓐ Ⓑ Ⓒ Ⓓ
7	P.O. Box 9162 Fouler, KS	64075-8714	P.O. Box 9162 Fowler, KS	64075-8714	Ⓐ Ⓑ Ⓒ Ⓓ
8	6827 Cutter Cir. Agate, MO	01120	6827 Cutter Cir. Agate, MO	01102	Ⓐ Ⓑ Ⓒ Ⓓ
9	2416 Nation Ln. Rialto, AK	26089	2416 Nation Ln. Rialto, AK	26086	Ⓐ Ⓑ Ⓒ Ⓓ
10	6234 Recital Rd. Clark, WA	27016-9529	6234 Recital Rd. Clare, WA	27016-0529	Ⓐ Ⓑ Ⓒ Ⓓ
11	451 Godey Ave. Artesia, MD	69102	451 Godey Ave. Artesia, MD	69102	Ⓐ Ⓑ Ⓒ Ⓓ
12	1133 Election St. Lody, CT	73497	1133 Election St. Lodi, CT	73497	Ⓐ Ⓑ Ⓒ Ⓓ
13	917 Elvis Ct. Clayton, NJ	24821-3534	917 Elvis Ct. Clayton, NJ	24021-3534	Ⓐ Ⓑ Ⓒ Ⓓ
14	351 Culture Ter. Fowler, TX	12090	351 Culture Ter. Fowler, TX	12090	Ⓐ Ⓑ Ⓒ Ⓓ
15	5527 Sun Pkwy. Arvin, MD	82069-0890	5527 Sun Pkwy. Arvin, MD	82069-0890	Ⓐ Ⓑ Ⓒ Ⓓ

Address Checking Practice Test 6 (cont'd): Continue to compare each pair of addresses for errors and mark the answer sheet as follows:

A. No Errors   **B.** Address Only   **C.** Zip Code Only   **D.** Both Address and ZIP Code

	Correct List of Addresses		Address List to be Checked		Answer Grid
	Address	**ZIP**	**Address**	**ZIP**	
16	2719 Fortune St. Harington, IL	68656-0807	2719 Fortune St. Harrington, IL	68656-0807	A B C D
17	4283 Jersey Way Center Hill, CT	20701	4283 Jersey Way Center Hill, CT	20101	A B C D
18	1176 Lerner Ave. Arcadia, RI	23989	1176 Lernur Ave. Arcadia, RI	23986	A B C D
19	3265 Country St. Woodvill, CA	77524-0066	3265 Country St. Woodville, CA	77224-0066	A B C D
20	545 Common Ave. Seaford, MN	80151	545 Comon Ave. Seaford, MN	80151	A B C D
21	931 Landon Ct. Maywood, NJ	98303-5057	931 Landon Ct. Maywood, NJ	98803-5057	A B C D
22	8765 French Ln. Gold Hill, AK	71350-7238	8765 French Ln. Gold Hill, AK	71350-7238	A B C D
23	1792 Culture Ln. Austin, MA	50561-7650	1792 Cuture Ln. Austin, MA	50561-7620	A B C D
24	4744 Osuego St. Gilroy, KS	15293	4744 Oswego St. Gilroy, KS	15293	A B C D
25	3822 Scenic Cir. Seaside, MD	38597	382 Scenic Cir. Seaside, MD	38591	A B C D
26	5251 Court Ter. Palisade, MD	65102-8160	5251 Court Ter. Palisade, MD	65102-8160	A B C D
27	6624 Colly Ave. Dover, SC	58216	6624 Colly Ave. Dover, SC	58219	A B C D
28	P.O. Box 7242 Belle View, VA	93523	P.O. Box 7242 Belle View, VA	93523	A B C D
29	7126 Famous Rd. Bristoll, OR	58562-9140	7126 Famous Rd. Bristol, OR	58562-9140	A B C D
30	3662 Metro Ave. Penrose, TX	11901	362 Metro Ave. Penrose, TX	11907	A B C D

Address Checking Practice Test 6 (cont'd): Continue to compare each pair of addresses for errors and mark the answer sheet as follows:

A. No Errors   **B.** Address Only   **C.** Zip Code Only   **D.** Both Address and ZIP Code

	Correct List of Addresses		Address List to be Checked		
	Address	**ZIP**	**Address**	**ZIP**	**Answer Grid**
31	5621 Tiger St. Bay Lake, FL	30431-9772	5621 Tyger St. Bay Lake, FL	30431-9772	A B C D
32	6817 Confer Ln. Gardena, OR	19533-5562	6817 Confer Ln. Gardena, OR	19538-5562	A B C D
33	3642 Sires St. Arcadia, RI	25986	3642 Sire St. Arcadia, RI	22986	A B C D
34	4522 Victory Way Grand, AR	79557-8998	452 Victory Way Grand, AR	79557-8998	A B C D
35	611 Pasada Rd. Avon, OH	95726	611 Pasada Rd. Avon, OH	95756	A B C D
36	7218 Startton Ct. Colton, IL	81757-3496	7218 Startton Ct. Colton, IL	81757-3496	A B C D
37	P.O. Box 5498 Madera, VA	72074	P.O. Box 5493 Madera, VA	72074	A B C D
38	9254 Graves Rd. Atwood, NY	27411	9294 Graves Rd. Atwood, NY	27141	A B C D
39	1876 Hockey Ln. Gill, MS	24596-6894	1876 Hockey Ln. Gill, MS	24596-6894	A B C D
40	852 Lane Ter. Galt, OR	20433-1274	852 Lane Ter. Galt, OR	20433-1214	A B C D
41	6372 Balker St. Atwater, MI	21718-0162	6372 Balker St. Alwater, MI	21718-0165	A B C D
42	455 Treasure Cir. Ross, WA	24760	45 Treasure Cir. Ross, WA	24790	A B C D
43	572 Classic Ave. Adelia, MA	74765-8634	572 Classic Ave. Adel, MA	74765-8634	A B C D
44	3129 Nation St. Commerce, KS	78213	3129 Nation St. Commerce, KS	78513	A B C D
45	865 Woller Ln. Ellerby, AR	86750-2354	865 Woller Ln. Ellerby, AR	86750-2354	A B C D

Address Checking Practice Test 6 (cont'd): Continue to compare each pair of addresses for errors and mark the answer sheet as follows:

A. No Errors   **B.** Address Only   **C.** Zip Code Only   **D.** Both Address and ZIP Code

	Correct List of Addresses		Address List to be Checked		
	Address	**ZIP**	**Address**	**ZIP**	**Answer Grid**
46	2741 Hockey Ln. Peyton, MO	76181-4278	2741 Hockey Ln. Peyton, MO	76181-4278	Ⓐ Ⓑ Ⓒ Ⓓ
47	1762 Lincoln St. Douglas, KS	17295	1762 Lincoln St. Douglas, KS	17295	Ⓐ Ⓑ Ⓒ Ⓓ
48	7467 Weller Rd. Arcadia, NJ	40401-3489	7467 Weller Rd. Arcade, NJ	40401-3489	Ⓐ Ⓑ Ⓒ Ⓓ
49	3962 Testor St. Davenport, MS	51425	3962 Testor St. Davenport, MS	51422	Ⓐ Ⓑ Ⓒ Ⓓ
50	4124 Bourne Ave. Shellman, OH	12471-1191	4124 Bourne Ave. Shellman, OH	12471-1191	Ⓐ Ⓑ Ⓒ Ⓓ
51	8111 Washer Ave. Gridley, NY	62138	811 Washer Ave. Gridley, NY	62138	Ⓐ Ⓑ Ⓒ Ⓓ
52	1824 Kisena Way Mill Valley, MN	10015-3302	1824 Kisena Way Mill Valley, MN	10015-3302	Ⓐ Ⓑ Ⓒ Ⓓ
53	5832 Gerry Road Clewis, IL	53582-5014	5832 Gerri Road Clewis, IL	53532-5014	Ⓐ Ⓑ Ⓒ Ⓓ
54	6810 Broad Ct. Avenal, VA	41145-5431	6810 Broad Ct. Avenal, VA	41142-5431	Ⓐ Ⓑ Ⓒ Ⓓ
55	882 Concert Pkwy Pleasant, MA	55415	882 Concert Pkwy Pleasant, ME	55415	Ⓐ Ⓑ Ⓒ Ⓓ
56	2734 Porter St. Shafer, OR	28016	2734 Porter St. Shaffer, OR	28019	Ⓐ Ⓑ Ⓒ Ⓓ
57	661 Mirror St. Dover, WA	43034-1341	661 Mirror Cir. Dover, WA	43034-1347	Ⓐ Ⓑ Ⓒ Ⓓ
58	P.O. Box 4251 Ambrose, FL	36461	P.O. Box 4251 Ambrose, FL	36491	Ⓐ Ⓑ Ⓒ Ⓓ
59	3135 Palmara Ter. Deltona, MI	38065	3135 Palma Ter. Deltona, MI	38065	Ⓐ Ⓑ Ⓒ Ⓓ
60	5515 Project Ln. Shiloh, MD	40196-1647	5515 Project Ln. Shiloh, MD	40196-1647	Ⓐ Ⓑ Ⓒ Ⓓ

Forms Completion Practice Test 6

This part of the test consists of 5 different forms and 30 questions relating to the 5 forms. Study each form and then answer the questions following each of the forms. (Time allowed: 15 minutes for 30 questions).

Answer questions 1 – 6 based on the following form:

HOLD MAIL (AUTHORIZATION)
1. This form authorizes the USPS to hold mail for a minimum of 3 days but not more than 30 days for the following individual(s).
2. Name(s)
3. Address (including number and street, Apartment or suite number, city, state, ZIP)
4. A. □ I shall pick up my mail upon my return. I understand that if I do not pick up my mail, then mail delivery will not be made until I pick up the mail. 4.B. □ I am authorizing the USPS to deliver all held mail and resume mail delivery on the ending date indicated below.

5. Beginning Date To Hold Mail	6. Ending Date To Hold Mail (This date can only be changed by the customer – in writing)	7. Signature of Customer

Shaded section is for Post Office (USPS) use only.		
8. Date this form received:		
9. Carrier name and ID Number receiving this form:	10. Carrier Name	11. Carrier ID Number
12. Clerk name and ID Number receiving this form	13. Clerk Name	14. Clerk ID Number
15. If option B was selected, complete this section: 16. □ All mail has been picked up on (Date)_____ 17. □ Regular mail delivery to be resumed on (Date) _____		
Signature of: 18. USPS Employee: _____ 19. Date Signed: _____		

	Question	Answer Grid
1	What would be a correct entry for box 13? A. 143428　　B. Clerk　　C. Abe Jones　　D. 24	Ⓐ Ⓑ Ⓒ Ⓓ
2	Where on this form should the postal employee sign? A. 2　　B. 10　　C. 13　　D. 18	Ⓐ Ⓑ Ⓒ Ⓓ
3	Where on this form should the customer sign? A. 2　　B. 7　　C. 13　　D. 18	Ⓐ Ⓑ Ⓒ Ⓓ
4	Which of the following boxes must be completed by the postal employee? A. 8　　B. 5　　C. 6　　D. 3	Ⓐ Ⓑ Ⓒ Ⓓ
5	How many names may be written in box 2? A. 1 only　　B. 1 or more　　C. 2 only　　D. None	Ⓐ Ⓑ Ⓒ Ⓓ
6	The maximum number of days that mail may be held is: A. 3　　B. 30　　C. 300　　D. 90	Ⓐ Ⓑ Ⓒ Ⓓ

Answer questions 7 – 12 based on the following form:

1. RETURN RECEIPT FOR DOMESTIC MAIL		
WHITE SECTION IS TO BE COMPLETED BY THE SENDER	**DARK SECTION IS TO BE COMPLETED UPON DELIVERY OF THE ITEM**	
2. ▶ Sender must complete items 1, 2, 3 (and 4 if Restricted Delivery is desired.) 3. ▶ Sender must print sender's name and address on the reverse side of this card so that card can be returned to sender. 4. ▶ Peel off glue protector strips on opposite side and attach to the back of the mail, or on the front if there is enough space.	7. Signature □ Addressee ▶ □ Agent	
	8. Received by (PRINT)	9. Delivery Date
	10. Is delivery address same or different from item 5? □ Same □ Different (If different, write delivery address below:	
5. Article addressed to:	Type of mail service:	
	12. □ Registered	15. □ C.O.D.
	13. □ Insured	16. □ Express
	14. □ Certified	17. □ Merchandise Return receipt
	18. Restricted delivery (Additional fee) $_____ □ Yes	
6. Article number (from service label)		

	Question	Answer Grid
7	The first and last name of the customer to whom the article is addressed to should be entered in box: A. 14　　　B. 6　　　C. 5　　　D. 7	Ⓐ Ⓑ Ⓒ Ⓓ
8	The person receiving the article should print his or her name in box: A. 8　　　B. 9　　　C. 5　　　D. 7	Ⓐ Ⓑ Ⓒ Ⓓ
9	Where on this form should the customer receiving the article sign? A. 8　　　B. 9　　　C. 5　　　D. 7	Ⓐ Ⓑ Ⓒ Ⓓ
10	Which of the following is a correct entry for box 9? A. done　　B. 7/12/10　　C. YES　　D. OK	Ⓐ Ⓑ Ⓒ Ⓓ
11	The sender may complete all of the following boxes, except box: A. 6　　　B. 5　　　C. 8　　　D. 12	Ⓐ Ⓑ Ⓒ Ⓓ
12	What would be a correct entry for box 9? A. None　　B. 26　　C. 10/5/2010　　D. Fri.	Ⓐ Ⓑ Ⓒ Ⓓ

Answer questions 13 – 18 based on the following form:

STATEMENT FOR PICKUP SERVICE			
1. Information (Product)		**2. Information (Customer)**	
Type of pickup service	**Quantity**	13. First and Last Name	
3. Priority Mail	8.	14. Company Name	
4. Express Mail	9.	15. Address 1.	
5. Parcel Post	10.	16. Address 2	
6.Global Express Guaranteed	11.	17. City	
		18. State.	
7. Estimated weight (total) of all packages (in pounds)	12.	19. Zip	

20. Affix stamps or Meter Strip in this space	Method of Payment		
	21. □ Metered Postage or Stamps		
	22. □ Postage Due Account		
	23. □ Express Mail Corporate Account Number		
	24. □ Check (Payable to Postmaster)		
	25. □ Label For Merchandise Return		
26. Signature of Customer	27. Signature of USPS employee		28. Pickup Date and Time

	Question	Answer Grid
13	There are 22 pieces of priority mail to be picked up. This should be indicated in box: A. 22 B. 13 C. 8 D. 4	Ⓐ Ⓑ Ⓒ Ⓓ
14	The stamps should be affixed in box: A. 8 B. 9 C. 20 D. 12	Ⓐ Ⓑ Ⓒ Ⓓ
15	Where on this form should the customer sign? A. 27 B. 28 C. 26 D. 13	Ⓐ Ⓑ Ⓒ Ⓓ
16	Which of the following is a correct entry for box 19? A. OK B. 10:10 a.m. C. $2.50 D. 10454	Ⓐ Ⓑ Ⓒ Ⓓ
17	The customer paid $19.00 in the form of a check payable to the Postmaster. Which box should be checked? A. 24 B. 7 C. 21 D. 22	Ⓐ Ⓑ Ⓒ Ⓓ
18	The pickup consists of 34 pieces of parcel post mail. In what box should this be indicated? A. 8 B. 9 C. 10 D. 11	Ⓐ Ⓑ Ⓒ Ⓓ

Answer questions 19 – 24 based on the following form:

CLAIM FOR DOMESTIC OR INTERNATIONAL MAIL					
2. Addressee Information			**3. Mailer Information**		
4. Last Name	5.MI	6. First Name	7. Last Name	8.MI	9. First Name
10. Business Name (if addressee is a company)			11. Business Name (if mailer is a company)		
12. Address (Number and Street)			13. Address (Number and Street)		
14. Address (Suite or Apartment Number)			15. Address (Suite or Apartment Number)		
16. City State Zip			17. City State Zip		
18. E-mail Address (Optional)			19. E-mail Address (Optional)		

20. Description of Missing Lost or Damaged Contents				
21. Item codes: 01 Jewelry, 02 Electronics, 03 Computers, 04 Animals, 05 Firearms, 06 Event Tickets, 07 Sports Equipment, 08 Collectibles, 09 Clothing, 10 Cash, 11 Other.				
22. Describe the contents and check off (L) for Lost or (D) for damaged				
23.Item	24. Description of contents	25.(L)or(D)	26.Item code	27.Value or Repair Cost in $
1		L ☐ D ☐		
2		L ☐ D ☐		
3		L ☐ D ☐		
		28. Total Value or Repair Cost in $		
29. The customer submitting the claim is the ☐ Mailer ☐ Addressee				
30. Payment is to be made to the ☐ Mailer ☐ Addressee				
31. Signature of Postal Customer submitting Claim		32. Date signed (MM/DD/YYYY)		

	Question	Answer Grid
19	The first name of the addressee should be entered in box: A. 6　　　　B. 4　　　　C. 9　　　　D. 2	Ⓐ Ⓑ Ⓒ Ⓓ
20	The middle initial of the Mailer should be placed in box: A. 8　　　　B. 9　　　　C. 5　　　　D. 20	Ⓐ Ⓑ Ⓒ Ⓓ
21	Where on this form should the customer sign? A. 4　　　　B. 7　　　　C. 13　　　　D. 31	Ⓐ Ⓑ Ⓒ Ⓓ
22	Which of the following is a correct entry for column 26? A. 07　　　　B. 12　　　　C. OK　　　　D. 13	Ⓐ Ⓑ Ⓒ Ⓓ
23	If the customer submitting the claim is the Mailer, this information should be stated in box: A. 31　　　　B. 29　　　　C. 24　　　　D. 22	Ⓐ Ⓑ Ⓒ Ⓓ
24	The E-mail address of the Mailer may be placed in box: A. 18　　　　B. 9　　　　C. 10　　　　D. 19	Ⓐ Ⓑ Ⓒ Ⓓ
25	What would be a correct entry for box 8? A. John　　　　B. Mary　　　　C. K　　　　D. 33	Ⓐ Ⓑ Ⓒ Ⓓ

Answer questions 26 – 30 based on the following form:

REPORT TO POSTAL INSPECTOR OF NON-RECEIPT OF CREDIT CARD

Dear Postal Inspector:

The addressee named below has informed the mailer that he/she did not receive the credit card mailed by the credit card company.

Addressee Information

1. Last Name	2. First Name	

3. Street Address	4. City	5. State	6. Zip

7. Telephone Number	8. E-mail Address (if any)	

9. Card type (Visa, American Express, etc.)

10. Were purchases made using this card? 11. ☐ YES 12. ☐ NO	13. If answer to 11 is "YES" where were purchases made? City State

Mailer Information

14. Mailer Name	

15. Street Address	16. City	17. State	18. Zip

19. Telephone Number	20. E-mail Address (if any)	

21. Mailed at Location	city	state	Zip

22. Credit card number	23. Credit card expiration date	

24. Date that purchases began (MM/DD/YYYY)	25. Total amount of purchases made with this credit card: $ _____

	Question	Answer Grid
26	Which of the following boxes does not contain information about the Addressee? A. 8　　　　　B. 9　　　　　C. 5　　　　　D. 20	Ⓐ Ⓑ Ⓒ Ⓓ
27	Where on this form should the customer indicate the expiration date of the credit card? A. 23　　　　B. 25　　　　C. 24　　　　D. 13	Ⓐ Ⓑ Ⓒ Ⓓ
28	Which of the following is a correct entry for box 2? A. None　　　B. Bill　　　C. 2400　　　D. 18	Ⓐ Ⓑ Ⓒ Ⓓ
29	Which of the following is a correct entry for box 24? A. 12　　　B. 1/18　　　C. 11/21/2010　D. 13	Ⓐ Ⓑ Ⓒ Ⓓ
30	The telephone number of the Mailer should be indicated in box: A. 8　　　　B. 19　　　　C. 10　　　　D. 11	Ⓐ Ⓑ Ⓒ Ⓓ

Directions for the following 36 Coding Questions

For each of the following 36 "Delivery Addresses" determine based on the coding guide whether the address belongs to Delivery Route A, B, C or D, and mark your answer grid accordingly. You have 6 minutes to code the 36 addresses.

Coding Practice Test #6:   Coding Guide

Range of Addresses	Delivery Route
200 - 1100 Hartford Street 100 – 1500 Neiman Ave. 1 - 1300 Reiker Lane	A
1101 – 2000 Hartford Street 1501 - 2000 Neiman Ave.	B
1301 – 2000 Reiker Lane 1 - 2100 Spiegel Circle 50 – 2700 Victory Ave.	C
All mail that doesn't fall in one of the address ranges listed above	D

	Delivery Address	Delivery Route				Answer Grid
1	346 Neiman Ave.	A	B	C	D	Ⓐ Ⓑ Ⓒ Ⓓ
2	2900 Victory Ave.	A	B	C	D	Ⓐ Ⓑ Ⓒ Ⓓ
3	145 Reiker Lane	A	B	C	D	Ⓐ Ⓑ Ⓒ Ⓓ
4	1575 Neiman Ave.	A	B	C	D	Ⓐ Ⓑ Ⓒ Ⓓ
5	1300 Hartford Street	A	B	C	D	Ⓐ Ⓑ Ⓒ Ⓓ
6	1301 Reiker Lane	A	B	C	D	Ⓐ Ⓑ Ⓒ Ⓓ
7	2200 Spiegel Circle	A	B	C	D	Ⓐ Ⓑ Ⓒ Ⓓ
8	1245 Neiman Ave.	A	B	C	D	Ⓐ Ⓑ Ⓒ Ⓓ
9	100 Spiegel Circle	A	B	C	D	Ⓐ Ⓑ Ⓒ Ⓓ
10	55 Victory Ave.	A	B	C	D	Ⓐ Ⓑ Ⓒ Ⓓ
11	200 Hartford Street	A	B	C	D	Ⓐ Ⓑ Ⓒ Ⓓ
12	1904 Neiman Ave.	A	B	C	D	Ⓐ Ⓑ Ⓒ Ⓓ
13	2400 Victory Ave.	A	B	C	D	Ⓐ Ⓑ Ⓒ Ⓓ
14	1300 Reiker Lane	A	B	C	D	Ⓐ Ⓑ Ⓒ Ⓓ

	Delivery Address	Delivery Route				Answer Grid
15	820 Hartford Street	A	B	C	D	Ⓐ Ⓑ Ⓒ Ⓓ
16	1775 Neiman Ave.	A	B	C	D	Ⓐ Ⓑ Ⓒ Ⓓ
17	100 Overton Street	A	B	C	D	Ⓐ Ⓑ Ⓒ Ⓓ
18	675 Reiker Lane	A	B	C	D	Ⓐ Ⓑ Ⓒ Ⓓ
19	1803 Spiegel Circle	A	B	C	D	Ⓐ Ⓑ Ⓒ Ⓓ
20	1801 Reiker Lane	A	B	C	D	Ⓐ Ⓑ Ⓒ Ⓓ
21	972 Hartford Street	A	B	C	D	Ⓐ Ⓑ Ⓒ Ⓓ
22	857 Lincoln Ave.	A	B	C	D	Ⓐ Ⓑ Ⓒ Ⓓ
23	1748 Hartford Street	A	B	C	D	Ⓐ Ⓑ Ⓒ Ⓓ
24	509 Victory Ave.	A	B	C	D	Ⓐ Ⓑ Ⓒ Ⓓ
25	998 Neiman Ave.	A	B	C	D	Ⓐ Ⓑ Ⓒ Ⓓ
26	555 Service Road	A	B	C	D	Ⓐ Ⓑ Ⓒ Ⓓ
27	1893 Reiker Lane	A	B	C	D	Ⓐ Ⓑ Ⓒ Ⓓ
28	1822 Neiman Ave.	A	B	C	D	Ⓐ Ⓑ Ⓒ Ⓓ
29	2000 Hartford Street	A	B	C	D	Ⓐ Ⓑ Ⓒ Ⓓ
30	1943 Jackson Ln.	A	B	C	D	Ⓐ Ⓑ Ⓒ Ⓓ
31	875 Hartford Street	A	B	C	D	Ⓐ Ⓑ Ⓒ Ⓓ
32	913 Reiker Lane	A	B	C	D	Ⓐ Ⓑ Ⓒ Ⓓ
33	2000 Spiegel Circle	A	B	C	D	Ⓐ Ⓑ Ⓒ Ⓓ
34	645 Spiegel Circle	A	B	C	D	Ⓐ Ⓑ Ⓒ Ⓓ
35	1588 Hartford Street	A	B	C	D	Ⓐ Ⓑ Ⓒ Ⓓ
36	598 Neiman Ave.	A	B	C	D	Ⓐ Ⓑ Ⓒ Ⓓ

Memory Practice Test #6:   Coding Guide

Range of Addresses	Delivery Route

You have 5 minutes to memorize the Coding Guide on page 198, then code the following 36 addresses based on your **memory** of the coding guide. (On the actual test you will probably have several minutes to practice answering coding questions. Those minutes can also be used, if you wish, to further memorize the codes.)

You have 7 minutes to answer the following 36 coding questions.

	Delivery Address	Delivery Route				Answer Grid
1	157 Reiker Lane	A	B	C	D	Ⓐ Ⓑ Ⓒ Ⓓ
2	2200 Spiegel Circle	A	B	C	D	Ⓐ Ⓑ Ⓒ Ⓓ
3	893 Hartford Street	A	B	C	D	Ⓐ Ⓑ Ⓒ Ⓓ
4	1899 Reiker Lane	A	B	C	D	Ⓐ Ⓑ Ⓒ Ⓓ
5	300 Neiman Ave.	A	B	C	D	Ⓐ Ⓑ Ⓒ Ⓓ
6	1201 Hartford Street	A	B	C	D	Ⓐ Ⓑ Ⓒ Ⓓ
7	2700 Kensington Street	A	B	C	D	Ⓐ Ⓑ Ⓒ Ⓓ
8	200 Hartford Street	A	B	C	D	Ⓐ Ⓑ Ⓒ Ⓓ
9	50 Victory Ave.	A	B	C	D	Ⓐ Ⓑ Ⓒ Ⓓ
10	1501 Neiman Ave.	A	B	C	D	Ⓐ Ⓑ Ⓒ Ⓓ
11	50 Spiegel Circle	A	B	C	D	Ⓐ Ⓑ Ⓒ Ⓓ
12	3100 Spiegel Circle	A	B	C	D	Ⓐ Ⓑ Ⓒ Ⓓ
13	1922 Reiker Lane	A	B	C	D	Ⓐ Ⓑ Ⓒ Ⓓ
14	2400 Victory Ave.	A	B	C	D	Ⓐ Ⓑ Ⓒ Ⓓ

	Delivery Address	Delivery Route				Answer Grid
15	993 Reiker Lane	A	B	C	D	Ⓐ Ⓑ Ⓒ Ⓓ
16	1287 Neiman Ave.	A	B	C	D	Ⓐ Ⓑ Ⓒ Ⓓ
17	1788 Hartford Street	A	B	C	D	Ⓐ Ⓑ Ⓒ Ⓓ
18	550 Borders Circle	A	B	C	D	Ⓐ Ⓑ Ⓒ Ⓓ
19	1555 Reiker Lane	A	B	C	D	Ⓐ Ⓑ Ⓒ Ⓓ
20	1249 Hartford Street	A	B	C	D	Ⓐ Ⓑ Ⓒ Ⓓ
21	1950 Neiman Ave.	A	B	C	D	Ⓐ Ⓑ Ⓒ Ⓓ
22	2244 Victory Ave.	A	B	C	D	Ⓐ Ⓑ Ⓒ Ⓓ
23	865 Reiker Lane	A	B	C	D	Ⓐ Ⓑ Ⓒ Ⓓ
24	782 Spiegel Circle	A	B	C	D	Ⓐ Ⓑ Ⓒ Ⓓ
25	2900 Victory Ave.	A	B	C	D	Ⓐ Ⓑ Ⓒ Ⓓ
26	1900 Hartford Street	A	B	C	D	Ⓐ Ⓑ Ⓒ Ⓓ
27	50 Alsace Lane	A	B	C	D	Ⓐ Ⓑ Ⓒ Ⓓ
28	1812 Neiman Ave.	A	B	C	D	Ⓐ Ⓑ Ⓒ Ⓓ
29	2245 Victory Ave.	A	B	C	D	Ⓐ Ⓑ Ⓒ Ⓓ
30	882 Reiker Lane	A	B	C	D	Ⓐ Ⓑ Ⓒ Ⓓ
31	4700 Victory Ave.	A	B	C	D	Ⓐ Ⓑ Ⓒ Ⓓ
32	555 Hartford Street	A	B	C	D	Ⓐ Ⓑ Ⓒ Ⓓ
33	450 Neiman Ave.	A	B	C	D	Ⓐ Ⓑ Ⓒ Ⓓ
34	2657 Victory Ave.	A	B	C	D	Ⓐ Ⓑ Ⓒ Ⓓ
35	1629 Hartford Street	A	B	C	D	Ⓐ Ⓑ Ⓒ Ⓓ
36	1745 Spiegel Circle	A	B	C	D	Ⓐ Ⓑ Ⓒ Ⓓ

Answers: Practice Test #6

Address Checking

1. B	7. B	13. C	19. D	25. D	31. B	37. B	43. B	49. C	55. B
2. A	8. C	14. A	20. B	26. A	32. C	38. D	44. C	50. A	56. D
3. C	9. C	15. A	21. C	27. C	33. D	39. A	45. A	51. B	57. D
4. D	10. D	16. B	22. A	28. A	34. B	40. C	46. A	52. A	58. C
5. A	11. A	17. C	23. D	29. B	35. C	41. D	47. A	53. D	59. B
6. D	12. B	18. D	24. B	30. D	36. A	42. D	48. B	54. C	60. A

Forms Completion

1. C	6. B	11. C	16. D	21. D	26. D
2. D	7. C	12. C	17. A	22. A	27. A
3. B	8. A	13. C	18. C	23. B	28. B
4. A	9. D	14. C	19. A	24. D	29. C
5. B	10. B	15. C	20. A	25. C	30. B

Coding

1. A	5. B	9. C	13. C	17. D	21. A	25. A	29. B	33. C
2. D	6. C	10. C	14. A	18. A	22. D	26. D	30. D	34. C
3. A	7. D	11. A	15. A	19. C	23. B	27. C	31. A	35. B
4. B	8. A	12. B	16. B	20. C	24. C	28. B	32. A	36. A

Memory

1. A	5. A	9. C	13. C	17. B	21. B	25. D	29. C	33. A
2. D	6. B	10. B	14. C	18. D	22. C	26. B	30. A	34. C
3. A	7. D	11. C	15. A	19. C	23. A	27. D	31. D	35. B
4. C	8. A	12. D	16. A	20. B	24. C	28. B	32. A	36. C

PRACTICE TEST 7

Part	Time Allowed	Number of Ques.	Description of Question
1. Address Checking	**11 minutes**	**60**	**Compare two addresses.**
2. Forms Completion	15 minutes	30	Correctly complete forms.
3. Coding	6 minutes	36	Find correct code for an address.
4. Memory (of coding examples, above)	7 minutes	36	Memorize address codes (which are same as codes in the "Coding" section part of the test.)

The first Part of this practice test is ADDRESS CHECKING.

(You have 11 minutes to complete this part of the test.)

When you are ready, turn the page and start the test.

Address Checking Practice Test 7: Below are 60 pairs of addresses. You have 11 minutes to compare each pair for errors and mark the answer sheet to indicate errors found as follows:

A. No Errors   **B.** Address Only   **C.** Zip Code Only   **D.** Both Address and ZIP Code

	Correct List of Addresses		Address List to be Checked		
	Address	**ZIP**	**Address**	**ZIP**	**Answer Grid**
1	5661 Rocker Ave. Red Cliff, AK	43121	5661 Rocker Ave. Red Cliff, AK	43241	A B C D
2	3712 Railroad Ln. Pueblo, RI	17295	3712 Railroad Ln. Pueblo, RI	17295	A B C D
3	7467 Weller Rd. Arcade, NK	40402-3294	7467 Weler Rd. Arcade, NK	40402-3294	A B C D
4	3962 Tertor St. Davenport, MS	51452	3962 Testor St. Davenport, MS	51422	A B C D
5	412 Bourne Ave. Shellman, OH	12471-1161	412 Borne Ave. Shellman, OH	12471-1191	A B C D
6	8111 Washer Ave. Gridley, NY	62138	811 Washer Ave. Gridley, NY	62138	A B C D
7	1824 Kissena St. Mill Valley, MN	10015-3302	1824 Kissena St. Mill Valley, MN	10015-3302	A B C D
8	5832 Gerrit Rd. Clewis, NY	53532-2014	5832 Gerrit Rd. Clewis, NY	53532-5014	A B C D
9	6810 Broad St. Arvenal, VA	41124-5431	6810 Broad St. Avenal, VA	41142-5431	A B C D
10	8241 Concert Ave. Pleasant, ME	55415	824 Concert Ave. Pleasant, ME	55415	A B C D
11	2734 Porter St. Shaffer, OR	28018	2734 Porter St. Shaffer, OR	28018	A B C D
12	661 Mirror Cir. Dover, WA	43034-1341	661 Mirror Cir. Dover, WA	43034-1347	A B C D
13	P.O. Box 4251 Ambrose, FL	36461	P.O. Box 4251 Ambrose, FL	36491	A B C D
14	3135 Palma Ter. Deltona, MI	38065	3135 Palma Ter. Deltona, MI	38065	A B C D
15	5512 Project Ln. Shiloh, MD	40196-1647	5515 Project Ln. Shiloh, MD	40196-1647	A B C D

Address Checking Practice Test 7 (cont'd): Continue to compare each pair of addresses for errors and mark the answer sheet as follows:

A. No Errors   **B.** Address Only   **C.** Zip Code Only   **D.** Both Address and ZIP Code

	Correct List of Addresses		Address List to be Checked		
	Address	**ZIP**	**Address**	**ZIP**	**Answer Grid**
16	2419 Delio St. Rush, RI	43165	2419 Dello St. Rush, RI	43165	A B C D
17	6102 Essex Ave. Dudley, TX	36250	6102 Essex Ave. Dudley, TX	36250	A B C D
18	847 Memory Ln. Avera, MN	59085-4708	847 Memory Ln. Avera, MN	59085-4703	A B C D
19	1117 Rural Rd. Montclair, ME	38452-2305	117 Rural Rd. Montclair, ME	38455-2305	A B C D
20	4734 Immagine Ln. Eastman, MS	32609-7117	4734 Imagine Ln. Eastman, MS	32606-7117	A B C D
21	5005 Pebble St. Hamilton, FL	60556-6112	5005 Pebble St. Hamilton, FL	60556-6112	A B C D
22	352 Captain Ave. Redvalle, AK	84645	352 Captain Ave. Redvale, AK	84645	A B C D
23	2184 Wayford Ct. Hasty, NY	76686-4541	2184 Wayford Ct. Hasty, NY	76606-4541	A B C D
24	1253 Temple Cir. Riverside, PA	93529	1253 Temple Cir. Riverside, PA	63529	A B C D
25	7470 Frank Ave. Doral, VA	36256	7470 Frank St. Doral, VA	36256	A B C D
26	5144 Island Ter. Bond, MD	39485-6156	5144 Island Ter. Bond, MA	39485-6156	A B C D
27	5268 Parks Ave. San Paolo, MA	32662-6587	5268 Park Ave. San Paolo, MA	32662-6582	A B C D
28	9832 Soccer Ln. Stanton, AK	64640	9832 Soccer Ln. Stanton, AR	64640	A B C D
29	P.O. Box 3182 Dunedin, SC	65664-7535	P.O. Box 3182 Dunedin, SC	65664-7535	A B C D
30	7912 Cotter Rd. Gretna, TX	88192	7912 Cotter Rd. Gretna, TX	88162	A B C D

Address Checking Practice Test 7 (cont'd): Continue to compare each pair of addresses for errors and mark the answer sheet as follows:

A. No Errors   **B.** Address Only   **C.** Zip Code Only   **D.** Both Address and ZIP Code

Correct List of Addresses   **Address List to be Checked**

	Address	ZIP	Address	ZIP	Answer Grid
31	374 Dotson Ave. Ashburn, FL	47501-2661	334 Dotsun Ave. Ashburn, FL	47501-2001	A B C D
32	671 Eledrts Ct. Brandon, OR	48311	671 Eledrts Ct. Brandon, OR	48311	A B C D
33	813 Teacher Ln. Culver City, NJ	95751	813 Teacher Ln. Culver City, NJ	95721	A B C D
34	6271 Corner St. Redstone, AK	62749-6211	6271 Comer St. Redstone, AK	62749-6211	A B C D
35	2712 Marton Rd. Hale, NY	71046	2712 Marlon Rd. Hale, NY	71049	A B C D
36	485 Canyon Ave. Hemet, NY	72049	485 Canyon Ave. Hemet, NY	71049	A B C D
37	8557 Ember St. Monterey, WA	83845-6787	8557 Ember St. Monterey, WA	83845-6787	A B C D
38	572 Sawyer Way Cypress, OH	41151-6518	575 Sawyer Way Cypress, OH	41151-6518	A B C D
39	6932 Pattern Ln. Corona, IL	96317	6932 Patter Ln. Corona, IL	99317	A B C D
40	742 Porter Pkwy. Morgan, MI	14312	742 Porter Pkwy. Morgan, MI	14312	A B C D
41	16 Planer Cir. Barstow, MD	14030-3243	16 Planer Cir. Barstow, MD	14030-3248	A B C D
42	3334 Mills Ter. South Gate, KS	47328	334 Mills Ter. South Gate, KS	47328	A B C D
43	9672 Exeter St. Corvina, MN	49829	9672 Exter St. Corvina, MN	49329	A B C D
44	2789 Series Rd. Bonanza, FL	17030-4243	2789 Seres Rd. Bonanza, FL	17030-4643	A B C D
45	P.O. Box 8261 Hartford, CA	72459	P.O. Box 8261 Hartfork, CA	72456	A B C D

Address Checking Practice Test 7 (cont'd): Continue to compare each pair of addresses for errors and mark the answer sheet as follows:

A. No Errors **B.** Address Only **C.** Zip Code Only **D.** Both Address and ZIP Code

	Correct List of Addresses		Address List to be Checked		Answer Grid
	Address	ZIP	Address	ZIP	
46	191 Papper Ct. Sargents, AK	12190	191 Papper Ct. Sargents, AK	12190	A B C D
47	5737 Cert Pkwy. Holly, NJ	03482-5235	5737 Cert Pkwy. Holly, NJ	03482-5235	A B C D
48	4647 Edison Ave. Gulf, CT	93065-9127	4647 Elison Ave. Gulf, CT	93065-9127	A B C D
49	P.O. Box 3210 Baldwin, OR	40412-9638	P.O. Box 3210 Baldwin, OR	40412-6938	A B C D
50	2141 Winters Ave. Davis, MO	13684	2141 Winter Ave. Davis, MO	13984	A B C D
51	5312 Franklin St. Sparta, MS	21142-3448	5312 Franklin St. Sparta, MS	21142-3448	A B C D
52	8928 Clifferd Way Buffalo, MN	21004	8928 Cliff Way Buffalo, MN	21004	A B C D
53	4110 Citizen St. Stockton, FL	20602-4919	4110 Citizen St. Stockton, FL	20602-4919	A B C D
54	7654 Kitten Rd. Hercules, KS	52678	7654 Kitten Rd. Hercules, KS	52978	A B C D
55	6784 Nativity St. Taft, IL	60843	6784 Native St. Taft, IL	60843	A B C D
56	3148 Volcanoe Ter. Sheridan, WA	41029-4762	3148 Volcano Ter. Sheridan, WA	41079-4762	A B C D
57	6142 Clement Ln. Sterling, TX	88761-3052	6142 Clement Ln. Sterling, TX	88761-3022	A B C D
58	4162 Control Ln. Islandia, MI	37348-6567	4162 Control Ln. Islandia, MI	37348-6567	A B C D
59	3528 Hamster Rd. Everett, MD	28078	3528 Hamter Rd. Everett, MD	28078	A B C D
60	92 Cooper Cir. Baden, SC	21091-8725	92 Copper Cir. Baden, SC	21091-8725	A B C D

Forms Completion Practice Test 7

This part of the test consists of 5 different forms and 30 questions. Study each form and then answer the questions following each of the forms. (Time allowed: 15 minutes for 30 questions).   Answer questions 1 – 6 based on the following form:

CUSTOMS DECLARATION	
FROM (SENDER): 1. Last and First Name (and Business Name, if any) 2. Street 3. City 4. State 5. Zip	11. Insured Amount 12. Insured Fees (U.S. $) 13. Importer's Name and Telephone Number

TO (ADDRESSEE):
 	
6. Last and First Name (and Business Name, if any)
 	
7. Strect
 	
8. City
 	
9. State   10. Zip
	14. Sender's instructions in case cannot be delivered:
	15. □ Treat as abandoned
	    □ Return to sender
	    □ Redirect to following address (#16):
	16.

17. Specific description of contents	18. Qty	19. Lbs.	20. Oz.

21. Comments

22. Check one	23. □ Airmail/Priority	24. □ Surface/Non priority

25. Check one   26. □ Documents 27. □ Merchandise 28. □ Gift 29. □ Other _____

30. Date Signed	31. Sender's Signature

Question	Answer Grid
1 The first and last name of the Sender should be entered in box: A. 6 B. 13 C. 9 D. 1	Ⓐ Ⓑ Ⓒ Ⓓ
2 Insured fees of $20.45 are being paid. This amount should be entered in which box? A. 17 B. 12 C. 11 D. 20	Ⓐ Ⓑ Ⓒ Ⓓ
3 Where on this form should the Sender sign? A. 1 B. 6 C. 13 D. 31	Ⓐ Ⓑ Ⓒ Ⓓ
4 Which of the following is a correct entry for box 19? A. ZIP B. 6/13/10 C. $3.50 D. 16	Ⓐ Ⓑ Ⓒ Ⓓ
5 If the article cannot be delivered, the Sender wishes the article to be returned to the Sender. This can be indicated by checking the correct box in section: A. 15 B. 7 C. 25 D. 22	Ⓐ Ⓑ Ⓒ Ⓓ
6 What would be a correct entry for box 9? A. Miami B. Las Vegas C. Naples D. NY	Ⓐ Ⓑ Ⓒ Ⓓ

Answer questions 7 – 12 based on the following form:

STATEMENT FOR PICKUP SERVICE		
1. Information (Product)		**2. Information (Customer)**
Type of pickup service	**Quantity**	13. First and Last Name
3. Priority Mail	8.	14. Company Name
4. Express Mail	9.	15. Address 1.
5. Parcel Post	10.	16. Address 2
6.Global Express Guaranteed	11.	17. City
		18. State.
7. Estimated weight (total) of all packages (in pounds)	12.	19. Zip

20. Affix stamps or Meter Strip in this space	**Method of Payment**
	21. ☐ Metered Postage or Stamps
	22. ☐ Postage Due Account
	23. ☐ Express Mail Corporate Account Number
	24. ☐ Check (Payable to Postmaster)
	25. ☐ Label For Merchandise Return

26. Signature of Customer	27. Signature of USPS employee	28. Pickup Date and Time

	Question	Answer Grid
7	Which of the following would be a correct entry in box 17? A. Vermont B. California C. Las Vegas D. Utah	Ⓐ Ⓑ Ⓒ Ⓓ
8	The stamps should be affixed in box: A. 21 B. 9 C. 5 D. 20	Ⓐ Ⓑ Ⓒ Ⓓ
9	Where on this form should the customer sign? A. 26 B. 28 C. 13 D. 27	Ⓐ Ⓑ Ⓒ Ⓓ
10	Which of the following is a correct entry for box 19? A. OK B. Priority C. $2.50 D. 10429	Ⓐ Ⓑ Ⓒ Ⓓ
11	The postal employee signs in which box? A. 13 B. 26 C. 20 D. 27	Ⓐ Ⓑ Ⓒ Ⓓ
12	The pickup date and time is entered in box: A. 8 B. 28 C. 26 D. 2	Ⓐ Ⓑ Ⓒ Ⓓ

Answer questions 13 – 18 based on the following form:

1. RETURN RECEIPT FOR DOMESTIC MAIL	
THIS SECTION IS TO BE COMPLETED BY THE SENDER	**THIS SECTION IS TO BE COMPLETED UPON DELIVERY OF THE ITEM**
2. ▶Sender must complete items 1, 2, 3 (and 4 if Restricted Delivery is desired.) 3. ▶Sender must print sender's name and address on the reverse side of this card so that card can be returned to sender. 4. ▶Peel off glue protector strips on opposite side and attach to the back of the mail, or on the front if there is enough space.	7. Signature □ Addressee ▶ □ Agent 8. Received by (PRINT) 9. Delivery Date 10. Is delivery address same or different from item 5? □ Same □ Different (If different, write delivery address below:
5. Article addressed to:	Type of mail service: 12. □ Registered 15. □ C.O.D. 13. □ Insured 16. □ Express 14. □ Certified 17. □ Merchandise Return receipt 18. Restricted delivery (Additional fee) $_____ □ Yes
6. Article number (from service label)	

	Question	Answer Grid
13	The date that the article is delivered is entered in which box? A. 14　　　B. 13　　　C. 9　　　D. 2	Ⓐ Ⓑ Ⓒ Ⓓ
14	If the article is being sent by certified mail, which box should be checked? A. 12　　　B. 14　　　C. 15　　　D. 16	Ⓐ Ⓑ Ⓒ Ⓓ
15	Where on this form should the person receiving the article sign? A. 7　　　B. 8　　　C. 13　　　D. 6	Ⓐ Ⓑ Ⓒ Ⓓ
16	Which of the following is a correct entry for box 9? A. Check　　B. 9/25/10　　C. $9.50　　D. March	Ⓐ Ⓑ Ⓒ Ⓓ
17	The customer paid $5.55 for restricted delivery mail service. In which box should this amount be entered? A. 17　　B. 18　　C. 15　　D. 13	Ⓐ Ⓑ Ⓒ Ⓓ
18	What would be a correct entry for box 15? A. $10.00　　B. 26　　C. check mark　　D. 7	Ⓐ Ⓑ Ⓒ Ⓓ

Answer questions 19 – 24 based on the following form:

CLAIM FOR DOMESTIC OR INTERNATIONAL MAIL					
2. Addressee Information			**3. Mailer Information**		
4. Last Name	5.MI	6. First Name	7. Last Name	8.MI	9. First Name
10. Business Name (if addressee is a company)			11. Business Name (if mailer is a company)		
12. Address (Number and Street)			13. Address (Number and Street)		
14. Address (Suite or Apartment Number)			15. Address (Suite or Apartment Number)		
16. City State Zip			17. City State Zip		
18. E-mail Address (Optional)			19. E-mail Address (Optional)		
20. Description of Missing Lost or Damaged Contents					

21. Item codes: 01 Jewelry, 02 Electronics, 03 Computers, 04 Animals, 05 Firearms, 06 Event Tickets, 07 Sports Equipment, 08 Collectibles, 09 Clothing, 10 Cash, 11 Other.

22. Describe the contents and check off (L) for Lost or (D) for damaged

23.Item	24. Description of contents	25.(L)or(D)	26.Item code	27.Value or Repair Cost in $
1		L ☐ D ☐		
2		L ☐ D ☐		
3		L ☐ D ☐		
		28. Total Value or Repair Cost in $		

29. The customer submitting the claim is the ☐ Mailer   ☐ Addressee

30. Payment is to be made to the ☐ Mailer   ☐ Addressee

31. Signature of Postal Customer submitting Claim	32. Date signed (MM/DD/YYYY)

	Question	Answer Grid
19	The three main sections of this form are numbered: A. 1, 2, 3 B. 2, 3, 20 C. 4, 7, 21 D. 2, 3, 4	Ⓐ Ⓑ Ⓒ Ⓓ
20	Which of the following information box is not under the "Addressee Information" section? A. 4 B. 6 C. 12 D. 13	Ⓐ Ⓑ Ⓒ Ⓓ
21	Where on this form should the customer sign? A. 7 B. 28 C. 4 D. 31	Ⓐ Ⓑ Ⓒ Ⓓ
22	Which of the following is a correct entry for box 32? A. OK B. 10/11/2010 C. $3.50 D. Jan.	Ⓐ Ⓑ Ⓒ Ⓓ
23	The E-mail address of the customer who mailed the article should be entered in box: A. 18 B. 19 C. 104 D. 13	Ⓐ Ⓑ Ⓒ Ⓓ
24	What would be a correct entry for column 26? A. 02 B. 26 C. 999 D. 675	Ⓐ Ⓑ Ⓒ Ⓓ

Answer questions 25 – 30 based on the following form:

REPORT TO POSTAL INSPECTOR OF NON-RECEIPT OF CREDIT CARD

Dear Postal Inspector:

The addressee named below has informed the credit card company that he/she did not receive the credit card mailed by the credit card company.

Addressee Information

1. Last Name	2. First Name	

3. Street Address	4. City	5. State	6. Zip

7. Telephone Number	8. E-mail Address (if any)	

9. Card type (Visa, American Express, etc.)

10. Were purchases made using this card? 11. ☐ YES 12. ☐ NO	13. If answer to 11 is "YES" where were purchases made? City State

Mailer Information

14. Mailer Name	

15. Street Address	16. City	17. State	18. Zip

19. Telephone Number	20. E-mail Address (if any)	

21. Mailed at Location	city	state	Zip

22. Credit card number	23. Credit card expiration date	

24. Date that purchases began (MM/DD/YYYY)	25. Total amount of purchases made with this credit card: $ _____

Question	Answer Grid
25 The first name of the person who did not receive the credit card should be written in box: A. 13 B. 14 C. 2 D. 14	Ⓐ Ⓑ Ⓒ Ⓓ
26 The date that purchases began should be entered in which box? A. 25 B. 24 C. 20 D. 10	Ⓐ Ⓑ Ⓒ Ⓓ
27 Where on this form should the credit card number be entered? A. 9 B. 22 C. 23 D. 25	Ⓐ Ⓑ Ⓒ Ⓓ
28 Which of the following is a correct entry for box 9? A. None B. Discover C. Lisa D. AOK	Ⓐ Ⓑ Ⓒ Ⓓ
29 The credit card expiration date should be entered in which box? A. 9 B. 22 C. 23 D. 10	Ⓐ Ⓑ Ⓒ Ⓓ
30 Which of the following is a correct entry for box 24? A. 11/12/2010 B. May 7, 2010 C. 5/7 D. 5/10	Ⓐ Ⓑ Ⓒ Ⓓ

Directions for the following 36 Coding Questions

For each of the following 36 "Delivery Addresses" determine based on the coding guide whether the address belongs to Delivery Route A, B, C or D, and mark your answer grid accordingly. You have 6 minutes to code the 36 addresses.

Coding Practice Test #7:   Coding Guide

Range of Addresses	Delivery Route
20 - 600 Grace Street 1 – 1000 Marcus Ave. 100 - 1200 Parker Lane	A
601 – 1200 Grace Street 1001 - 2000 Marcus Ave.	B
1201 – 2500 Parker Lane 30 - 400 Layton Circle 10 - 800 Wycoff Ave.	C
All mail that doesn't fall in one of the address ranges listed above	D

	Delivery Address	Delivery Route				Answer Grid
1	145 Marcus Ave.	A	B	C	D	Ⓐ Ⓑ Ⓒ Ⓓ
2	601 Grace Street	A	B	C	D	Ⓐ Ⓑ Ⓒ Ⓓ
3	438 Parker Lane	A	B	C	D	Ⓐ Ⓑ Ⓒ Ⓓ
4	100 Wycoff Ave.	A	B	C	D	Ⓐ Ⓑ Ⓒ Ⓓ
5	1010 Marcus Ave.	A	B	C	D	Ⓐ Ⓑ Ⓒ Ⓓ
6	900 Wycoff Ave.	A	B	C	D	Ⓐ Ⓑ Ⓒ Ⓓ
7	205 Grace Street	A	B	C	D	Ⓐ Ⓑ Ⓒ Ⓓ
8	1290 Parker Lane	A	B	C	D	Ⓐ Ⓑ Ⓒ Ⓓ
9	40 Layton Circle	A	B	C	D	Ⓐ Ⓑ Ⓒ Ⓓ
10	650 Layton Circle	A	B	C	D	Ⓐ Ⓑ Ⓒ Ⓓ
11	732 Wycoff Ave.	A	B	C	D	Ⓐ Ⓑ Ⓒ Ⓓ
12	1200 Parker Lane	A	B	C	D	Ⓐ Ⓑ Ⓒ Ⓓ
13	400 Layton Circle	A	B	C	D	Ⓐ Ⓑ Ⓒ Ⓓ
14	2200 Parker Lane	A	B	C	D	Ⓐ Ⓑ Ⓒ Ⓓ

	Delivery Address	Delivery Route				Answer Grid
15	375 Grace Street	A	B	C	D	Ⓐ Ⓑ Ⓒ Ⓓ
16	367 Layton Circle	A	B	C	D	Ⓐ Ⓑ Ⓒ Ⓓ
17	988 Marcus Ave.	A	B	C	D	Ⓐ Ⓑ Ⓒ Ⓓ
18	689 Grace Street	A	B	C	D	Ⓐ Ⓑ Ⓒ Ⓓ
19	3500 Parker Lane	A	B	C	D	Ⓐ Ⓑ Ⓒ Ⓓ
20	529 Marcus Ave.	A	B	C	D	Ⓐ Ⓑ Ⓒ Ⓓ
21	833 Parker Lane	A	B	C	D	Ⓐ Ⓑ Ⓒ Ⓓ
22	2000 Marcus Ave.	A	B	C	D	Ⓐ Ⓑ Ⓒ Ⓓ
23	1201 Sonora Drive	A	B	C	D	Ⓐ Ⓑ Ⓒ Ⓓ
24	600 Grace Street	A	B	C	D	Ⓐ Ⓑ Ⓒ Ⓓ
25	543 Wycoff Ave.	A	B	C	D	Ⓐ Ⓑ Ⓒ Ⓓ
26	1100 Grace Street	A	B	C	D	Ⓐ Ⓑ Ⓒ Ⓓ
27	1548 Marcus Ave.	A	B	C	D	Ⓐ Ⓑ Ⓒ Ⓓ
28	993 Parker Lane	A	B	C	D	Ⓐ Ⓑ Ⓒ Ⓓ
29	798 Marcus Ave.	A	B	C	D	Ⓐ Ⓑ Ⓒ Ⓓ
30	1577 Parker Lane	A	B	C	D	Ⓐ Ⓑ Ⓒ Ⓓ
31	776 Grace Street	A	B	C	D	Ⓐ Ⓑ Ⓒ Ⓓ
32	300 Layton Circle	A	B	C	D	Ⓐ Ⓑ Ⓒ Ⓓ
33	457 Grace Street	A	B	C	D	Ⓐ Ⓑ Ⓒ Ⓓ
34	437 Wycoff Ave.	A	B	C	D	Ⓐ Ⓑ Ⓒ Ⓓ
35	1332 Marcus Ave.	A	B	C	D	Ⓐ Ⓑ Ⓒ Ⓓ
36	665 Parker Lane	A	B	C	D	Ⓐ Ⓑ Ⓒ Ⓓ

Memory Practice Test #7:   Coding Guide

Range of Addresses	Delivery Route

You have 5 minutes to memorize the Coding Guide on page 218, then code the following 36 addresses based on your **memory** of the coding guide. (On the actual test you will probably have several minutes to practice answering coding questions. Those minutes can also be used, if you wish, to further memorize the codes.)

You have 7 minutes to answer the following 36 coding questions.

	Delivery Address	Delivery Route				Answer Grid
1	254 Parker Lane	A	B	C	D	Ⓐ Ⓑ Ⓒ Ⓓ
2	900 Wycoff Ave.	A	B	C	D	Ⓐ Ⓑ Ⓒ Ⓓ
3	644 Marcus Ave.	A	B	C	D	Ⓐ Ⓑ Ⓒ Ⓓ
4	1564 Marcus Ave.	A	B	C	D	Ⓐ Ⓑ Ⓒ Ⓓ
5	690 Grace Street	A	B	C	D	Ⓐ Ⓑ Ⓒ Ⓓ
6	444 Parker Lane	A	B	C	D	Ⓐ Ⓑ Ⓒ Ⓓ
7	300 Layton Circle	A	B	C	D	Ⓐ Ⓑ Ⓒ Ⓓ
8	1000 Marcus Ave.	A	B	C	D	Ⓐ Ⓑ Ⓒ Ⓓ
9	10 Ryder Ave.	A	B	C	D	Ⓐ Ⓑ Ⓒ Ⓓ
10	1201 Parker Lane	A	B	C	D	Ⓐ Ⓑ Ⓒ Ⓓ
11	124 Wycoff Ave.	A	B	C	D	Ⓐ Ⓑ Ⓒ Ⓓ
12	210 Grace Street	A	B	C	D	Ⓐ Ⓑ Ⓒ Ⓓ
13	800 Wicker Ave.	A	B	C	D	Ⓐ Ⓑ Ⓒ Ⓓ
14	993 Grace Street	A	B	C	D	Ⓐ Ⓑ Ⓒ Ⓓ

	Delivery Address	Delivery Route				Answer Grid
15	332 Grace Street	A	B	C	D	Ⓐ Ⓑ Ⓒ Ⓓ
16	10 Arbor Road	A	B	C	D	Ⓐ Ⓑ Ⓒ Ⓓ
17	124 Marcus Ave.	A	B	C	D	Ⓐ Ⓑ Ⓒ Ⓓ
18	2500 Parker Lane	A	B	C	D	Ⓐ Ⓑ Ⓒ Ⓓ
19	800 Wycoff Ave.	A	B	C	D	Ⓐ Ⓑ Ⓒ Ⓓ
20	554 Parker Lane	A	B	C	D	Ⓐ Ⓑ Ⓒ Ⓓ
21	100 Barber Street	A	B	C	D	Ⓐ Ⓑ Ⓒ Ⓓ
22	1200 Grace Street	A	B	C	D	Ⓐ Ⓑ Ⓒ Ⓓ
23	378 Layton Circle	A	B	C	D	Ⓐ Ⓑ Ⓒ Ⓓ
24	590 Grace Street	A	B	C	D	Ⓐ Ⓑ Ⓒ Ⓓ
25	2200 Parker Lane	A	B	C	D	Ⓐ Ⓑ Ⓒ Ⓓ
26	710 Brown Avenue	A	B	C	D	Ⓐ Ⓑ Ⓒ Ⓓ
27	840 Parker Lane	A	B	C	D	Ⓐ Ⓑ Ⓒ Ⓓ
28	321 Tyker Lane	A	B	C	D	Ⓐ Ⓑ Ⓒ Ⓓ
29	825 Marcus Ave.	A	B	C	D	Ⓐ Ⓑ Ⓒ Ⓓ
30	245 Layton Circle	A	B	C	D	Ⓐ Ⓑ Ⓒ Ⓓ
31	1311 Marcus Ave.	A	B	C	D	Ⓐ Ⓑ Ⓒ Ⓓ
32	567 Wycoff Ave.	A	B	C	D	Ⓐ Ⓑ Ⓒ Ⓓ
33	600 Grace Street	A	B	C	D	Ⓐ Ⓑ Ⓒ Ⓓ
34	224 Elser Avenue	A	B	C	D	Ⓐ Ⓑ Ⓒ Ⓓ
35	965 Grace Street	A	B	C	D	Ⓐ Ⓑ Ⓒ Ⓓ
36	1289 Marcus Ave.	A	B	C	D	Ⓐ Ⓑ Ⓒ Ⓓ

Answers: Practice Test #7

Address Checking

1. C	7. A	13. C	19. D	25. B	31. B	37. A	43. D	49. C	55. B
2. A	8. C	14. A	20. D	26. B	32. A	38. B	44. D	50. D	56. D
3. B	9. D	15. B	21. A	27. D	33. C	39. D	45. D	51. A	57. C
4. D	10. B	16. B	22. B	28. B	34. B	40. A	46. A	52. B	58. A
5. D	11. A	17. A	23. C	29. A	35. D	41. C	47. A	53. A	59. B
6. B	12. C	18. C	24. C	30. C	36. C	42. B	48. B	54. C	60. B

Forms Completion

1. D	6. D	11. D	16. B	21. D	26. B
2. B	7. C	12. B	17. B	22. B	27. B
3. D	8. D	13. C	18. C	23. B	28. B
4. D	9. A	14. B	19. B	24. A	29. C
5. A	10. D	15. A	20. D	25. C	30. A

Coding

1. A	5. B	9. C	13. C	17. A	21. A	25. C	29. A	33. A
2. B	6. D	10. D	14. C	18. B	22. B	26. B	30. C	34. C
3. A	7. A	11. C	15. A	19. D	23. D	27. B	31. B	35. B
4. C	8. C	12. A	16. C	20. A	24. A	28. A	32. C	36. A

Memory

1. A	5. B	9. D	13. D	17. A	21. D	25. C	29. A	33. A
2. D	6. A	10. C	14. B	18. C	22. B	26. D	30. C	34. D
3. A	7. C	11. C	15. A	19. C	23. C	27. A	31. B	35. B
4. B	8. A	12. A	16. D	20. A	24. A	28. D	32. C	36. B

For the FREE samples of the questions online, please visit:

www.PostalTest.com

For FREE INTERACTIVE Access Code, see Page 83)

<u>Good luck!</u>

Other books by Angelo Tropea:

Pass the New Citizenship Test 2009 Edition

Pass the New Citizenship Test Kindle Edition

Pass the New Citizenship Test Questions and Answers

Pass The New York Notary Public Exam 2010 Edition

Pass The New York Notary Public Exam Kindle Edition

Pass The New York Notary Public Exam Questions and Answers

Notary Public Journal Of Notarial Acts

7645718R0

Made in the USA
Charleston, SC
26 March 2011